I0423467

WITHDRAWN FROM LIBRARY

THE

Secret Lives

OF

Married Men

WITHDRAWN FROM LIBRARY

THE
Secret Lives

OF

Married Men

DAVID LEDDICK

alyson books
los angeles

© 2003 BY DAVID LEDDICK. ALL RIGHTS RESERVED.

MANUFACTURED IN THE UNITED STATES OF AMERICA.

THIS TRADE PAPERBACK ORIGINAL IS PUBLISHED BY ALYSON PUBLICATIONS,
P.O. BOX 4371, LOS ANGELES, CALIFORNIA 90078-4371.
DISTRIBUTION IN THE UNITED KINGDOM BY
TURNAROUND PUBLISHER SERVICES LTD.,
UNIT 3, OLYMPIA TRADING ESTATE, COBURG ROAD, WOOD GREEN,
LONDON N22 6TZ ENGLAND.

FIRST EDITION: OCTOBER 2003

03 04 05 06 07 **a** 10 9 8 7 6 5 4 3 2 1

ISBN 1-55583-774-3

LIBRARY OF CONGRESS CATALOGING-IN-PUBLICATION DATA
LEDDICK, DAVID.
    THE SECRET LIVES OF MARRIED MEN / DAVID LEDDICK.— 1ST ED.
    ISBN 1-55583-774-3
    1. GAY MEN—BIOGRAPHY. 2. GAY MEN—RELATIONS WITH HETEROSEXUAL
WOMEN. 3. BISEXUALITY IN MARRIAGE. I. TITLE.
HQ75.7.L43 2003
305.38'9664—DC21   2003052255

CREDITS
COVER PHOTOGRAPHY BY AIREDALE BROTHERS.
COVER DESIGN BY MATT SAMS.

Contents

for Andrew Sargent

Introduction

We were sitting at Plouf, the restaurant of the moment in San Francisco, on a Friday night. Plouf has the cutest French waiters outside of France—perhaps even *in* France. Lights flickered on the terrace where we were eating, the noise was loud, the food was good, and the wine flowed freely.

My friend Ray was telling us about his encounter with the famous English actor Charles Laughton. Ray had been a handsome young actor in Hollywood right after World War II. Things were not moving particularly well for him then, and he said to his agent very insistently, "I want to do a play."

Bertolt Brecht was still in Hollywood, having passed the war there, and plans for the first production of his play *Galileo* were in the hands of Charles Laughton. When Ray's agent called, he was told that, unfortunately, the play was already cast. The agent said, "But you really must see this young man." Brecht agreed.

Ray's reading for the second lead pleased Brecht and particularly impressed Brecht's wife, Helene Weigel. Ray and Helene Weigel bonded on sight. She felt strongly that he was right for the part, and both Brecht and his wife insisted that Laughton see Ray for the part.

The following day Ray returned to the Brecht home. Soon the large, shambling figure of Charles Laughton appeared at the door, his arms filled with books. As he entered, a book fell to the floor. Ray attempted to pick it up, and Laughton glared down as him. "Leave it there," he said and proceeded to the next room.

While Ray read, Laughton sat sunken in a large chair, his large jowly face equally sunken in depression. When Ray finished, Laughton's baggy countenance opened and he said, "Beautiful."

Ray was added to the production. While in rehearsal Laughton invited Ray to his home one evening and read Walt Whitman's poems to him for hours. Ray was intimidated by Laughton's overwhelming presence. He clearly understood that Laughton wanted some kind of physical relationship, so Ray responded only with an actor's interest. While Ray was reading, Laughton paused at one point to say, "You resemble a young blacksmith. I don't mean that to reflect on your class background."

After the reading Laughton said, "You know, the other day on stage you made a gesture that was slightly effeminate. The director said to me, 'Do you think he's one of *those*?' and I assured him that you weren't, couldn't possibly be."

He then added, "I have a streak of that myself, you know. About a yard wide."

I then told everyone at the table the story about the time Laughton's wife, the actress Elsa Lanchester, returned home one evening to find her husband and a young man entwined on the couch. She rushed upstairs and spent the entire night fretting about what she should do about the situation. In the early dawn she decided. She went downstairs and got rid of the couch.

Ray Unger's story was not new. He was eventually gotten rid of, too.

As opening night approached, rehearsals became more intense. Many young actors in the Hollywood community began to attend them. At a break one day a young actor Ray knew slightly came backstage and introduced himself. He asked Ray whether they could take a short walk. Ray agreed, and as they walked the actor told him, "You're very good in the part and I just wanted to ask you if Mr. Laughton has ever invited you to his home." Ray told him he had been there four or five times. "Has he asked you to stay over?" the young actor asked. Ray said that he had been asked and had always refused.

"I just couldn't." Ray told our table.

Then the actor said, "My boyfriend is out front. He's going to replace you."

So Ray did not open in *Galileo*. He never had the opportunity to be seen by all Hollywood, which would have surely set him on the path to true stardom.

This story got me thinking about the many gay men married to women. I asked my dinner companions whether they knew any. Two handsome young who were a couple replied simultaneously, "We were both married to women." And so the ball began to roll.

As I set to work on this book, many people asked me about my next project. I would say, "I'm working on a book about gay men who are or were married to woman."

The next question was always the same. "But where do you find them?"

And my response was always the same: "They're everywhere."

One or two of the more astute would then respond, "We just don't know it, right?" And I would assure them they were right.

Among the men I interviewed for this book was one young man who told me that he felt he had to explain himself to his parents upon his divorce from his wife. He had only been married a few years and there were no children, but his wife had suffered several miscarriages, which his parents had deeply regretted. When he told them he was getting a divorce because he was homosexual, his mother replied, "But how can that be? You're capable of fathering children!" That fact alone has long been society's gauge of heterosexuality, as many men in this book can attest.

This book is an attempt in a series of interviews to explore this little-known—to many, unknown—phenomenon: the homosexual man who is or has been married to a woman. Writing this book has been a fascinating experience. My own preconceptions of these men, why they married and what they wanted were swept away after the first few interviews. Each man was different from the next. Broad generalities were obviously not going to be in order. And once all 40 interviews had been completed, I allowed myself to draw some modest conclusions included at the end of this book.

These interviews cannot truly be called research, but I have tried to balance the interviewees by age group, economic situation, and geographic position. Likewise, I have tried to make the book somewhat international in scope.

Many of the men I interviewed knew very little about other men who'd had experiences similar to theirs. Nor, surprisingly, did they seem very interested in finding out more. They were largely unwilling to admit they were not alone.

I frequently brought up Alexander the Great, a married homosexual who had conquered much of Mediterranean and the Middle East by the time he died at the age of 33. Sometimes I added that Frederick the Great—enlightened emperor of 18th-century Prussia, friend of Voltaire, and lover of many men—had as his wife a stiff little Teutonic princess whom he scarcely knew and rarely saw.

Louis XIV's infamous brother, Philippe, who was known simply as Monsieur, was unknown to any of the interviewees. In the licentious 17th century, he was famous for his love of handsome men, yet he married the beautiful Henrietta, sister of the King of England. Upon her death he married a large German-speaking princess. (There always seemed to be plenty of foreign princesses to go around in those days.) And that marriage produced a number of children. Monsieur seemed to like his wife just fine and she him. Those were more adult times.

The men I interviewed were all quite knowledgeable about one well-known married gay men: Malcolm Forbes. His dallyings with young men while raising a family of five were no secret to any of the men. And other contemporary names frequently came up: Calvin Klein, Oscar de la Renta, John Cheever, designer Russell Wright, museum director Everett "Chick" Austin, and others.

The fact that many gay men have once been married to women is little understood or recognized in the gay community. And the heterosexual world ignores that many of the sober, industrious men living right next door are gay. The desire to shed some light on the shared histories of these men is what prompted me to write this book.

A very longtime friend, now a widow, said to me when we discussed this book, "You must realize that there are many happy heterosexual marriages. Not everyone is hiding some kind of sexual feeling, running around doing things their spouses don't know about. You don't want your book to look like sour grapes, like a homosexual saying that no heterosexual is really happy behind the facade of their marriage." Her point was well-taken. But I do think there is value in sharing these stories, if only to reassure some men that they are not alone. What the straight world may think of these revelations I do not conjecture upon.

So here are the stories of men who for reasons of culture, career, parental compulsion, fear, or guilt—often a complex of many reasons—found themselves denying their own sexuality. And for most, these are stories of how they fought their way out of denial and forged the lives they live today.

Out of respect for the privacy of certain individuals, some names have been changed. Interviews for the profiles were conducted from 1998 to 2002.

The Hidden Generation: 60 and Up

What can one say about the group of men aged 60 to 88 who were interviewed for this book? Are there any common threads that bind them together?

Certainly, one can say that they come from an era when men who wanted to be successful in an upper-middle-class way could not conceive of not being married. In the wealthy suburbs of the major cities there was no place for a successful single man—and certainly no place for two men making a life together.

Curiously, society condoned two unmarried women living together. This was called "a Boston marriage" and was regarded as a satisfactory solution for two spinsters who could not find spouses.

But two "perennial bachelors," as *Time* magazine used to call single men with no plans of marriage, were not allowed this domestic arrangement without much looking askance. In the Victorian period Dr. Watson and Sherlock Holmes lived together without comment, but in mid-20th century America even the most naive thought this arrangement a little "funny."

Gay men could remain single if they escaped to New York, Hollywood, or Europe to work in the trades of theater, fashion, advertising, or in the newly burgeoning television industry. But most gay men did not aspire to this. It was too threatening and too unknown a world. Most people were not brave enough to go far away from the familiar to work at things they knew nothing about.

Like most American men of their generation, these men wanted to follow the same safe path their parents had chosen—or had been taught to choose This way of life required marriage. Indulging a desire for sex with men was possible only in the context of a rigidly concealed extramarital life, if at all.

During the post–World War II period, the role of women was greatly different than today. Few women aspired to have careers. Women went to college largely to equip themselves to be suitable wives for the men they met there.

In the social strata that didn't attend college, there was a similar theme. Boys and girls dated, they became serious, and the girl often became pregnant—hopefully at about time her boyfriend was finishing his high school education. They usually married after graduation.

This was the established pattern, and few resisted it. The women themselves made it difficult for the men in their lives to avoid marriage. There was nothing to redeem the dreaded fate of being a single woman who had finished her education but wasn't at least engaged. Marriage was the only road to take. This social philosophy led to many loveless marriages because it imagined true compatibility as a happy accident rather than as a precondition for union. And when the husband had known or unknown homosexual tendencies, it led to profoundly unfulfilled sexual relationships.

Many times interviewees from this age group revealed that outside of marriage to a woman there was simply no concept of a happy and fulfilled life for a single man. This group rarely voiced a great desire to have children. And on the other hand, members of this group most often prided themselves on marrying women of social position and a monied background.

In this mid-century world, social ascension was paramount; accordingly, these men were certainly the most ambitious of any of the age groups interviewed. They achieved more in the world of money and power than the men in the other groups.

This group also included the only men who would not have chosen a different life than the one they had led. Several would have preferred that their wives had not left them when they discovered their husband was homosexual. Widowers would in no way have traded in their country clubs and suburban parties to live with another man.

Those interviewees who did end up living with another man usually made an effort to replicate in a gay context their former heterosexual upper-middle-class lives. I should also note that men in this group most often requested they be given pseudonyms, or that I alter the details of their stories to ensure their anonymity.

These are the men who most feared being outed, being called homosexual, and being shunted aside by the society they so aspired to be part of. They have for the most part pursued their sexual satisfaction as a concealed subtext to an apparently heterosexual life.

One final note: There remains today a high level of denial among these men. We have all heard, "Denial: It's not just a river in Egypt." That aphorism is all too true in most of these cases. Even someone long divorced and sharing a life with an antique dealer in San Francisco wants to believe that no one back in his old home town is going to figure out that he is gay.

While some of these men are in contact with the gay world that was born in the 1960s and 1970s, most have chosen to live only on its fringes.

Carl Elliott:
FROM RICHES TO RAGS AND BACK

Unlike some of the interviewees, Carl Elliott has no problem with me using his real name. "If my children object to my using my real name for this interview, they'll just have to object," he says.

Carl is now a successful real estate agent and architect in Miami Beach. He has been married three times and has two children. He was born into money, inherited money, and earned lots of money. Now much of it is gone, but his life has been wild; he is rich in experience.

As a small child, Carl was raised in Washington, D.C., and New York City. His father was a well-to-do Washington lobbyist, who celebrated his 65th birthday eight days after Carl was born. As a young man, Carl's father had invested his inheritance in land in Texas. He had planned to raise cattle, but instead he struck oil. "Once he hit oil, the family was never the same," Carl says.

Carl grew up in a gilded, at times sinister-seeming household staffed by 15 servants. "There were more of them than there were of us," he recalls. When Carl was very young, a black manservant slept near him in his bedroom. This was to protect Carl from his older sister, who had tried to kill him several times—once by attempting to smother him in his sleep. "In old family movies of that time," Carl remembers, "as soon as the camera moves to me toddling across the lawn, suddenly my sister is there between the camera and me. She really hated me."

Carl assumed that the socialite he thought was his mother loved him. But she always seemed to be so busy and had little time for him. Carl was never told he was adopted, although he he remembers his mother saying to him as child, "Behave or we'll send you back." He never inquired where.

One of Carl's wives later said of Carl's mother, "She wasn't really beautiful, but she thought she was, so it added up to the same thing." Carl's mother had married Carl's father at the end of World War I, when she was 18. The newlyweds promptly moved to Washington, where she became a pillar of society. Carl wryly adds, "When she died, she still had an 18-inch waist."

Carl was 37—the year was 1976, and his mother had just died—when he first discovered that this distant woman was not his biological parent. He learned his own history when her will was read: Carl was the child of his father's mistress, who had been very young at the time of Carl's birth. She placed her baby in an orphanage and "returned to her life as a virgin in Palm Beach." But before she returned to Palm Beach, she had the foresight to have a million-dollar trust fund set up for her baby and another million-dollar trust fund set up for herself.

Already very successful in New York, Carl flew down to Palm Beach in his private plane to see his biological mother. She came to the airport to meet him, though it was not the meeting Carl had hoped for. "She came aboard the plane, stayed about 13 minutes, and made it very clear she did not want to know me, would never recognize me as her son, and that this was to be our only meeting. She had done her part in settling a trust fund on me. There would be nothing else. And she left." When asked whether she had at least handled this difficult interview elegantly, Carl answered, "She was beautifully dressed. That was about as far as the elegance went. I was crushed."

This meeting also changed Carl's view of his father. Carl discovered that had been rescued from the orphanage where he had been placed when he was 10 months old. Of course, he remembers nothing. "Now I think my father came to get me only because he wanted his money back," Carl says. "As long as he had me with him he could handle my trust fund."

But this history didn't play any obvious role in his early interactions with his father. "I adored him," Carl says. "He took me to the Oak Room at the Plaza Hotel in New York and sat me up on the end of the bar and gave me a Roy Rogers to drink while he was with his pals." Carl's father frequently took his young son with him to the office and spent a good deal of time with him.

However, at the age of 8, Carl was sent to military boarding school. He was in and out of many such schools throughout his teen years. When asked whether his sexual explorations with other boys began at this time, he replies, "You could say that was one of the reasons I changed schools a lot." He adds, "I think I was a very scared kid."

Carl feels that in some ways his father liked his craziness and bad behavior and rewarded him for it. Upon finishing military academy at 18, Carl had a heart-to-heart conversation with his father, telling him he feared he was homosexual. His 83-year-old father replied in a jocular manner, "That makes a lot of sense. You've been a sissy since you were 2."

Carl was enraged by his father's reaction, and two days later ran off with a girl he refers to as "a local redhead." His family had numerous homes, one of them in Huntington, West Virginia, where wealthy Kentuckians maintained vacation residences. He says, "Both of my parents were from Kentucky, but there was nowhere good enough in Kentucky for them and other people like them. They all kept homes in Huntington, and where my parents went, I went."

The redhead was the daughter of a beauty shop owner and the same age as Carl. They married at 18 and consummated their union in a nearby motel. But Carl's father had the marriage promptly annulled. "It was as though it had never happened," Carl remembers. "There was no trace of it left in the records. Later the girl's father wanted some money from my father and he was told, 'I don't spend money on damaged goods.'"

Carl then entered college. He chose the University of Cincinnati because he wanted to study architecture and the school offered a program that allowed students to alternate study semesters with work semesters. Carl was determined to not be totally reliant on his father for his education. "Although my father paid for the first two years, I was on my own after that."

It was in Cincinnati that Carl had his first real relationship with another man. He became the lover of an older man who owned a gay bar across the Ohio River from Cincinnati, where wilder living was permitted. Carl says, "I've always liked older men, but finally he became so possessive and jealous I had to leave him." Carl never lived with this man but, "we spent a lot of time together in a motel he also owned."

When asked if he had loved this man, Carl says, "I don't think I was in love. I think it was a kind of experimentation. We didn't live together because I lived in a fraternity. I had one gay fraternity brother, and he knew what was going on. We used to go to gay bars together. He was a good friend. But finally I just left town on one of my work semesters and I never saw my lover again."

Not long afterward Carl married a second time. And again he proposed to a young woman from Huntington whom he had met while he was living there with his parents. "She had the worst disposition of anyone I ever met," recalls Carl. "Why in the world I married her I have no idea. I was screwing her. It was the early 1960s. I guess that's what you did then."

Carl adds that his fiancée's periods were very irregular and that while they were dating she was repeatedly convinced she was pregnant. But she was still not pregnant when they married. At the time Carl still had to finish two more years of his six-year architectural program. Carl and his new bride both planned to work and agreed to have children later in life. But their married life soon took a different course: "She promptly got pregnant for real. She never worked. My daughter was born while I was still in college."

Carl and his wife remained married for ten years and had two children. The family remained in Cincinnati until Carl received his degree. Then Carl suddenly developed tuberculosis. He withdrew to his parent's farm in Kentucky and went to bed for six months.

Although Kentucky required all TB patients to go to a sanitarium, Carl's records were altered with the help of his adoptive mother's cousin, Louis Mayo, founder of the Mayo clinic. After six months of bed rest Carl was declared cured.

The young couple then moved to New York City and took up residence in the Plaza Hotel, where Carl had once sat on the Oak Room bar when he was a child. When queried about how all this was paid for, Carl revealed that at 21 he had come into his trust fund, so money was not a problem. The small family remained at the Plaza Hotel and later moved to the Stanhope Hotel to be nearer a satisfactory school for their daughter. Meanwhile, Carl had started litigation to take occupancy of his father's 14-room apartment, which had been decorated by Dorothy Draper and had a fixed rent of $1,000 a month. Carl won his case, and the young Elliott family moved in.

During this same time, Carl opened an architectural firm that specialized in planning and building office space in skyscrapers. The business had romantic perks, too. "I met a major developer who was also a married man, and we had a little affair. He was older than I was but, like I said, I always liked that. Through him, my business went crazy."

When I wryly suggested that perhaps Carl had fucked his way to the top, he laughed and said, "Not at all. I didn't sleep with him for career reasons. I have always devoted myself to doing my best. I don't worry about the money. I try to be honest and fair and that's how it always worked. My company was the best in New York for planning how to organize office space when companies moved into a new building. We did it right and it was very successful."

Carl soon met Geraldine, a very talented young American who would become his third wife. She was still working in Italy when they first met. She then went to work for Carl, rejected his amorous advances for four years. Finally, in 1969, Geraldine married Carl after he had divorced his second wife.

Before the divorce, Carl's second wife had been unhappy in New York and insisted on moving to Chicago. Carl had four very successful offices—in New York, Chicago, Los Angeles, and San Francisco—so relocating his family to Chicago posed no great problem. However, in Chicago Carl's wife began an affair with a man who lived across the hall from their apartment in the John Hancock Center. The end result was that Carl and his second wife each filed for divorce at the same time in the late '60s.

Carl doesn't see dishonesty—at least on his part—as one of the factors that contributed to the divorce "I had always been up front with my [second] wife about what I called my bisexuality. During my marriage to her, I fooled around very little, but if I was out on a business trip I might drop in at a gay bar or a bathhouse. I'm what I call a 'sexual opportunist.' I don't really pursue it. I'm not a predator. But if it was right there, I would go for it." He adds, not without a tinge of irony, "I think she'd just as soon that I took it somewhere else instead of bringing it home to her. None of my wives liked sex very much. But they were all very glamorous. My father had a quote, and he's the only one I ever heard use it: 'Sleeping with your wife is too much like incest for me.'"

Carl's second wife used her knowledge of her husband's extra-marital sex life to her benefit in the divorce settlement. Because Carl admitted to being bisexual, he was denied any visitation rights to his children. The wife was awarded $250,000, and each child was allotted $600 a month (a hefty sum 35-odd years ago). Carl would never see his children again. His ex-wife promptly married her neighbor and disappeared from Carl's life—only to reappear some ten years ago badly in need of money. Carl then gave her another $40,000 and also bought an apartment building for each child. Though they have accepted his generosity, neither child has seen fit to reconnect with Carl.

The year 1970 was a major turning point for Carl—and one with mixed blessings at best. He had sold his business for a great deal of money, and he had just married Geraldine the year before—and he was drinking very heavily. He says, "I told myself it was about not getting any visitation rights." But he admits his drinking could also have been related to his not hidden, but unresolved, homosexuality.

Carl and Geraldine then decided to take two years off. They rented a yacht and wandered about the Mediterranean and Aegean Seas. Of those days, Carl reminisces, "I had too much money and no one around me except takers, including my wife, who was very good at squirreling things away for herself. I had no one to give me advice."

After two years of carousing and drinking about the Mediterranean, Geraldine decided she'd had enough and returned to New York, where Carl still had his 14-room apartment. Carl soon followed her, but still couldn't control his drinking. "I was doing what I was doing to escape life," he now admits. "I used to say, 'I drink for transportation.' Fortunately for me, cocaine hadn't come into great use, so I was only escaping into alcohol and sex."

Eventually, Geraldine had Carl declared incompetent and took possession of his money—to which Carl said, "Screw that, I can drink without you." And for the next four years he lived as a New York City street person. "I was kicked out of a men's shelter in New York for messiness and bitchiness," he recalls. Carl's tone of voice is almost astonished as he thinks about those years. "It was really self-imposed. I didn't have to do it."

A woman friend happened to run into Carl on the Bowery and engineered his rescue. "I expected to drink myself to death, but you can't count on that." Carl says. "My friend took me home, detoxed me, cleaned me up, and loaned me a bicycle to get to AA down the street. That was October 1976. I haven't touched alcohol or drugs since."

Carl then went back to Geraldine. He gives her credit for saying when she saw him, "Welcome home."

"I thought she was the greatest person for doing that." Carl says.

Carl and Geraldine created a new life for themselves, buying a farm near Washington, D.C. Geraldine painted while Carl began to launch a new career in the city. They only met on weekends, when they were always surrounded by many friends and acquaintances in their country home. They never resumed an intimate relationship, since Carl had forsworn being heterosexual or even bisexual "As soon as I got sober, I never slept with another woman."

In Washington Carl began a pattern of having both an older boyfriend and a younger boyfriend. These were sexual relationships that came and went. Finally, when he was 54, Carl decided to come to grips with his homosexuality and face it squarely. He says, "I didn't really decide to deal with it until I had been 18 years sober. I never really wanted a gay lifestyle. It was nothing I thought I would enjoy. After my first couple of boyfriends I thought the gay world was very cruel. It's a difficult world to enter at 54 when you don't have the looks or the charisma or the magnetism to attract in an obvious way. I've had to depend on the openness of my personality since I don't have the magnetism or the looks."

At that time his wife and he had decided to move to a warmer climate. They investigated Miami Beach, Key West, Venice (California), and Palm Springs. They opted for Key West, where Carl opened a small gallery to display his wife's paintings and those of selected friends. It was the first time that his wife and he had actually lived in the same house on a permanent basis during their marriage—and it didn't work out. After nine months Geraldine departed for a summer holiday on Mykonos and Carl moved to Miami Beach. Returning after a month away, his wife appeared in Miami Beach and wanted to move in with him. Carl refused. Their marriage was over. Geraldine returned to her hometown of Detroit.

Carl explains that his decision to be on his own was largely based on his wife's constantly pushing alcohol his way. She would serve him wine at dinner, and she herself drank heavily and indiscriminately used prescription drugs and mood enhancers. "I would probably be with Geraldine today," Carl says, "but she was just too crazy."

Carl now has a Florida real estate license and is a well-respected professional in the Miami Beach area. He lives alone but is embarking on a friendship with a younger man that may develop into something. Or it may not. Carl is cheerily ready for anything. But through these many ups and downs, has Carl Elliott ever been in love? Has he ever felt the kind of love that wrecks your life when it falls through? "I think I'm as close to that with the friendship I'm building now as I ever have been before," he says. "But I'm not sure. Usually when something goes wrong, I feel bad for three or four days, and then I get up and get going again."

Colonel Brendel Mixer:
THE MAN WHO WOULDN'T HAVE IT ANY OTHER WAY

Colonel Brendel Mixer is 88. He stands straight, walks briskly, and may well be as handsome today as he ever was.

He came out of the closet to his gay friends in Tulsa, Oklahoma, two years ago—the year his wife died. He is a curious combination: a raconteur who discusses his sexual interests with people he trusts, yet he is also an official personality who has spent his life associated with the military.

The Colonel retired to Tulsa almost 30 years ago. He had served as a recruitment officer there several times in his career. Both his wife and he liked Tulsa and had made many friends there. Curiously, Tulsa ranks second only to San Francisco in the percentage of male homosexuals in its population.

In this covert but strangely overt city, the Colonel feels comfortable. It is a place where his long career in the military is respected. It is a place where the American military's "don't ask, don't tell" policy has long prevailed in everyday civilian life, as it still does in many less urbane parts of the country. If anyone in Tulsa who knows the Colonel well suspects that he is not entirely heterosexual, they do not ask.

On the other hand, there are plenty of restaurateurs, bar owners, bookstore managers, store clerks, and blue-collar workers in Tulsa who make no bones about their preference for other men.

They readily accept the Colonel as one of them and encourage his enthusiasm for the beauty of men.

Brendel Mixer was brought up in upper-middle-class circumstances in St. Paul, Minnesota. He worked in the family banking firm in his early years, dated proper young women, and attended the requisite balls and dinners that formed a prelude to marriage in that milieu. Brendel's failure to marry while he was still young raised no eyebrows during the Great Depression. Most people thought he was just waiting for the right girl.

Not yet 30 when World War II began, Brendel entered an officer training program open to college graduates and joined the Army Air Force. Although he was trained to fly, his talents were administrative; he spent the war as a staffer for several different generals.

The Colonel is close-mouthed about his sexual adventures during World War II, but as was true of so many other men in the military, he must have been thrown into many situations where men who were drawn to other men could meet without detection and share their bodies. The Colonel thrived in the military atmosphere, perhaps because his rather formal personality served him well there. And certainly, he must have been excellent at his work, since he advanced rapidly in rank.

At the close of the war, the Colonel decided to remain in the service, which did not particularly disturb his well-bred Minnesota family. When the separate branch of the Air Force was formed in 1947 he transferred to it—an intelligent move for an officer who was not a West Point graduate.

Above all, the Colonel has been a highly social creature, his somewhat aloof demeanor notwithstanding. Despite his closeted homosexuality and the restrictions of bourgeois living, he seems to have suffered very little. He has always resolved to make whatever adjustments he had to make in order to fit his sexual orientation into the world he chose to inhabit.

In the tradition of the British aristocracy, repression was not a consideration for him. If he needed sexual release, he pursued it as an activity outside of and concealed from his conventional life.

With turning 40 not too far off, the Colonel married a young woman of good family from his hometown. Alicia Mixer wasn't particularly young herself. In her early 30s, she must have been thought an appropriate choice. This may not have been a dramatic or romantic love match, but the Colonel was sincerely fond of his wife and enjoyed the many years he spent in her company. They had two sons and two daughters.

There seems to be no reason to believe that Alicia did not enjoy her life as an officer's spouse. Always popular and well-respected, the Colonel was not a negligent husband. If he indulged in sexual escapades when his military assignments took him away from home, there was no readily apparent reason for Alicia to suspect any shenanigans.

After Alicia's death, the Colonel, then 86, began to allow himself a much more open social life among his homosexual acquaintances. But in this aspect, too, Tulsa was far from St. Paul, Minnesota, as well as the military world where he had spent much of his life.

It does not strike the Colonel as peculiar that his innermost needs were never truly known to his wife or his children. But in his world, confidences of any sort are often seen as potentially embarrassing. Husbands and wives who share the Colonel's mindset often maintain a certain distance with each other—and even with their children. Fathers in particular rarely express any real emotions, which are considered unmanly. As a rule, American men, heterosexual or homosexual—and especially the Colonel's contemporaries—don't tell their wives how they feel, nor do they share their feelings with their children.

Colonel Mixer has never wished this lack of familial closeness wasn't the case. A lifetime without what many people would consider true marital intimacy does not seem to have disturbed him. And to be sure, he is proud of his heritage. In his home he displays to visitors the family portraits that link him to the early pioneers of the Middle West. One portrait of a female ancestor shows an extremely good-looking woman, her beautiful face gazing out between two wings of dark hair. On the mantelpiece in his living room are other photographs of his dashing and stylish mother, his beetle-browed and aggressive businessman father, and Alicia in her youthful and ladylike loveliness. Military awards and framed newspaper clippings are in the Colonel's bedroom—all testimonials to a long military career, of which he has every right to be proud.

But one of Colonel's sons is gay. He has violated the taboo against intimacy and wants his father to come out as a homosexual. The Colonel is irritated by this—and in some ways understandably. To officially notify old friends and acquaintances in the Twin Cities and the military would serve no purpose in his eyes and only embarrass both him and them. Socially, it would not be the correct thing to do, as it would only alienate old friends of his now-deceased wife.

On the other hand, the Colonel is totally out to the group of friends with whom he spends most of his time in Tulsa. He makes no pretense of not being interested in other men and seems at ease when younger men kid him about his sex life.

Ultimately, the fact that openly admitting his homosexuality to the world might result in a new level of closeness to his children and old friends does not seem to be of great interest to the Colonel. He feels he has been as close to people in his lifetime as he has wished to be.

There is something of the 18th century about Colonel Brendel Mixer. As was the case with the Marquis de Sade's father, who was repeatedly arrested in the Tuileries gardens in Paris for consorting with other men in the shrubbery, the Colonel dismisses the details of his life as inconsequential. He regards his sexual interests as a kind of eccentricity to be indulged, but in no way will he allow it to interfere with family connections and social intercourse, let alone control over money.

The Colonel doesn't talk about homosexuality in physical terms. Issues such as whether one is a top or a bottom or whether one likes to give or receive blow jobs are technicalities he is unwilling to discuss. It may be that his physical experience with other men has been limited and that much of the sexual satisfaction he receives takes the form of fantasy. As with some of the Victorians, his sexual attraction may be internalized and poeticized.

When asked if at any point in his life had he ever wished to have a permanent, long-term relationship with another man, Colonel Brendel Mixer says very firmly and very clearly, "No. In no way. I liked my life exactly as it was. I would not want to have changed it in any way."

Henry Rednell:
HE WAS NEVER ASKED AND NEVER TOLD

Henry Rednell is from the Texas-Louisiana border country. The Rednells were early settlers in this fertile, rolling part of the South. His father's ancestors were from Scandinavia and came to the area shortly after the Civil War to farm and run a smithy for the reshoeing of horses. His mother's family was a mixture of French settlers—not Cajun, but New Orleans aristocrats—and more recent Italian immigrants, but deeply Catholic on all sides. His father's family were casual Protestants; there was little or no protest when Henry was brought up in the Catholic faith.

It has been a long voyage from the small-town life of the border area where Henry was born immediately after World War I to his present position as the director of a prestigious drama, dance, and art center in the Pacific Northwest. Now, at 81, his life has been neatly divided into two completely different halves.

When Henry was a young boy, his mother did not feel that the education offered in his hometown was adequate, and at 10, Henry was sent to a Southern military boarding school. He remained in this academy until he was ready for high school, when he transferred to a college preparatory military school in another part of the South. He spent his college years at a Catholic university near Washington, D.C. He graduated with a degree in science, although it was understood that he would return to Louisiana to take over his father's businesses, which included not only major land holdings but also a highly successful chain of hardware stores that had evolved from the family's blacksmith days.

Not having great enthusiasm for the family business, and with war in the offing, Henry Rednell enlisted in the Army, or more specifically, the Army Air Force, where he trained as a bomber navigator. Because of his years in military schools, Henry was an apt student. When he finished his training he was assigned to remain at his training station as an instructor in his own specialty. He eventually taught advanced science courses. When his own students began to return to the base after seeing action in Europe, Henry began to get itchy to fight in the war himself.

Through school friends he was able to apply for duty with the O.S.S., a military group drawn from all the services to infiltrate and work behind enemy lines. This organization was the predecessor of today's C.I.A. Henry's bilinguality (he was brought up speaking French as well as English) may have counted for something in this change of duty.

The war in Europe was winding down when his training was completed, and he was assigned to duty in India. He remained at an O.S.S. office there until VJ Day arrived. He liked his duty so much that he contrived to stay on, even though the British were eager to get American armed forces out of India as rapidly as possible.

While at his teaching post in the United States, Henry had fallen in love with his commanding officer's daughter. A handsome young man, even more so in his officer's uniform, he had vied for and captured the young woman's affections, but her father convinced them not to marry until after the war. The older man reasoned that, as soldiers were being lost in great numbers, it would be better for his daughter not to be a widow, perhaps with a child, at the war's end.

By a great coincidence the father of Henry's fiancée was assigned as commanding officer to the military base in India where Henry was stationed. His potential father-in-law suggested he remain there as an aide-de-camp on his staff, which Henry did.

In due time the older officer was transferred back to the United States, and Henry accompanied him as part of his staff. There he married his fiancée, and he remained on her father's staff for several years until his own father's retirement loomed and Henry was pressured to return to Louisiana to take the helm of the family business.

He and his wife had three children in the early years of his managing the family stores and land. His mother had died while he was in college, but his wife followed in her footsteps by finding the local educational facilities inadequate for their growing family.

His wife's solution was to take up residence in New Orleans so that their children could attend school there. Henry would commute for long three-day weekends to be with them.

Henry doesn't say specifically that one reason for his wife's change of residence was boredom with small-town living. But he does say that she soon became active in arts activities in New Orleans and quickly formed an interesting new group of friends.

The family business became extremely successful under Henry's management. There was plenty of money for a relatively lavish lifestyle in New Orleans and plenty of time for the young couple to interest themselves in museum committees, local theater groups, and touring dance companies.

One of these touring ballet groups brought a young Russian émigré dancer to the attention of Mr. and Mrs. Rednell. He was to become Henry's first male lover.

Henry admits that one of the reasons he became interested in ballet was the beauty of the male dancers. Both of the Rednells became extremely friendly with the talented young Yuri, who frequently stayed with them when he was on tour. On one of the ballet company's swings through the South, the Rednells thought it would be fun to travel with the dancers on their tour through the nearby states. They did this, sharing a suite of rooms in hotels with Yuri as they traveled.

Finding himself so squarely in temptation's way couldn't have been an accident. Henry's destiny arrived one day when he was in the shower between their two bedrooms in a hotel suite and Yuri slipped into the shower with him.

Henry says that this was the first time he had truly made love with another man. He was 35.

When asked what kind of homosexual preliminaries he might have had, he remembers that before he went to boarding school the family gardener once kissed him in the garage. He told no one and found it puzzling. In boarding school he had a single experience when another student slipped into his room and bed one night and masturbated him. He remembers thinking, *I'm not doing anything so I'm innocent.*

Further along in school he had a handsome, sports-playing friend who used to invite him home on holidays. There they showered together and masturbated each other. But that was as far as it went.

While in the military, he spent time with an enlisted man—an artist who loved to visit temples and bazaars in India. But their relationship was filial, not sexual.

His relationship with Yuri convinced him that he had to pursue his interest in men, but he soon met with disappointment. Henry told his wife about his sexual encounter with Yuri, and she was sympathetic. Perhaps she had even anticipated something of the like for herself. But she asked that he not repeat the experience.

However, when Yuri passed through New Orleans again, they did repeat the experience. And more than once. Henry was very much in love, but Yuri explained, not unkindly, that a relationship wasn't possible. He had always been promiscuous and intended to continue to be. Henry took this very hard. Henry remarks that if it hadn't been Yuri it certainly would have been someone, as he was ready to explore his own sexuality.

After Yuri's departure from his life Henry made some homo-sexual acquaintances in the cultural world of New Orleans. Through them he met other men whom he permitted to perform oral sex on him. He considered himself to be "trade" and not truly homosexual, but one of his partners said, "Henry, you're just kidding yourself."

Meanwhile his life continued, with his wife and children living in New Orleans and his commuting in from his business out of town. It was through his wife that he met his first more permanent lover. She had made the acquaintance of a young man recently out of the Navy whom she found very interesting. "You must meet him," she told her husband. One can't help wonder whether she wasn't subconsciously trying to place a lover in his path, or perhaps even delegating him to have the sexual adventures she was perhaps too timid to have.

His new lover was to precipitate his divorce. The young man fell deeply in love and was unhappy only seeing Henry surreptitiously on his weekend visits to New Orleans. He announced that he planned to move to the small town where the Rednell family businesses were. Henry forbade him to do so, but the young man came anyway and moved into the family home. Henry was able to pass him off as an old acquaintance on a visit for a short while, but inevitably his wife heard about the affair and demanded a divorce, which they obtained very amicably. His family knew the reason for the divorce and regretted it, but they never discussed it and never treated Henry differently.

After the divorce Henry changed his life completely. He sold the family businesses, settled a large income on his wife and the children, and returned to school to study theater and art.

He enrolled at a Texas university, where he got a Master's degree in the history of theater and art. He was older than the other students and quickly managed to have three male lovers and a girlfriend on the side. His first lover was a graduate student who was married and had children. To him he added another male graduate student and an undergraduate. Henry recounts that at the end of one day he had slept with all three of them at different times during the school day. He also dated a sorority girl whom he slept with occasionally, "to keep up appearances."

At no time did he live with any of his lovers, nor did he wish to. He says, "In fact, I enjoyed my life very much. I wanted to eat when I felt like it, sleep when I felt like it, make love when I felt like it. Of course, that doesn't mean I didn't feel jealous of some of them." One of these lovers eventually moved to Paris, and Henry has continued to see him through the years.

Upon graduation he taught at the university for several years. Then an opportunity arose for him to head an arts center in Fort Worth. He took the job, and was very successful in creating a real interest in the arts in Fort Worth. He became a local personality of some note, and in only a few years was contacted by a much larger arts center in a large city in the Northwest. He didn't seriously consider the possibility at first, but during his interview he realized there was a major opportunity for him in the center's plans for expansion in both size and activities. He accepted the offer and remained there. He is now 81.

Sexually, Henry has had a series of long-term lovers, but he doesn't acknowledge any of them as a true companion. As the director of an important arts center, much of his life has been a combination of social and fund-raising activities. He has had to squire about the wives and widows of tycoons, and his position has required, in his own eyes, that he be single and available. He admits that in some ways he is in denial. He says, "Things have changed so radically in my lifetime I realize that I don't have to maintain any facade. But I don't enjoy the company of groups of gay men, I don't like their gossip, and I don't like being identified with them. I also realize that people probably do know about me, but I don't recognize it. I guess that's where the denial comes in."

Henry has had a series of younger lovers who have lived in the same house with him, but they were always identified as young men earning money for a college education by working as his houseboy. He has occasionally gone to the movies with them but never to any kind of official social activity. Of these young men he says, "I was always the dominant partner. I've never been screwed."

He no longer has a young man living in his house with him, and he plans to retire soon from the directorship of the arts center. It has consumed many years of his life, and he has been eminently successful in expanding it and making it a powerful force for the arts in his part of the world. His last lover was one of his much younger gardeners. He says that after a recent session of lovemaking he decided that he would put an end to his sex life. He told the young man, "This interferes with your gardening, and I feel silly. It just seems inappropriate." Henry Rednell died in early 2003.

Bill Rangle:

THE MAN WITH THE WIFE UPSTAIRS

Bill Rangle is still married, although he has had a number of lovers and many one-night (or less than one night) stands in the last 30 years. In that fact alone he is in the minority of the men interviewed for this book. As did many of the older men, he solved the problem of his sexual need for other men by living a kind of double life, preserving a domestic family life with wife and children. But his life differs in that, though his wife knows he prefers men, he has remained married.

Bill explains his situation by saying, "I always felt that I should have a domestic life with a family. It never occurred to me that I could live otherwise." When asked whether his own home life as a child was pleasant and whether his parents were happily married, he replies in the negative. However, his maternal grandparents (and aunts, uncles, and cousins) did provide an example of close kinship. There were plenty of family gatherings filled with joy, humor, and kisses.

Born and raised in Toronto in a traditional upper middle-class family, Bill particularly liked summer vacations as a child, which he usually spent with his mother's parents, who lived in a very small town on the shore of Lake Ontario. There his grandparents were demonstrative and affectionate with him.

As a child he was allowed to study tap dancing and with a girl partner always starred in his dancing school recitals. But as his teen years approached he got the message that this was not something that a boy's boy did. His dancing stopped.

He didn't completely abandon his interest in art, and in his eighth and ninth grades he had a teacher who strongly encouraged him to study art and plan a career as an artist. His family agreed to this on the condition that he pursue a teaching degree rather than plan to be a "serious" artist. His parents imagined him living in some garret, barely eking out an existence.

He attended a Midwestern college in the United States, the same one that his influential teacher had attended. He graduated in 1959 and taught for a year in an elementary school in the college town.

He realized that the demands of teaching were draining his creativity. But, since he was about to be drafted, he was able to abandon his teaching career without any parental disapproval by enlisting in the Army.

Before enlisting he married his college sweetheart, a young woman with a creative imagination from a much more liberal and—to him—interesting background than his own. He liked her parents and he liked her, although he says that he was never in love with her. He says, "You know how you are at that age, put close to warm flesh you can always get sexually excited."

His new wife did not accompany him when he was sent to Japan after being trained as a technician in security for the Army. Instead she remained in her parent's hometown in Wyoming, where she worked as a teacher.

In time she joined him in Japan and was hired to teach in a school for military dependents. They were able to live together in a small house near his base. At first his wife did not like living in a foreign country, but soon she made friends among her fellow teachers and came to like their life in Japan.

His military work also allowed Bill to work as a librarian, which enabled him to do research and gather information about the world of commercial art in New York. He greatly admired the work of a famous New York designer and decided that when he left the Army he would try for a career as a commercial artist himself.

When his military service was over he and his wife embarked for New York, where Bill enrolled in an art school to hone his skills as a commercial artist. After six months his teacher felt that Bill's goal of working as an advertising art director was within his grasp, so Bill prepared a portfolio and quickly had a job in a major advertising agency.

He didn't like his new career at all. His boss kept telling him not to waste so much time on sketches he was doing for his layouts, and it became clear to the young art director that what he really wanted to do was illustration.

Pursuing this, he enrolled in evening classes taught by the artist whom he had long admired. Bill's solutions for class assignments impressed the designer enough that at the course's conclusion he offered Bill an entry-level position at his studio. After a number of years with this internationally known studio, where much of his work won praise from the clients he served, Bill Rangle decided to become a freelance illustrator.

He moved to San Francisco, and he and his wife had a child. On the surface things looked good as his career moved forward satisfactorily in California. But below the surface his long-suppressed sexuality was stirring.

He remembers his sexual history as having begun with an incident in kindergarten. Another little boy and he were discovered playing with each other sexually by a horrified Miss Tannenbaum, who dragged Bill into a corner and hissed, "Do you want your mother to know about this?" Bill was petrified by the idea and repressed any thoughts of sex-play activities from then on.

In sixth grade he was playing in the woods behind his home when an older boy accosted him and wanted to know if he ever jacked off. Bill had no idea what this meant, and when the boy illustrated his meaning with gestures, Bill ran home deeply disturbed.

In high school he became fascinated with a handsome boy he saw in the locker room. Bill's budding lust must have communicated itself in some way; the boy taunted him about being effeminate after that. Although he did have some mutual masturbation encounters with another boy who lived in his neighborhood, he had extremely limited sexual experiences during his high school years. He dated a girlfriend and tamped down any feelings he had for men.

In college he continued to notice boys who titillated him but continued to repress those feelings. He dated a number of girls until he met the woman who would become his wife.

In the Army he encountered enlisted men who made no great effort to conceal their homosexuality. He became very friendly with one man who planned to become an actor after he left the service, but this was someone whose company he enjoyed very much, not someone who was sexually interesting.

There were a number of men among the teachers working with his wife who also made little attempt to conceal their gayness. One man rented a house near the base, which he shared with his sailor boyfriend. The two couples socialized, and through them Bill met other gay serviceman with whom he could have had affairs, but he chose not to do this.

The closest he came to a sexual encounter was with a Marine officer who ran the officers' club at the base. This officer invited Bill to his quarters for a drink on one occasion and inquired whether he would like to get intimate. Bill fled. One of the reasons, he explains, is that he has just a "sliver" of types that interest him sexually. One of these was a good-looking young Italian on the base who was a bodybuilder. Bill was fascinated with the dark young man and went to the gym with him occasionally, and he did invite him and his blond workout partner to go out on the town one evening after he won a prize in a military art contest. But this rendezvous led to nothing but frustration.

The years of repression began to take their toll. In New York Bill began to notice dark young men, whom he occasionally followed. In Times Square a young Puerto Rican he had been following, whom he'd thought hadn't noticed him, suddenly turned and said, "You want to go see a movie? I've got the biggest dick in New York City." In the darkness of a 42nd Street motion picture palace Bill Rangle began another phase in his sexual life. He was 28.

He saw the young Puerto Rican on a number of occasions. The young man wanted to be paid in some way, but theirs was a casual relationship and payment was often dinner or clothes.

After the Puerto Rican was a man from British Honduras. In addition to their sexual relationship, Bill helped the man to find a job and improve his English. On one occasion he told his wife he had to travel out of town, and indeed he did: to visit his friend's family with him in Honduras.

After moving to San Francisco, he began a relationship with a Mexican man who was the major romance of his life. They were lovers for ten years—until the other man died of lung cancer in 1984.

Through this period, Bill's life with his wife and family continued uneventfully. He slept with his wife from time to time, although theirs had never been a passionate relationship. He says of her, "My wife was a summa cum laude graduate. She was beautiful. I married her thinking of the potential of our lives together. I thought I would become passionate about her. And I wanted a family. I had never thought of myself in anything but a family setting."

It seems that his wife was never passionately in love with Bill either, which he discovered when their life together suddenly exploded. They were living in San Francisco. They had a child and had decided to adopt a second one—an Asian orphan who was a year and a half old at the time.

Precisely at the time that this new child was entering their lives Bill's wife discovered that he had a lover: the Mexican man he had been seeing for a number of years. In their angry discussions it came out that while in Wyoming before joining him in Japan, his wife had joined an older woman friend in weekend rounds of bar-hopping and picking up cowboys, with whom they had sex. In Japan she had also been infatuated with a pair of gay male teachers, with whom she had a ménage à trois.

Bill says, "This was the time when it would have been logical for our marriage to have broken up. I wanted to leave, but then I thought of my child and the newly adopted baby. I just couldn't leave those children in the lurch like that. So my wife and I decided to stay together and weather it out."

He went into psychoanalysis for two years "to straighten out," as he puts it. This was a time when homosexuality wasn't considered a disease but a "personality disorder." His doctor encouraged him to be more assertive and aggressive. Following this advice led Bill to get into fisticuffs with an imperious neighbor while walking his dog and to his being overly confrontational with various acquaintances. He abandoned his analysis just as his wife began hers of six years.

Her analysis resulted in her wandering off by herself for days at a time, leaving Bill to mother and father his two children by himself. Always a very capable artist and crafts worker, his wife began to isolate herself in a world of quilt making, a world she continues to inhabit today. Traveling, teaching, and corresponding with fellow quilt makers occupy most of her life, and she remains at arm's length from her husband. They both live and work in their own spheres.

Bill's two boys are grown up now and have lives of their own. One is married and has a child, and the other is living with a girlfriend he plans to marry.

Bill has never wished to have a long-term domestic relationship with another man, which he says falls outside his fantasies about men. He has always only been able to imagine a male-female domestic life with children, although his sex life has been elsewhere.

Since his Mexican lover died, Bill's sex life consisted of casual pickups and assignations with street hustlers. He discovered last year that he is HIV-positive. He felt that he had to offer his wife a divorce at the time of this discovery, but she has preferred to stay with him for the sake of preserving the family unit. Bill thinks her decision is influenced primarily by the fact that he supports her and provides the home she lives in. In her reclusive lifestyle she prefers to remain in the home they have shared for many years, though they work and live on separate floors and share a severely limited social life.

When asked whether he sees any pattern in his life, Bill Rangle says, "I never wanted to disappoint anybody. I always did my homework, and practiced the piano. I wanted to do what people expected of me." He feels that any success he has had in his life is linked closely to his wish to do what he saw was expected of him, more than any strong desire to compete.

He says that he does not feel guilty about betraying his wife. And quite unexpectedly, at the end of his interview he says, "I have a good many close friends who don't know about me. I have some friends who do know, but there are many others who don't, and those two groups of friends don't know each other." He explains further that he thinks his sons don't know or don't wish to know. He remembers a conversation with his older son, who was en route to Mexico City. Bill said, "Oh, I've been there." His son asked when and Bill replied, "Visiting with a friend."

His son said, "Don't tell me any more. I don't want to know anything more." This conversation led Bill to believe that his son is aware of Bill's gay tendencies and doesn't want to know any details or have any conformation of his suspicions.

Bill also added that at one time he belonged to a gay dad's association that to him seemed mostly dedicated to its members getting out of their marriages and outing themselves. Since he didn't want to do either of these things, he didn't remain with the organization, but he was very surprised at the large number of men who belonged to it.

At the close of our conversation Bill admits he suspects that many of his friends whom he assumes don't know about his homosexuality actually do know but simply are too embarrassed to broach the subject with him. So Bill Rangle, after many years, still lives a life of some pretense, more for his own comfort than for that of those around him.

Geraldo:
The Quintessential Gay Dad

Still strong-looking and still darkly handsome, Geraldo cuts a noticeable figure as he strolls down Lincoln Road Mall or sits sipping coffee in front of Books and Books bookstore in Miami Beach. He is a colorful, swashbuckling character, known to many in this tropical town where glamour is everything.

Geraldo is very forthright about his past. He grew up near Boston, married the daughter of a wealthy and prominent local man, had a son, separated from his wife after only a few years of marriage, gained custody of his son, whom he brought up, and now is retired. He has had a series of fun but short-lived careers in Miami Beach.

This thumbnail biography has more meat on its bones than one might suspect, once he elaborates on the details. He was aware of an attraction to other boys and men at an early age, and as a Catholic he felt compelled to bring his feelings into the confessional. However, he was very aware that in his hometown information could leak out of the confessional, so he traveled into Boston to a church where he was a stranger to admit his feelings to a priest.

He was about 14 at this time. The priest to whom he confessed said that it wasn't easy to be sure what these feelings meant and that Geraldo needed to have a private interview with the priest to discuss it.

Later, at the interview, the priest told him that he had to look at

Geraldo's private parts to determine whether he was truly homosexual, as there was a visible difference between heterosexuals and homosexuals. Geraldo, crying and embarrassed, dutifully dropped his trousers. The priest proceeded to fellate him.

Geraldo believes that his father was homosexual and that his father's constant derision of his young son was really motivated by the man's own guilt. Some years later, on entering a notorious bathhouse, Geraldo noticed his father's signature on the list above his. He believes that his father's constant suggestions that Geraldo was homosexual added to his determination to marry.

Geraldo's good looks and ebullient personality captured the attention of the daughter of a wealthy family. They had a long engagement, and before their marriage he found work in a large Connecticut town on Long Island Sound. His fiancée insisted that he contact one of her friends there, who had recently married and moved to this same town.

Geraldo says that the moment he met this young couple and saw the husband, fireworks exploded. He and the husband immediately became lovers. Shortly thereafter, when he was married, Geraldo and his new wife moved into a house down the block from their friends. While living there he became a father, enjoyed his new job, and met with his lover/neighbor regularly—usually once a week. They became shopping buddies and spent a lot of time together.

Geraldo's lover would have been content to leave their situation as it was, but after a few years Geraldo couldn't handle it. He wanted to leave his wife and hoped he and his lover might go away somewhere together, but his lover was unwilling to do this. Both men were Italian and lived in a web of family: parents, grandparents, brothers, sisters, in-laws, cousins. Geraldo was willing to turn his back on all this—perhaps even eager, considering his poor relationship with his father. But his lover could not imagine living outside this familial support system, so Geraldo left on his own. He moved to the West Coast and cut himself off from his former life.

However, the separation was not to be as simple as that. Through friends he heard that his wife, who had moved back to

Boston, had a very busy social life with other men, and that their child was being seriously neglected. He sued for custody in Boston and won, which required him to set up serious housekeeping as a father.

His son's growing up took place in Arizona, where Geraldo had found a new job. Although he never made any attempt to disguise his sexual orientation from his son and his son's school friends, he didn't "flaunt it" either. Geraldo maintained a solid home atmosphere with regular meals, help with lessons, much parental presence, and discipline when necessary.

In his teen years Geraldo's son had many friends who liked to hang out at his home. His son's having a gay dad gave him a certain cachet in his high school and was certainly never a source of unpleasantness, Geraldo says.

As his son entered adolescence Geraldo felt that it was necessary that they have a sit-down discussion about his own homosexuality, which Geraldo dreaded. On a flight to Boston he finally overcame his qualms and found the courage to have a heart-to-heart with his son. As he searched for words over Chicago, his son interrupted him: "Dad, are you trying to tell me that you're gay?"

Geraldo said that was exactly what he was doing. His son responded, "Aw, I've known about that for years." And the conversation was over.

When his son left for college Geraldo moved to Miami Beach. This was at a time when the town was just forming its new identity and was still very much a mix of old Central European retirees and new hippies. A few Art Deco hotels were being renovated, and a handful of investors were beginning to realize that the acres of empty beach and the low rents made a very attractive combination.

Geraldo's newly adopted career at this point was interior decorating. He rented an inexpensive space on Lincoln Road Mall to showcase some of the furnishings and decorations he had to offer. He also began to do inexpensive interior design for some of the new people who were beginning to buy houses and apartments in the area then called the Art Deco District, now called South Beach.

He had an Italian-style coffeemaker in the shop for himself and whoever was helping him as an assistant. One day a woman, smelling the aroma, walked in and said, "I'll have a cup of coffee."

Geraldo replied, "We're not a coffee shop, we're a decorating and antique shop."

The woman looked around at the tables and chairs and said, "Well, you certainly look like a coffee shop."

Geraldo gave her a cup of coffee and immediately launched a new and more lucrative business.

A few new restaurants were beginning to open on Lincoln Road Mall, many gay men were beginning to relocate to the area, foot traffic was picking up, and a coffee shop was just what everyone was waiting for. The little café did a brisk business. Geraldo had only to put a few tables and chairs out on the sidewalk to shift his business into its new persona. The swags, mirrors, and pillars inside made for a chic decor and remained for sale if anyone was interested.

In 1991 Hurricane Andrew trashed Geraldo's restaurant, which turned out not to be a catastrophe. The quick-witted entrepreneur decided to transform his business from a bohemian café into a black-leather bar, and within 24 hours he had reopened with a new nighttime identity. With the help of friends, the entire interior of the shop was painted with black enamel, and a secondhand bar was installed along one wall. As quickly as he reopened, Geraldo was a success. There were few gay bars in the area, and none catered to men in black leather outfits posing as toughies.

Geraldo's new business—his third in the same space—went roaring forward for several months, until city officials began to tell Geraldo that he did not have the kind of bar the citizens of Miami Beach approved of. Again thinking quickly, Geraldo's changed the name of his bar from the Bulldog to Peacock Alley and reopened his space as a piano bar. At this point he sold the business.

Although he has lately had some problems with his heart, Geraldo is still a social presence in Miami Beach. During his days as café owner and bar impresario he made friends with everyone in his community. He continues to enjoy the company of these many acquaintances, even though Lincoln Road Mall is now host to the Gap, Williams-Sonoma, Banana Republic, and a host of chic and up-market restaurants filled with chic and up-market people.

His son is happily married and living in Japan, where he teaches English. The relationship between father and son remains as loving as it has always been, but the fact that he lives halfway around the world may indicate something that does not come up in Geraldo's conversation. However, they do visit each other with regularity.

Geraldo recently had contact with the married lover of his early years. The man and his wife had tried to reach Geraldo through relatives. When they finally reached him they revealed that Geraldo's aunt had steadfastly refused to tell them of his whereabouts throughout the years, despite their frequent entreaties. Finally the aunt died. Her husband—Geraldo's uncle—had no problem with giving them Geraldo's address and phone number in Miami Beach.

Geraldo flew to Connecticut to visit the couple. He says that from the moment he left the plane it was clear that the electricity of the early romance still existed. His lover's wife, very seriously ill with emphysema, had been the determining factor in their finding Geraldo again, and he couldn't help but wonder whether she wanted her husband to reconnect with Geraldo before she died.

During dinner the first evening no one mentioned the earlier relationship. But after the wife, weak from her illness, excused herself to go to bed, Geraldo and his former lover took a walk through the Connecticut night. As they were walking the other man turned and said, "Why did you ever leave me?" They were immediately back on their old footing. But there was not to be a happy ending to this rekindling of old love.

The lover's wife did die before long, but her husband did not want to resume his relationship with Geraldo in an open way, which was the only way that Geraldo would accept. Geraldo's lover had children and grandchildren and couldn't handle having to confront them with the fact that Grandpa was gay. Despite this additional setback, the two men remain good friends.

Now Geraldo is a single retired man in Miami Beach, where he has a busy social life. He has a penchant for lost men, and from time to time takes someone home in an effort to domesticate them, but this has not proven to be successful. However, hope remains in Geraldo's heart. He is still ready for love and still on the lookout, his enthusiasm for life and romance undiminished.

Peter Blanc:
THE ACCIDENTAL MILLIONAIRE

Peter Blanc and I have a mutual woman friend: a German dealer in very beautiful Art Deco furniture, paintings, and drawings. Of Peter she says, "He's not really gay. *You're* gay. You always were. You never pretended otherwise. But Peter and [she names several other gay male friends who have been married] are not really gay. I don't know what they are thinking of!"

Regine has put her finger on something that is difficult to discuss and define. Seated at a table with half a dozen men, Peter Blanc would be the last you might single out as gay. Gray-haired, handsome (he was once a stand-in for the actor Peter O'Toole), affable, and thick-armed, he is everyone's picture of the ideal husband and father. Indeed, he is formerly married and the father of two daughters. His slowly shifting sexual direction as the years have passed seems not to have produced any great drama.

He was born in New York City and raised by unusual parents. His father, of a well-to-do German family, had been sent to Australia to study before World War I. When hostilities were declared with Germany, the young student moved in with his aunt's family and changed his name to avoid incarceration. His Australian aunt of German descent had married an Englishman, Mr. Blanc. From then onward her nephew was known as Blanc also.

After the war Peter's father became involved in unionizing activities and had to leave Australia for his own safety. He shipped out on a freighter for San Francisco, jumped ship, paid a midwife to swear she had been present when he was born in that city, and obtained an American birth certificate. He spent the rest of his life in America as an American. While in San Francisco he continued his interest in the labor movement and spent part of his life working in or negotiating with labor unions. He became a civil servant after settling down in marriage.

Peter's mother had an almost equally adventurous life for a woman of her era. She was born to a well-to-do Jewish family in Chicago and followed the usual paths for a nice, well-brought-up girl of the 1920s. But upon finishing college she wished to work, become the secretary of a very successful businessman and moved with his offices to New York. Although still a young woman, she was already a highly paid executive secretary living by herself when she met Peter's father—very unusual for a young woman of this time. It would only have been possible in a handful of the largest American cities.

So these two independent, intelligent people met and eventually set an example for married compatibility and admirable parenting any child might wish to copy. They knew a great mix of political and otherwise accomplished people of their day, whom they entertained frequently in their home. Peter and his younger brother were always treated as intelligent entities by these friends and were also thoroughly exposed to all New York could offer in the way of museums, theater, and sports events.

Peter attended the Bronx High School of Science, which was jammed to the gunwales with the brightest students in New York and the boroughs. He also had the advantage of having a highly social aunt. She was living in Argentina, married to an Englishman, and was traveling to Europe through New York after World War II. She took a special interest in her young nephew and made sure he attended dancing classes and met his peers in society. How his very liberal parents regarded this we don't know, but as Peter got older he was invited to social events of New York society, where his good-looking blond presence was appreciated.

From high school he proceeded to the Georgetown School of Foreign Service in Washington, and from there, always alert to adventure, he took a job as an overseer on a copra plantation in the interior of Panama. From there he was drafted into the army and was sent to Korea, where the war had just ended. After the Korean War he was separated from the army in Japan and embarked upon a two-year jaunt with a friend, returning slowly to the United States via lengthy stays in Asia and the Middle East. Slowly making his way through Thailand, India, and then Iran, he eventually found himself in Europe. In Seville he was an extra with the production of *Lawrence of Arabia,* which was filming interiors and some outdoor locations in Spain.

Since his height and coloring matched those of the film's star, Peter O'Toole, he became his stand-in and occasionally accompanied the actor upon some of his many collisions with the bottle.

Peter was also asked to model for *Playboy* fashion pages while he was in Barcelona, but it never occurred to him that either acting or modeling might be a possible civilian direction. The art director for *Playboy* took a fancy to Peter, but this came to nothing. Peter doesn't come right out and say he had secret fantasies about other men at this time, nor does he claim that he was completely unaware of his attraction. What he will say is, "I always wanted to have a family. I couldn't imagine not having family life. It just didn't occur to me to pursue anything else."

In a turn of events lifted from the pages of the book *The Talented Mr. Ripley,* Peter's parents encouraged a young friend to go to Spain to see Peter and suggest he return to New York and begin earning a living. Peter complied.

Upon his postwar return Peter discovered that jobs were not easy to find. He finally was employed by the realtors Webb and Knapp and became the assistant manager of the Graybar Building, adjacent to Grand Central Terminal and then home to the Condé Nast magazines.

He also found a girlfriend: the sister of a previous girlfriend with whom he had exchanged postcards during his wandering around the world. He had met his new girlfriend briefly while attending school in Washington. She was now living in New York as a divorcée with a small daughter. Blond, attractive Renée was the daughter of an extremely wealthy Canadian family and worked for the theatrical producers Feuer and Martin. She lived an exciting New York life. The young couple began living together, and when Peter was offered a job as manager for a building complex built by Webb and Knapp in Washington, D.C., he accepted it. And he asked Renée to marry him. They then took up residency in the capital.

The conventional flow of Peter's life was soon interrupted when Webb and Knapp declared bankruptcy. His job was gone, he was in a city where he knew few people, and he had a wife and child to support.

In a curious turn of events, he had answered an advertisement for tutoring in current events while he was in college in Washington. The woman who had placed the advertisement was a very pretty, newly divorced woman who was dating some of Washington's heaviest hitters. She needed to be briefed in order to carry on intelligent conversation. Peter was hired to do the briefing. He was 18 years old and well suited for the job. An extremely successful entrepreneur was among this beauty's suitors.

While waiting for his young lady friend to get ready for an evening out, the entrepreneur frequently discussed with Peter the capital and its affairs. They became good friends, and he remained a mentor to Peter for many years. It was he who helped Peter after he lost his job, hiring him to manage an old inn he owned in Virginia.

In addition to the historic inn, Peter and his mentor started the Wayside Theater. Through this enterprise Peter made many friends in the theater business.

By his late 30s, he and Renée had had a daughter, but they found their private life was slowly collapsing. Peter says that he was always more eager to make love than his wife, and that she wanted out of the marriage. Was it the possibility of making a more financially successful marriage that prompted Renée to want a divorce? Or did she sense that there was something not right at the core of it? Renée's own statement is: "I felt there was more to life. Peter didn't have enough passion for me." So she departed, and Peter was a bachelor again. Their divorce was amicable and he remained in very regular contact with his daughter and stepdaughter and continues to this day to supervise his ex-wife's business affairs. She did not re-marry and lives in Miami, where Peter now resides, and they see each other regularly.

After the work of renovating and managing the Wayside Inn, Peter was prompted to move back to Washington. There he launched a contractor's business that specialized in renovating old homes.

His older mentor reappeared in his life once again and asked him to manage a restaurant in a hotel building that he owned. There had never been a successful restaurant in this location, but Peter conceived a restaurant and bar that would appeal to the Washington crowd that was interested in the arts. This worked very successfully; it became one of Washington's premier restaurants throughout the 1980s. Without really meaning to, he became wealthy. He says, "It was just by accident."

He also began to experiment with male lovers during this time. One young man entered his life when his car broke down at a party on a snowy evening and he had to spend the night at Peter's. They became public lovers, and Peter took him everywhere with him in Washington. All of Peter's friends seemed to accept this with no problem, but of the relationship Peter says, "I think I was infatuated with the idea of having a love affair more than that I was in love with him."

Asked if he has ever really been in love, Peter admits to one true great romance with a younger man in his post-marriage period—a romance in which they exchanged love letters and he wrote poetry. Unfortunately the man was drafted, and while he was separated from Peter in the army, they drifted apart emotionally. He later died of leukemia.

During this time of experimenting with men, Peter also was having affairs with woman. When asked whether he ever felt guilty about playing both sides of the fence, he answers with a resounding no and adds that he had no idea whether the women knew he also slept with men from time to time. "If they did, they certainly didn't seem to care," he muses.

Peter is a curious person. In his relationships with women he often is the pursued person. Women *want* him, and he allows himself to be grabbed up; he doesn't do the grabbing. He thinks that way of dealing with personal relationships may come from his parents, that perhaps he is rather like his mother in this.

As for his relationships with men, he says that he would like a long-term relationship with someone he cares for but he doesn't "know how to engineer it." There is a younger man he sees from time to time who likes older men, but this man is not at all interested in any kind of exclusive relationship with him. Peter voices the feeling that he's not so sure he does either.

Peter gives the impression that perhaps there are emotions yet to be unleashed within him—experiences he desires that he has yet to have. He is a man whose social world, in the best sense, has been very important in his life. He has been a family man, he has been an important player in the Washington arts scene, and he has always taken his responsibilities as an adult and as a citizen very seriously. From his parents he acquired a great interest in the political and social world in which he lives.

Perhaps he has not explored his interior world and what he might want to achieve there as energetically as he has explored the business and social world. Perhaps he is preparing for this adventure even now.

In more recent years Peter Blanc's real estate interests led him to Miami, a city he visited occasionally throughout his life. Now he divides his time between Miami Beach and Washington. Whether he will continue to divide himself emotionally remains to be seen.

Tony Rhodes:
LIKE FATHER, NOT LIKE SON

Tony Rhodes was in the hospital having minor surgery. He was 18 years old. The first day in recovery, his phone rang: His cousin Carmen was on the line. "I don't know how to tell you this, Tony, but your father was just arrested in the men's room at Weibold's department store." Tony laughed and laughed. "Gosh, Carmen, that's just what I needed. A good laugh. I feel better already."

"It's no laughing matter, Tony. He really was." Carmen said. And so Tony found out that was father was gay.

His father never knew that Tony was told. His mother was never told. And to this day his parents have only touched upon the subject with him very briefly.

Tony's father was born in Cuba in 1915. He is now 85 years old. He married an extraordinarily beautiful woman in 1948 and moved with her and his two children to the United States from Cuba in 1964.

In Cuba he had been the sales representative for a company that manufactured household products and had traveled around the country from store to store. In the United States he was never to reach this level of job stature and had to work as an employee in an airport bar until his retirement. With his family he had come to Chicago, where he had relatives, and there he stayed until moving to Florida in his retirement.

Tony had some early inkling of his father's sexual interests when as a teen he was asked to translate something for his father. His father showed him a handwritten note and was very intent on knowing the meaning of every word. The note, in essence, said, "Yes, you can go down on me if you pay for it." His father said it had been slipped to him under the dividing wall of a bathroom stall. Upon learning the exact meaning he said to his son, "Some people are crazy."

Tony reports that his relationship with his father was never warm and affectionate. His father reserved those feelings for Tony's older sister. Tony, who has been openly gay since his late teens, believes his father has always felt resentment and even jealousy toward him.

His father is very "old-fashioned," as he puts it, rigid in his ideas and with highly moral opinions. Everything in his father's Catholic Cuban background would have been in opposition to his sexual interests, in Tony's view. Which made him extremely repressed.

Even when Tony was a child, when his father would lie on the bed and balance his daughter on his upraised feet in a kind of acrobatic act, he would refuse to do the same thing with his even smaller son. Tony remembers shouting, "Me, play with me, me." And his father refused to do so. It is possible that Tony's father kept his physical distance for fear that he might kindle sexual feelings toward his son, who was growing more attractive every year.

During the interview Tony began piecing together fragments of memories, which added up to some more solid thoughts about his father. "My father had a very good friend, Tito. They were inseparable. And often on their days off they would go away together, antiquing and things like that. My father was always a very reliable dad and husband. He came home promptly from work. He was meticulous about keeping accounts and had a horror of ever owing anyone a penny. But he also was strict about having private time to himself. And much of that time was spent with Tito, who was single and very effeminate."

Tony also remembers experiences with his brother-in-law that tied into those with his father. "When my sister was engaged to be married, her fiancé came to live with us for about three months prior to their wedding. He was Colombian and had to go home and tell his parents first, so they didn't marry immediately, even though my sister was pregnant.

Tony recalls: "Alberto moved in with us and slept in my room, which had single beds that met in a corner with a table between them. Every evening he would reach under the table and drag me into his bed. I was about 15. We slept together every night until he married my sister. After their marriage they continued to live with us, and when we had the opportunity we had sex again." Tony adds firmly, "There was nothing romantic about this. He was my sister's property. It was just a fun thing to do. Also Alberto was an obvious alcoholic and beat my sister from time to time.

"The reason I tell you all this is that Alberto also had a best friend, who was *really* a screaming queen, and they used to hang out with my father and Tito. The four of them would spend a lot of time together."

When asked whether his mother ever had an objection to this, Tony says, "She would make a comment from time to time, but it is not the Latin way to criticize the head of the family. Or to do anything that would destroy the family structure." This was to change markedly later.

Despite these kinds of clues, Tony was not to know for certain that his father was gay until his cousin's call to the hospital. But it was not Tony who went to bail out his father, nor was it he who appeared in court with him. That was left to his cousin Carmen, a young unmarried woman in her 20s whom his father evidently felt was mature and trustworthy enough to deal with the situation. During that period Tony remembers his father being very tense at home and behaving "as though he was walking on eggshells," as Tony puts it. He also adds that at that time he realized that whenever he was in a department store with his father, his father always had to go to bathroom.

And he also remembers as a very small child in Cuba going to a large restaurant with his father, who took Tony to the men's room and left him there for some time while he disappeared. From that time Tony has always found the smell of a men's room equally sexy and disturbing.

In his later teens Tony had a local boy as a boyfriend. He says that he invited the good-looking boy home one evening when no one was there and very deliberately gave him screwdrivers to drink. The young man said, "Tony, you're trying to get me drunk." And promptly went to bed with him. He subsequently spent most of his nights in Tony's bedroom, which aroused no comments from the parents on either side.

Not long after, Tony met his lover Bruce and fell very seriously in love. They have now been together 25 years. He says that he has never discussed his homosexuality with his parents but that it was never objected to and always accepted without comment. There was never any negative reaction to his lover Bruce or his presence in Tony's life.

Only once did Tony confront his father directly—about ten years ago, when Tony was in his mid 30s and his father in his mid 70s. "Are you gay?" Tony asked his father.

"You know that I like everything," the older man replied.

Tony is not so sure that his father's tastes are so very broad, however. Tony ran into him repeatedly when Bruce and he went to a well-known gay beach on Chicago's Lake Michigan shore.

Tony remembers that at one point before his father retired his parents were not on good terms and scarcely spoke to each other, though they lived in the same house. He believes his mother had had enough of her husband's activities and this was her way of dealing with it.

Now his parents are once again on friendlier terms and have moved to Tampa, where they live in the same neighborhood as Tony's sister. Tony finds this inevitable, as his father always seemed to prefer her to any other member of the family.

Of his father he says, "Now he is riding his bike around Tampa, swimming every day, as my mother says, 'Like a little raisin with legs,' and I just want him to say, 'Yes, I'm gay.' He's such a hypocrite. He's very opposed to single mothers, he's racist, and he's

Republican to the bone. Once he saw me being dropped off by a very handsome black guy I was seeing before Bruce and told me, 'I'd rather you just masturbated to take care of your needs than to see someone like that.'

"Now I don't ever plan to have him admit anything. Now he's very nervous, very frail. He's getting smaller all the time. He is no longer the handsome 5-foot-11 he once was. No, I don't think I will ever see that happen."

David Tartcloche:
I Was a Sissy From the Moment I Was Born

David Tartcloche has been HIV-positive for 19 years. Despite this, he remains fit and has very little gray in his hair, even though he is in his mid-60s. His keen intelligence and quick wit are easily detected behind his eyeglasses, and his demeanor and movements are those of a man quite a bit younger. Now retired with a family of friendly dogs in a house in a small California city, he is one of the most appealing men I interviewed for this book.

He commences the interview by saying, "I was a sissy from the moment I was born." Born in Denver, Colorado, but raised in various parts of the United States, his story could have taken place 50 years earlier.

His father was, as he says, a roustabout: a man's man who made a stab at being a professional baseball player and subsequently worked as a cowboy, miner, and day laborer. His paternal grandfather, an Englishman, was a schoolteacher; David was to spend a lot of his younger years with his grandparents.

His mother was the daughter of a formidable woman who had spent her early life living in a tent and cooking meals for oil rig workers all over Oklahoma. She amassed enough money doing this—dragging her children with her as she went—to eventually own apartment houses in Denver.

The marriage of his parents effectively came to an end when David was still in the eighth grade. He returned home after school one day to find that his mother had had a mental breakdown and the family was in an uproar. Separated from his older brother and younger sisters, he was sent to live with his aunt and grandmother in the small Nebraska town where his grandfather taught school.

The only member of his generation to graduate from high school, he did so while living in Nebraska. He remembers their simple country life there with affection. The large garden provided much of their winter fare, canned by his grandmother. A 30-gallon barrel buried in the side yard was filled with ice in the summer to make a rustic refrigerator. He says, "We lived at a subsistence level, but it was very pleasant."

Upon graduation from high school he immediately began teaching at a country schoolhouse in Nebraska with eight students, ages 5 to 14. He was 18. Although it was very like the 19th century, it was in fact the school year of 1952–1953.

After a year of this he went to Omaha to join the army. Arriving there he discovered that the army recruitment center was closed. However, a Marine recruiter was still open for business in a mobile home parked nearby, so he joined the Marines.

David became a legal clerk and court recorder in the Marines, but it was not an easy time for him. It was the toughest chapter yet of the lifetime of abuse he had already suffered for his effeminacy. David remembers, "I was a sissy always. I was the butt of all jokes from the very beginning. It was terrible for my father, to have this sissified son that had come from him."

His older brother was "Father's little man." He was assigned the job of fighting when someone attacked David. There were many such fights, even when they were attending school in the relatively big city of Denver.

He remembers that when his father went to see a teacher about the constant abuse of his son, he was told "He brings it on himself." He adds, "I didn't know why I was getting into so much trouble." On his first day at one school, he recalls being told, "Alan Nagel is going to beat up on you on the way home from school." He didn't even know who Alan Nagel was.

His brother preceded him into the armed services and was a tank commander in Korea at the age of 17. He told his younger brother, "Don't ever go in the service. You'll never be able to cope."

David did cope, but it was tough. In boot camp he was called "Percy" and then "cunt." He remembers having some 20 fights while in boot camp over being called that name. When mail was delivered, the men had to run into a small gulch and up the other as their names were called out. His well-meaning aunt sent the hometown weekly newspaper. David's sergeant once demanded, "What do you get every week?"

Some wiseacre from the platoon hollered "Kotex." A roar of laughter followed the gibe.

One night in his Quonset hut barracks David heard muffled laughter from one corner. One of the men tried to slip into his cot with him after lights were out, saying, "Move over." David slipped out the other side and waited until the intruder went away. The barracks had been waiting, holding their breaths, to see if David would let the man stay. And who knows how many of those men would actually have liked to crawl into his bed?

Of his sexual history in high school David Tartcloche says, "I was always trade. There was sucking. And also some fucking. But I was never the recipient. I tried once but it was a total disaster."

One friend of that time told him later that he had been very much in love with David. He had joined the Navy and had therapy there. He told his therapist that he had been in love with a man who wasn't "that way." David laughs when he tells this story.

In the Marines there were no sexual contacts, and David says, "I could never figure out what *not* to do to keep men off my back. Finally I started copying a super-macho guy in my platoon. In a funny way I became him, and then I could hide very well."

After three years in the Marines David left the service and went to a Missouri college, where he got a teacher's certificate. This qualified him to teach high school, which he did while getting a master's degree in night school and on summer vacation.

Of this period he says, "I had two sexual experiences in college, and I was very strongly drawn to both of these men. But I felt I had to resist those feelings because I couldn't spend the rest of my life being persecuted. I also had no idea that there was any way to connect with other gay men. I had no idea that there were bathhouses or gay bars."

After a brief stint teaching high school, David was one of the first people to sign up for the Peace Corps, recently created at President Kennedy's instigation. He says, "I had a sense of wanting to give, of wanting to contribute to other people's lives."

He was scheduled to go to Nigeria to teach in the town of Nsukka. The president of Nigeria had created a land grant school there, with the aim of teaching his people practical things like agriculture and mechanical skills. The English had instituted very formal schools in Nigeria, which were thought to be impractical by the government.

All those to be sent to Nsukka were enrolled in a training program at Michigan State University in East Lansing, Michigan. They were mostly young people, some of whom had been teachers prior to joining the Peace Corps. The young woman David was to marry was in the group. They fell in love and were married shortly after arriving in Nigeria. Soon they were parents-to-be.

Although the young couple would have been happy to go to a Irish nun gynecologist who supervised the native hospital in Nsukka, the Peace Corps officials felt this unwise, and they were transferred to a community in Southern Nigeria. There was a hospital there, run by British Petroleum, near the missionary boarding school for girls where the young couple were employed as teachers.

They became unpopular when they taught their male servant to drive their rickety little car, a dream of his. Other servants soon wanted to learn also, as driving was a valuable skill in Nigeria. The English community in which they were living opposed this dissemination of knowledge. Many people had as many as five servants, and they didn't want to bother to train anyone to do anything other than menial work. Before the couple left, many of the school staff had relented and were teaching their servants to drive.

David and his wife returned to the United States, after two years abroad, with a daughter and another child on the way. David was unable to find work, as they had returned in the autumn when school staffs were already complete, so he returned to graduate school. The following year he also had trouble—a number of schools told him they felt that someone who had been in the Peace Corps in Africa "wouldn't fit in."

He finally found work at the high school where he had initially taught after college. He taught history and hated it. The school had instituted new experimental TV teaching systems, which the students disliked. And they transferred their dislike to their teachers. After two years supervising unruly students David decided to quit teaching. He also says that he was beginning to "get frantic sexually."

Although his wife and he dreamed of taking their family to a small mountain town and raising them in idyllic conditions, this kind of job never materialized. They decided to move to Seattle, where David studied library science with the goal of becoming a librarian. After two years and an additional degree he found work as a university archivist in Bozeman, Montana.

Of this time in his life, David says, "When I went to library school I began to feel that I had made a terrible mistake. There was just something missing. I had learned about bathhouses and gay bars. I said to myself, 'There *is* a way to meet other gay men, and here I am trapped with my family, these victims of my own foolishness.'

"I felt suicidal, but I decided I couldn't abandon them. I had a plan to jump off a bridge with bricks in my pockets so I could just disappear and there wouldn't be a terrible disgrace for anyone. The university sent me to a psychiatrist in Seattle, but I didn't *want* to get used to myself. I wanted to change my needs, and this psychiatrist supposedly could turn men around.

"He told me that I felt I had been a failure as a teacher and I wanted to punish myself and part of that was being gay. If I could turn my career around I'd get over being gay.

"I thought that no matter what I do, no matter how successful I feel I am, this will never go away."

While he was in Seattle the head of his department sent David to Denver for a month of archival management courses. On his own in Denver, he went to a gay bar. He was now in his mid-30s. He says that within minutes, "I got picked up by the hunkiest guy, who took me to his apartment. Strangely enough, it was right next door to a building my grandmother had owned. We did everything. Afterward I said, 'You were in bed with four virgins.' The man replied, 'I can't believe that.' And I told him, 'If you fantasize enough, you're ready for anything.'"

He had a number of other sex partners while in Denver, and upon his return to Bozeman he came down with mononucleosis. He feared that he had syphilis, too, so he told his wife about his experiences in Denver. She said, "I never would have guessed."

Of this he says, "Even with my most intimate partner I had concealed my true nature."

Upon consideration his wife told David, "You're the best father our children could possibly have." They tried to work out a plan to stay together.

They left Seattle, their ideas about an idyllic country life crushed. They moved to Los Angeles in 1970 and remained together for another 13 years. David found work in a public library, and then with a nearby community college, where he remained for 20 years until his retirement.

Going to gay bars in Hollywood, then to bathhouses, David met a man who fell very much in love with him. They soon had a permanent liaison. David says, "It made it easy for me. I could go see him once a week. On his vacation we could go away together. We'd go camping. Sometimes we went to a dude ranch for gay men. I finally broke off with him after seven or eight years because I felt he deserved better. If I were out of the picture he'd find somebody else. He thought that if he stayed with me until my children were out of school I would leave my wife and we could be together all the time. But that wasn't my plan at all. I planned to be married all my life.

"But then I got symptoms of AIDS. It was 1981. One of my wife's best friends, a fellow teacher, had just died. One of the earliest cases.

I decided that I just couldn't stay with her and risk infecting her, so I moved out. I didn't expect to live very long."

Doctors in those days of primitive testing told David he didn't have AIDS or he would be dead already. So for a time he returned to a life of visiting bars and bathhouses.

In 1984 the University of California, Los Angeles started testing T-cells. These tests showed that David's system was becoming less robust; he *had* been infected since 1981.

David defines his private life since leaving his wife as "a string of short-term disasters. I was always picking people who were the most vulnerable, who needed protection. I always ended up doing all the giving, and they did all the taking. A friend of mine said, 'David's 50 going on 16.'"

His children were informed of his homosexuality when his daughter was 18. They were very accepting. His son's only comment was "I know." He remains close to them and also to his wife, who lives in the Northwest with a new companion. David whittles amusing and sexy wood carvings as a hobby and keeps busy with friends and his pets.

When we spoke on the phone several weeks after our initial interview, David said, "I just had a final epiphany. I just remembered a conversation I had while I was in the Marines. Some guy called me 'queer' and I said, 'Bill, why would you say that? I've never done anything that would make you call me queer.' And he said, 'You don't have to *do* anything to be queer.'"

Paul Steele:
I'm Gay Everywhere Except Philadelphia

There is something of the Old World about Paul Steele. He has the air of an 18th-century Irish or English aristocrat. He is tall, has a ruddy complexion and a prominent nose, and, although not heavyset, he is full-bodied. One can easily imagine him in a portrait by Romney or Gainsborough. Or even more accurately, a rowdy drawing by Rowlandson. There is a sparkle in his eye that indicates a lively interest in the world and the wish to savor it.

Of all the men interviewed for this book, Paul is among the few who are still married, and certainly he must be considered the most successfully married. He has accomplished this by essentially living his life in several spheres simultaneously.

He was born in Philadelphia in 1940. He has no siblings. His parents were also Philadelphians. His father, a successful engineer, did not want his wife to work; he wanted his only son to have the best possible upbringing. Paul was raised with a strong sense of entitlement.

The family lived in Bryn Mawr, a suburb of Philadelphia, where Paul attended public schools through the 12th grade. From there he was accepted at Yale. He began a liberal arts program but then decided to pursue an architectural degree. He remained at Yale for five years, until he received his degree.

He says, "I lost my virginity in my sophomore year to a girl from Smith." But at the time he was also visiting New York and going to

56

gay bars. This interest began when he was taking the train from Philadelphia to New Haven during college. Paul says, "I realized I was attracted to men when I was about 16 or 17. But I couldn't accept it. I was from a religious home, as religious as Presbyterians get, and I felt it wasn't right.

"On a train my freshman year, going up to Yale, I saw a man get on at the North Philadelphia station. He asked me to join him in the men's room, and there he knelt down in front of me. I got an erection immediately, and it felt really good. When I got to New Haven I felt so guilty I burned my underwear.

"At first I was very guilty about those feelings for men. But then I was visiting friends in New York on weekends, and I realized that many people were doing this. I started going to bars. I had my first adult drink, a gin and ginger ale, at the Mais Oui, a gay bar on West 74th Street. I was staying with a friend who attended Columbia.

"I met guys, but I never dated. It was all anonymous. I never used my real name. There was none of that 'Jonathan and David' stuff. There were no romances.

"I used to go to a place called Mary's on West Eighth Street, too. Tennessee Williams tried to pick me up there. They had wonderful meatloaf and mashed potatoes and boiled corn in a little back room restaurant. I was eating and someone came over to me. I was 18, so it was legal for me to be in Mary's in New York City. This man said, 'Mr. Williams wants to see you.' I said, 'Who is Mr. Williams?' He said, 'The famous writer. Tennessee Williams.' I said, 'Why does he want to see me?' He answered, 'All I can tell you is that Mr. Williams said, "I want that boy."'

"So I went over and talked to him. I told him my name was Paul Reynolds. I used that name a lot. People assumed I was either a member of the aluminum family or the tobacco family. All these store clerks used to want to buy me a drink. When I insisted on buying my own, they said I was so *gallant*. Anyway, Tennessee Williams and I chatted, and he was very interested when he learned I went to Yale. But then I told him I had to go. He said, 'Honey, can't I have your number?' I said, 'No, my parents would kill me.' He said, 'Honey, your parents would never know.'

"I had a lot of experience by the time I finished my undergraduate years. Most of it in cheap hotel rooms. There was the Carter near Times Square. They didn't care if you only used a room for a few hours. They just turned the mattress over, made up the bed, and rented it again."

Upon finishing his undergraduate studies Paul took a grand tour of Europe. He had worked as a draftsman for local New Haven architectural firms, some of whose architects were on the faculty at Yale, and had saved money. He'd also been given a traveling fellowship.

He says of this trip, "To have officially visited a country I had to have had sex with a national there. Other tourists or other nationals didn't count. My rule was that I hadn't really been there unless I had sex with someone who lived there. A man, obviously. I went everywhere.

"I got all my shots and vaccinations in London, even went back to get more so I could travel to all kinds of places. It was great."

Upon leaving college Paul had to do an apprenticeship with an architectural firm; he got a position with the Kahn Company in Philadelphia. He planned to live at home and told them, "You can pay me less and let me finish my apprenticeship sooner." Which they did, allowing him to finish his allotted time with them in two years.

Once he was a licensed architect in Pennsylvania, Paul had a plan. There were many rundown houses in once-good areas in Philadelphia, some available for as little money as $2,000. Always interested in rehabilitation, Paul began buying these houses, fixing them up, and reselling them. As both architect and contractor he could keep a tight hold on expenses. Local banks were sympathetic to what he was doing, so loans were not a great problem. He also bought property between town houses—where houses had been torn down—and built new houses that fit into the neighborhood.

Paul adds, "I never bit off more than I could chew, so I was never overextended financially. Also, I was never discriminatory in any way about my employees. Not on the basis of race or sex. I had lots of black employees and a female carpenter. She was a lot tougher than I was."

He was successful enough at this that in a few years he was able to buy a town house for himself, which he renovated and refurbished. This was 1970.

While he was doing this, he continued his sexual exploits, but he says, "Never in Philadelphia. I went to New York and other cities, but I never had a reputation in Philadelphia for being gay."

Paul met his wife in almost predestined circumstances. He had bought a single ticket to the Philadelphia Symphony. A young woman, who was also alone, was seated next to him. They chatted. She was a law student, attending Temple University, in her first year of advanced study. She seemed very knowledgeable and interesting, so Paul asked her to accompany him to nearby Schrafft's after the concert. The young woman suggested they meet again, so Paul invited her to lunch.

When she arrived at his town house and was shown around she said to him, "Now you're going to think I want to marry you for your money."

Paul remembers that he blushed as she went on, "But I do want to marry you."

He says, "You have to remember that this was our second meeting. We had never had sex, never even thought about it."

Paul explained to her that he was gay. That he had slept with perhaps 125 men and two women. She felt that they should try nevertheless. When Paul said, "But what if I'm thinking of some guy while I'm sleeping with you?" she replied, "Some men think of other women. There's not much difference."

They married soon after, to the delight of his parents. His wife interrupted her law studies to have their child and then returned to school after giving birth. Paul was able to spend a lot of time at home, as he had a drafting studio on the upper floor of his house, so he could baby-sit. They were able to organize their lives well. He says of his wife, "She was not a great student, but she is an excellent lawyer."

Paul says that he did not stray for the first two years of their marriage. But then, after an argument, he went to New York and picked up a man. Returning home, he told his wife, and she was upset. He said to her, "It's difficult for me." She then established that he was not to do anything in Philadelphia, and that there was to be no full-time lover or boyfriend. "This is an agreement I have kept," Paul says.

He has, however, sometimes organized his life so that his wife gets to know someone with whom he has been involved, without her realizing it. He will buy tickets for a concert or play, two on a credit card for his wife and himself and one with cash. All seats adjoining. The third ticket is given to a lover who is visiting from out of town. The lover then becomes friendly with his wife, who believes that she and her husband are making his acquaintance for the first time. They often retain these men as friends for long periods of time. Other than this, she has no contact with his other life, which is conducted during Paul's frequent travels. He says, "I don't think she'd divorce me if she found out—she'd kill me."

Of his manner of living, Paul says, "It's not ideal, but it's better than any alternative I can think of." He admits that the idea of having a live-in relationship with another man holds interest for him, but he does not want to trade in the life he has now.

He is helping to support his son, a struggling writer, "but only to age 25," he points out. He adds, "Yes, I probably married partially to please my parents. And yes, I do have my guilt. I know that in part I want to conform for my wife's sake. I would never want to humiliate her in any way. I consider my life to be in many ways similar to former president Clinton's. He has his sins, but they're only part of his life. And his big error was in dropping Jennifer Flowers. She was good enough to be the mistress of a governor, but not good enough for a president. That was why she took her revenge upon him. I'm careful to avoid those kinds of situations.

"My modus operandi is to take men I like to foreign countries when I travel, or to distant cities. There we can have an adventure together, distanced from both our home locations. And I'm always willing to help them."

He tells a story of a handsome bathhouse attendant in Boston who refused to consider him for any kind of sexual encounter but who needed help paying for an automobile repair. Paul went to the garage, intimidated the owner, and rescued the repaired car for a small fee. His actions prompted the car's owner to say, "How can I ever repay you?"

Paul replied, "I think you know the answer to that." And adds, "He was the ultimate fuck. I still tell him that to this day."

In Palm Springs he met another man, a photographer at a gay party, who also rejected Paul's advances. Nevertheless, they became friends. Paul helped him buy an expensive part for a camera. Again, the young man said, "Is there anything I can do for you?"

Knowingly, Paul replied, "Jeremy, don't say that." He took Jeremy on a much-desired scuba diving trip to Fiji, which resulted in a physical encounter between them. Paul considers this an important achievement.

When asked whether he's ever truly been in love, Paul says, in a manner worthy of a Don Juan of 200 years ago, "I've been in love so many times. With so many people. I'm almost in love with you."

He says he has never "kept" anyone, though he has *helped* some seven men start their first year in college. He believes he has avoided AIDS because, "I was injured when I was screwed in 1964. So I never did that again. And I believe that is what saved me."

He finishes the interview by saying, "You must remember that I spend perhaps 15% of my time with gay friends and 85% of my time with my wife. She's happy with me. I'm happy with her. Heterosexual or gay relationship, it finally is just two mammals living together. Living with another human being is a difficult thing in the long term. And we managed it. We will stay in this framework of life."

He says, "There has been a great excitement and pleasure for me in feeling a man's heartbeat in his cock, whether it was in my hand or my mouth. But perhaps I will phase out of the sexual aspect of life soon. I've had so many conquests, so many relationships.

"And my wife and son have always come first. Any obligation

to my wife will come first. I will always fulfill her requests to attend the symphony, theater, going to New York for the theater. That's why I am gay everywhere except Philadelphia. And perhaps the idea that no one in Philadelphia knows I'm gay is a fiction. A fiction that only I believe."

He makes a final reflection on life: "Obviously, something or someone has organized this world we live in. But it's beyond me. I don't understand it. But I do understand an orgasm. And a good meal. And I just say, 'Forgive us our trespasses as we forgive those who trespass against us.'"

As he walks away, after a final snapshot of his interviewer, he calls back, "I'm not living a lie. I'm living a fiction."

Ted Blumenstein:
As Bad as It Was, It Wasn't All That Bad

One could say, perhaps, that Ted Blumenstein has spent his life trying to do the right thing, which has led him down some unusual paths.

Born in Cincinnati in 1930, he attended public schools there and then went to the University of Michigan. He chose his alma mater partially because of its reputation as the best Midwestern university and partially to put some distance between himself and Cincinnati.

Neither of his parents finished high school before they married, which was not at all unusual at that time. His mother was to finish school in her middle years.

His father, who had a successful tire retreading business, had a lifelong suspicion that too much education was not a good idea for a hard-driving businessman. But he sent his only son away to university anyway. At Michigan Ted majored in sociology and economics, joined a fraternity, and was certainly looked upon by the coeds as a cute guy and a very eligible marriage partner. However, marriage was to wait until later for Ted.

From university, having been declared 4-F because of a congenital back problem, he returned to join his father in his business. He planned to stay there for a year or two before pursuing a "real" career but wound up staying for five.

During that period he met his wife, when a Cincinnati group

took an organized tour of New York City. They met on a Circle Line boat, in 1955. Ted had been out of school for three years. His fiancée was a senior at the University of Cincinnati. Ted says, "I thought I was in love with her. Later, when I did fall in love, I found out what falling in love really was."

He goes on to say, "I married out of social pressure. Pressure that was internalized and entirely of my own doing. My family never put pressure upon me. It was what a successful person did. And it was very important to me to be successful."

After his marriage Ted and his wife attended the Episcopal church regularly; he had been brought up in that church, if only in a very fringe way. But his new wife, who had been brought up as a Baptist, wanted to transfer her faith to his church. And in attending this church with its young clergy, Ted discovered to his great surprise a reawakening of an earlier interest.

While in college he had attended a seminar on group dynamics and had become convinced its theories were extremely important. He says, "It became my religion. It was going to save the world. It was the resolution for all the problems of government, business, and family. And when I started going to this particular church I discovered that they called this same kind of theory the Holy Spirit. I was hooked. I left my father's business and went to seminary to find out more about it."

His wife had no problem with this change of career, as she had always thought she would marry a clergyman. Together they went off to the Virginia Theological Seminary in Alexandria, Virginia.

Ted says his thinking was, "Clergy don't get wealthy, but they are never poor. They have comfortable lives. It was a commitment on my part to join the intellectual poor."

He attended the seminary for three years, and in that time both of his sons were born. Ted and his wife enjoyed their life in Alexandria and the company of the many other young couples who were also involved with the seminary. Finances were tight; the assistance that the church had said would be forthcoming never materialized. But with savings and Ted's father's help, the young couple launched a new life and a new family at the same time. Of this Ted says, "It was fun. It was a neat community."

On leaving the seminary they went to Columbus, Ohio, as it was the Episcopal practice to return to your diocese upon finishing seminary training.

After three years at St. Mark's Church, in a very upwardly mobile suburban parish, the Blumensteins went to Vandalia, Ohio, to organize a new congregation in what was essentially a blue-collar community. Ted's new adventure was highly successful.

He says of that time, "I was Mr. Social Action." He was a local chairman for the Human Rights Committee and was known as "the nigger-loving Jewish preacher." He was the rector of this parish for nine years, until the other side of his life required some agonizing reappraisal.

Discussing his private feelings, Ted says, "I always knew I was attracted to men. As a child I was fascinated by a photo of bare-chested men in prison irons. I never realized that I was feeling sexual excitement. In junior high I started experimenting with other boys and didn't realize what it was all about.

"Later when it began to dawn on me I told myself, 'I'll grow out of it.' And even later I told myself, 'I'm gay, but I can overcome it.'

"I was strongly motivated to be successful. My parents represented the idea for me that to be happy you had to be successful. My father often said to me, 'You will never make it financially. You're too smart for your own good.' The fear of not making it financially was a great driving force."

Returning to his private life, Ted talks more about his earlier sexual development. "Delmer and I were sex partners. He was a childhood friend. And the boy across the street and I used to go off into the woods together. Then when I was in college I met a guy in my first year and we went to work in the same summer camp. We got together sexually.

"There were also a couple of guys in the dormitory. There was one I would be sure to let know when my roommate was going to be away for the weekend so he could drop in."

During the same period Ted also dated girls and was pinned to a woman from Pi Phi sorority, which had to have given him prestige in the eyes of his fraternity brother.

There were also casual male pickups around his hometown after he finished college. And he continued much the same thing in a very limited way after his marriage. He says, "I knew I desired it. I tried to resist it but couldn't. The only person I could trust was a gay Episcopalian priest. It was so sad, because I didn't like him. I like to be with someone who is fun, someone I like. This was never the case with him. What a sad way to have sex."

While attending seminary Ted was arrested in a plainclothes police entrapment in a men's room in Jackson Square, the park across Pennsylvania Avenue from the White House. And also right across from the Episcopal Church of St. John. This rest room had been a male pickup place for decades. The man who picked him up suggested to Ted that he had a place they could go and on the way there arrested him. He was set free without trial. He says, "I got by with lies and luck, and my wife didn't find out. I felt great shame and guilt, but even at that time I knew it was society who was wrong, not me. I knew the shame was their fault. It pushed me into a period of shame, fear, and tightening of the closet door, but somehow I knew what I was desiring was not evil."

After serving as rector of the Vandalia parish for nine years, Ted left to open a consulting business that operated on the principles of group dynamics. He remained an Episcopalian priest and sometimes worked with parishes that were having organizational or intergroup problems. But for the most part his work was helping large companies like Procter & Gamble with organizational development. When new teams were organized to work on new products, Ted's job was to help them understand and analyze how they were working together and how to make it work better.

In 1974 Ted learned he had a brain tumor, which was removed and found to be benign but which caused him to lose hearing in his left ear. The recovery was long, and after a year Ted discovered that his business partner had done nothing in his absence and was waiting for him to return to work. Ted, already saddled with a very dependent wife, felt he didn't need an equally dependent partner and closed his business.

He returned to full-time church work, at first working in the coordination of 15 parishes in Dayton, Ohio. This did not last very long, and he eventually took an interim position in a very wealthy church in Glendale, Ohio. He then moved to Marion, Ohio, as a traditional pastor, leaving Vandalia, where he had lived for 17 years. He was to remain in Marion for 16 years, until his retirement. He says that he never felt accepted in Marion, even though he received the city's Distinguished Citizen award. He feels he was always seen as "a pushy New York Jew." This was certainly in part because of his involvement in creating a free medical clinic, a homeless shelter, and a free meal program, and transforming the Marion AIDS Task Force. Although the town liked all these social programs, there were members of the church who didn't approve of them.

But in addition to all of this involvement, Ted found that his involvement with men was increasing also.

Ted was entrapped again during a trip to Cincinnati, where his work for Procter & Gamble frequently took him. This time he had to go to court, get a lawyer, and pay a fine. Again he was able to keep his trouble from his wife by telling her that it was his work—not his court dates—that repeatedly took him to Cincinnati.

Ted's first brush with real romance was with a heterosexual friend in Vandalia, to whom he never revealed his love. A member of his church, Art and he had sons who went to summer camp together. They became buddies, and at times Art would say, "Ted, you're closer to me than any of my brothers." This touched Ted deeply—for the first time he was understood what all the poetry was about. "This is what love is," he told himself. But Ted never told Art, and his love for Art became a life-long friendship.

His interest in a new acquaintance, Dave, went further. Dave was a psychiatrist whom Ted knew socially in Vandalia. Dave was in the process of coming out as a homosexual when Ted met him. Dave and his wife were attempting to continue their marriage as friends and decided to give a party where homosexual friends and heterosexual couples could meet and mingle. Ted laughs, "I was invited as part of one of the heterosexual couples."

Dave and he became friends, and one evening when they were alone together Ted initiated sex. When they fell in love they were both 48 years old. It was 1978. Dave had already come out to his children and was separating from his wife. He was becoming a role model for Ted.

Finally, after they had attended a Unitarian Universalist conference together and were returning to Dayton that night, Ted decided that if he was ever going to truly have this man, with whom he was very much in love, he, too, was going to have to come out.

It was a complete surprise to his wife, who found it a horror and an abomination. For her it was a sin that stirred the latent Puritanism in her Southern Baptist background. In 24 hours she had moved out, leaving Ted with the house and furniture. Ted's sons, who were both in college, then had to be called. That their parents were getting a divorce was not a surprise to either of them. The reason for the breakup *was* a surprise, but they handled the news with acceptance and have remained close to their father.

Of this time, Ted says, "The marriage wasn't really over because of my homosexuality. I married a very dependent woman. At first the glue was strong. I wanted someone to be dependent upon me. But later, when I pushed her to be more independent, she felt she was being deserted. She became even more dependent. I felt I had an albatross around my neck.

"Our problems were aggravated by her alcoholism. She had started drinking at dinner parties we gave, to ease her feeling of being awkward and dull. When we parted she got into a 12-step program on her doctor's insistence—her liver was giving out—and she did get better. Her memory came back. The kids started seeing her again.

"But when I attended one of my sons' wedding a few years after our divorce, she came up to me and said, 'You must be the bride's father.' And I said, 'No, Paula, I'm Ted, your ex-husband.'

"With my kids, after the breakup, our relationship actually got better. When I told them they immediately began talking about all the kids in their school and neighborhood they had known who were gay. If you had said that coming out would cause your relationship with your children to be better, I would have laughed. But it has."

Ted started coming out in Marion. A gay clergy friend advised him, "Just let it happen. Those who can handle it will accept it. Those who can't will deny it." Ted adds, "And they did. Even though I went to the gay March on Washington and it was publicized, many people just ignored it. They knew I had close gay friends but they would say, "He's an Episcopal priest, he has children. He can't be gay.""

Unfortunately, although Ted began to like himself a lot more, he found that his new love for Dave was not reciprocated. Dave explained that Ted was just not his type, and on a vacation that they took together Dave met the man with whom he is now living. Although greatly disappointed, Ted has remained close to Dave.

Since then Ted has a close but nonsexual attachment to a much younger man, whom he has helped to get a medical education. This young man has been very supportive emotionally of Ted.

They attended the March on Washington together in 1987, and Ted remembers ruefully that the marchers gathered on the lawn of St. John's Church. His friend Michael had to use the toilet, and Ted indicated the public men's room across the street. Michael asked, "How did you know that it was there?" to which Ted replied, "I was arrested there."

He says, "At that earlier time I thought I was worthless. I was desperate. And here I was 15 years later in a pride march on the same spot. I had gone from being lost in the depths of homophobia to the heights of freeing myself from it."

Of his lifelong attachment to his church Ted says, "Since I have become a gay activist I've been punished many times for being a church professional. Many gay people say, 'You've joined the enemy, you work for the enemy.' But my thinking through the years always was, 'I know I must never reveal my awful secret or I will be rejected, but should someone find out, my church will always accept me, no matter what.' And despite the many stories about rejection by the church, this has never been my reality."

Now retired in Columbus, Ohio, Ted has been the chaplain at the Hospice of Columbus, a post he only very recently resigned. He has remained politically active in the Episcopal church, where he was Midwest regional vice president on the Board of Integrity (an organization for gay Episcopalians). He says, "My high energy level lets me know how much energy went into maintaining the closet wall for all those years." His ex-wife died a few years ago. He and his sons remain close.

To summarize his life, Ted remarks that once when he interviewed for a job, the interviewing board asked, "What has been the biggest success of your life?"

Ted replied, "Parenting."

Ted Blumenstein died in 2002.

The Confused Generation, 50 to 60

For men between 50 and 60, born during World War II or immediately thereafter, social striving has been important, but the wild and druggy '60s and '70s also played a large role in freeing them sexually and offering alternatives to conventional lifestyles. Curiously, most of them report they experienced a lot of repression nevertheless.

Marriage as a key ingredient in upwardly mobility played a role in some of these men's lives, but to a somewhat different degree than it did for interviewees just a half-generation their elders. Whereas the older men saw upward mobility as adding to their prestige and importance in the eyes of others, for this group, enjoying the pleasures of an upscale lifestyle was of prime importance. They enjoyed the fine restaurants, travel, and the beautiful homes that their upward climb brought. In this way they were less puritanical than their elders.

That is not to say this group is entirely made up of unrepentant hedonists. Indeed, this group is most importantly characterized by their contributions to society. They are movers and shakers. Many are active in improving their community's social and educational facilities, and they involve themselves in cultural activities. And often they continue to share deeply in their children's lives.

Men in this group would not have preferred to lead a lives of sexual ambiguity, hiding their true interest in other men. Surprisingly, many had not even realized they were interested in other men until relatively late in life; often, they had considered their sexual predilection an annoying personality flaw to be discounted and ignored. There was a high level of what could be called numbness or self-deception in this group.

But once these men had to confront their sexuality, once they understood that sex and love with other men was important for them, they have moved with alacrity to assert their true selves. Several admitted that losing themselves in very demanding jobs and filling their spare time with activities had been ways of keeping themselves from thinking about their sexual preference, although invariably this recognition has come with hindsight.

The childlike enthusiasm of the 1960s and the "anything goes" atmosphere of the 1970s strongly colored the personalities of these men and their ways of relating to the world. Oddly enough, their immediate seniors were more aware of their emotional needs and took steps to meet them halfway with hidden agendas, whereas men in this group hurled themselves into very active, very group-oriented activities. Often, they had epiphanies, in which suddenly they realized they preferred men to women.

Overall these men seem less cynical than those in other age groups and less determined to find a place in the upper-middle class through the security of heterosexual marriage. One could say they are more honest and quicker to adapt themselves to their new orientation Once they recognized their sexual orientation, they were honest with themselves and quickly adapted to a new gay lifestyle. But it was left to the age group that immediately follows them, the men in their 40s and 50s, to take public stands on issues of equal rights for homosexuals.

Katzen Hammerer:
HE CAME OUT AND STAYED HOME

Tall, blond, rangy, and still good-looking, Katzen Hammerer is in his 50s and has spent much of his working life as the director of a private school for boys in Germany.

Like many of the men interviewed for this book, Katzen remembers his first engaging in homosexual sex as a teenager with his friends—experiences he assumed would be forgotten as he progressed through life. For his friends, they were, but not for him.

Trained as a teacher, Katzen took a post in a well-known private school upon his education. He enjoyed his job and felt he was good at it. Which must have been the case, as he was advanced to the directorship of the school before too many years had passed.

The school, located in a small rural town in Germany, offered few distractions. As a single man, Katzen was soon a source of interest to the young unmarried women of the village. "There were six of them," Katzen remembers, "and I married the prettiest one." He still has no qualms about his marriage; at the time he saw it as a natural progression in the life he had planned for himself.

The young couple enjoyed their life together. After some ten years of marriage they had three children—two boys and a girl.

Katzen saws he rarely thought of other men during this period. When he did find a man attractive, he quickly dismissed his feelings as quirky behavior that found it a little strange perhaps, but not distressing.

An elderly woman had befriended Katzen during his earliest days as teacher. She owned a summer home in Mallorca and one year invited him to spend his vacation there with his family. He was then about 35. Although all Northern Europeans prize the sun, Katzen is particularly devoted to getting a tan. He accepted his elderly friend's invitation with pleasure. He was then about 35.

For some reason—perhaps jealousy—Katzen's wife did not like the older woman and tried to make the vacation unpleasant by sulking and staying in her room. Mrs. Hammerer was the daughter of a wealthy farming family, who were disappointed that she had not married into another landed family. Katzen Hammerer's world of education, books, and culture was not theirs and not one they valued. Very likely, her husband's shared interests with his elderly female friend woman made his wife feel like an outsider. But this was nothing in comparison with what was to come.

Because his wife didn't want to come along on outings, Katzen often found himself alone with the children on hikes, trips to the beach, and picnics. One day, while he and the children were all in their swimsuits, they noticed that there was a guided tour of a large cave near their beach. With the children in tow, Katzen decided to join the tour group and explore the cave. A handsome young local man led the tour. Wandering through the stalactites and the stalagmites, the group came to an aperture in the cave wall that opened onto a path down to a very secluded beach. The children darted through the opening and ran quickly down to the shore to plunge into the sea, while Katzen and the guide watched from above. The guide reached out and touched the front of Katzen's bikini trunks. Katzen says, "It was like a current of electricity hit me. I woke up. Suddenly, I knew what I really wanted." The guide proceeded to give Katzen his first experience with oral sex.

Katzen saw the guide a number of times before he and his family left the island. Upon his return to Germany he realized that his life had to take an extreme turn.

For a time Katzen remained married but began to seek out sex partners in nearby cities. Finally, he felt a confrontation with his wife was necessary. A small-town bourgeoise, her shock was total and her rage enormous. She was completely unaccepting of Katzen's situation and immediately demanded a divorce. Curiously enough, she did not "out" Katzen to the townspeople. Both Katzen and his ex-wife remained in the village. He also retained his position as director of the boy's school. His life went on, although now he was a single man again.

Although Katzen Hammerer has retired from his school directorship, his home is still in the same small town. He has built a modern house for himself that includes space for an art gallery—he has a new career as a gallery owner and promoter of young artists. His career also includes dealing in rare books, which was always an interest and has now become a vocation as well.

Once divorced from his wife, Katzen found a great interest in the bawdier aspects of sex with men. His book dealing and art representation leads him to many countries, where his pleasures and experiences have been great and varied. When asked whether his small-town neighbors disapprove of his lifestyle, he says, "I'm a dealer. They are used to many people coming and going at my home on business."

Katzen has explored having a long-term relationship with another man. But his lover lived in France, and that complicated matters. Their relationship didn't last. Katzen does not seem to be unduly dismayed by this and enjoys his continuing sexual adventures in Paris, New York, Miami Beach, and many other cities.

Interestingly, Katzen represents a definite type of homosexual or bisexual male who married and had children. As a young man, he had planned to follow the path of job, wife, and children. It had not occurred to him to do otherwise. Then, the awakening.

Many homosexuals may not accept that some men are in their mid 30s or later when they realize they are homosexual and become seriously interested in pursuing passionate relationships with other men, as was the case with Katzen Hammerer, Yet there are situations where a man has simply dismissed or ignored his feelings for other men for many years. It isn't necessarily guilt that leads such men to set aside their attraction to other men. More often, it is because paying greater attention to these feelings would not have fit neatly into their life plans; therefore, men like Katzen often suppress any gay desire.

For Katzen and others like him, the attraction to other men begins to resurface once other mileposts have been passed. Once such men have found fulfillment in their careers and successfully started to raise a family, deep-seated emotions begin to arise. Like several other interviewees, Katzen enjoyed sex with his wife and did not avoid it. "It just wasn't as exciting or powerful as sex with men." he says.

Katzen regrets that his wife has never abandoned her outrage. But he has remained on very good terms with his children, all of whom have benefited from his adventurousness as a dealer in books and fine art. They live in large cities in Germany and the United States and accept their father as he is without criticism or comment—and always enjoy his visits.

Jerry Chasen:
I Hope You Don't Mind Me Telling You That You Have a Beautiful Body

Jerry Chasen is a perky bundle of energy. Peppiness exudes from his compact muscular body, his curly hair, and his bright glance. As he tells it, he was always like this. His parents and his two sisters always had a tough time keeping up with him—particularly the rate of speed with which he talked. According to them, he spoke almost from the moment of birth.

Jerry was born in Brooklyn a little over 50 years ago and attended grade school on Long Island. By the time he reached junior high school his family had moved to Miami, and he finished high school there. He attended Tufts University in Boston for his undergraduate degree and went to law school at New York University. In more recent years he received a degree in estate planning from the University of Miami. His quick and perceptive brain has been very well educated.

Jerry married before his last year of law school. He first met Sheila, the young woman who later became his wife, when he was a freshman at Tufts. At the time she was dating a handsome young man who soon became Jerry's roommate—a roommate on whom Jerry developed a very big crush.

Sheila and Jerry broke up once during their somewhat prolonged dating period, although by the time Jerry was an undergraduate senior, they were back together again. Curiously enough, Sheila had been briefly married to another man during this interim period.

Looking back, Jerry does not think he was ready for marriage, emotionally or sexually: "I was *so* inexperienced sexually on both fronts at the time of my marriage. I used to kiss my friend Michael on the cheek when we passed in the hall in 6th grade. But it didn't send any message."

What sexual awareness Jerry had at the time was derived from images generated by the mass media. "I remember seeing a *Mad* magazine at my grandmother's house in Brooklyn when I was about 7. There was a very sexy drawing of this beefy Italian guy. There may not even have been a visible face, but I just kept looking at it. I remember seeing a *Life* magazine cover of Sophia Loren bursting out of her bodice when she was in the film *Two Women* and saying, 'Oh, she's kind of fat.' My father stared at me and said, 'What?' I used to search out Charles Atlas ads in the back of comic books, too. I was already working out in 9th grade."

That's not to say Jerry was entirely inexperienced with sex. "I fooled around with boys. All through my teens I had 'jack-off' dates with guys. I thought this was just a phase. That's how much I knew. And I have to add, at the time of my marriage I functioned very well with my wife. I did all those things that straight guys did."

Like several other interviewees, Jerry admits that pleasing his parents and his own desire for upward mobility prompted him to marry so early. "I got married because it was 'the program.' I was trying to do 'the program.' I went to law school. I'm suited for law, but that's just been by chance. Programming is part of an immigrant family's climb into a different position in society. It worked for others, and that wasn't lost on me. The day before I went to work for a prestigious law firm, I visited Ellis Island and was impressed that my grandparents had arrived there with very little. And there I was: working for an important legal firm.

"Also, one year my parents took the whole family skiing to Snow Mass in Vermont and *Roots* was being shown, which we all saw together. Afterward my parents asked me an unusual question.

They said, 'What are you so angry at?' And, you know, I have no memory of being difficult. But evidently, I was acting out being very dissatisfied with the prospect of the life I must have felt I was expected to lead. And that I thought I wanted to lead.

"I wanted to please my parents. My father was successful. It would have been very difficult to say to my parents, 'I just can't do it that way.' And it would have been even more difficult with my mother than my father.

"When I split up with my wife, I called my parents and told them that my marriage was over and I thought I was gay. My father said, 'I don't care. I love you. Is there anything we can do?' My mother said, 'Oh, we wondered.' That was all. It was extremely difficult for her to accept my new life.

"I tried to explain to her when we were having lunch in New York shortly after the breakup. I said, 'When I die, I want my life canvas to have a lot of bright colors. I don't want a lot of straight lines.'"

There were limits to Jerry's parents' level of acceptance. Later on, Jerry's lover, Dwight, happened to be passing through Miami when Jerry was there visiting his parents. Jerry suggested they all have dinner together. His parents refused.

But soon afterward Jerry's mother sent him a ticket to come to Miami and enclosed this note: "Dear Jerry, let's talk. Love, Mother."

For the entire weekend Jerry spent with his parents, nothing was said. Then on Sunday afternoon, not long before he was to leave, Jerry was sitting on the lawn reading a collection of gay short fiction: *Stories from Christopher Street*. His mother came out and asked, "What are you reading?" Jerry showed her and said, "It's really wonderful to read something like this and not have to translate it into my own experience."

Looking back, Jerry says, "I could see the lights go on. I think at that point she began to realize my being gay wasn't about her. It wasn't something I'd done to hurt her."

Sometime later Jerry's grandmother was dying from injuries

incurred during a freak accident. She had fallen in her bathtub and had hit the hot water handle as she fell. Unable to rise, she was so seriously scalded she died three weeks later. Jerry visited her when she was no longer able to speak. She scrawled on a note pad "I know" and smiled.

Jerry's maturation as a gay adult was slow in coming, though, even after he had started the coming-out process. "There came a point when my own development took over. I was about 23 years old. During that period I was an editor of the law review, and when a friend mentioned me to an acquaintance, he replied, 'Oh, is he that gay guy?' Which surprised me—I was the last to know. And even as a straight guy I was a SNAG: Sensitive New Age Guy. Perhaps that's a veil for many men. I thought about romance with a man but that never happened so I thought it couldn't happen. If the guy who'd introduced me to my wife had wanted to run away with me, I would have done it. What a body! What a dick! And a perfect butt.

"But at the time of my marriage I thought, 'This is how you have a happy life.' We lived at 22 Grove Street in Greenwich Village in New York. My wife had a degree in occupational therapy, but that wasn't high-toned enough for me, so I had her studying clinical psychology at the New School for Social Research. Altogether, we were married for three and a half years.

Emotional support for Jerry eventually came from an unusual source. "Finally, it was the best man at my wedding who led me out. Cary had been my best friend since high school. In our first phys ed class in high school, we were on opposite sides playing touch football. When the word 'hike' was said, we both started giggling and immediately became friends. This was the girlfriend I always wanted. We went shopping. We gossiped. We were two little homosexuals. And we didn't even know it.

"I was the best man at Cary's wedding. He was the best man at my wedding. We decided to go on a camping trip together. I was about to start a one-year apprenticeship to a federal judge who was very difficult to work for. I wasn't looking forward to it.

"In our tent Cary and I had sex. When I got up, I knew that if he had said, 'Let's go away together,' I would've. The job and the marriage would have been history. But he didn't. One of us said, 'I don't know what to do. I'm married, but I still have feelings for men.' It was probably me because Cary split with his wife soon after and went to live in a house in the woods.

"I went to visit Cary several times, but he made it clear that he didn't want to continue with our sexual relationship. His take was, 'I married my high school sweetheart. Now I don't want to marry my high school best friend.'"

Things began to shift for Jerry at this point. Once he had a brief run-in with a man in the gymnasium showers, he opened up to Sheila and tentatively discussed his situation with her. Noting how Cary had handled his own situation, Jerry began to feel that something else was possible.

"I'd gotten strong enough to realize that what was right for me wasn't necessarily what was right for the rest of the world. My wife said, 'We can have an open relationship.' So I had an affair with another law student." Meanwhile, Sheila had an affair with a man who thought Jerry was gay and suggested that she "get fucked by a real man." Sheila told Jerry this and demanded he come home from the office, where he was working late. He says, "I came home. We had fabulous sex. And that was it. We didn't discuss it further."

Not long afterward, Jerry's friend Cary came from Boston to visit him in New York. It was February 1979. They went together to see the play *Gemini,* in which one of the characters came to terms with being gay. On the bus home Jerry said to his friend, "I need to leave Sheila." And Sheila left. Jerry has no idea where she is. He knows that she subsequently married and divorced again. The last he heard of her, she was living with a Yugoslavian.

Jerry was now a 27-year-old single man living on Grove Street in Greenwich Village. He met an older man at the gym who had just broken off an 18-year relationship. This affair was short-lived. Then, while visiting Cary in Boston for a weekend, he attended a party and met "the handsomest man I ever saw in my life."

This was Dwight. Their Boston–New York long-distance relationship lasted two years.

In 1981 Jerry was spending a summer holiday on Fire Island. While out dancing, a blond man with blue eyes stopped him and said, "I hope you don't mind me telling you that you have a beautiful body." This was Walt, an architect. "I have a thing for architects and designers," Jerry admits, pointedly adding that Walt was Southern "with all *those* problems." They were together for seven complicated years. During this period they moved to Santa Fe together, and there they went their separate ways. Walt later died of AIDS, refusing to let his mother visit him on his deathbed at the end.

From 1988 to 1994 Jerry was single. He moved to Miami in 1993 and returned to school, getting a degree in estate planning from the University of Miami. While visiting Fire Island again, he met yet another Southern man with a degree in architecture. This man moved to Miami to be with Jerry but never really put down roots there. Their fitful relationship ended in 1999.

Jerry is now in a firm relationship with Mark Kirby, another designer. of course. They met in the summer of 2000 at an Ellen DeGeneres benefit. Later that same season they ran into each other again on the dance floor. "I was so not ready for another relationship," Jerry says, "but it was just too sweet to not do it. And Mark told me later that when he first met me he had told himself, 'It's just a matter of time.'"

In the autumn of 2001, Mark hosted a lavish 50th birthday party for Jerry. On hand were Jerry's parents, his sisters and their husbands, and a great many friends. It was exactly the kind of splendid evening many upwardly mobile couples—gay, bi, or straight—would have greatly enjoyed, with no hint of unease among the family members, relatives, in-laws, or business acquaintances in attendance. It has taken a while, but Jerry finally has the life he has always wanted.

Bill Frampton:
THE PATIENT WHO WASN'T SICK

A native of Toronto, Bill Frampton now divides his time between that city and Miami Beach, where he has had an apartment for about ten years.

Bill's story differs from the experiences of many interviewees: he spent many years strenuously trying to correct his homosexuality through psychotherapy. "If Canada hadn't been so far behind the United States in the practice of psychotherapy," he explains, "I probably wouldn't have wasted so many years trying to be straight."

Bill's father was killed in a freak water-skiing accident on a lake north of Toronto when Bill was a child. His memory of his father is slight. Bill's mother began working in unskilled jobs immediately after his father's death, and Bill subsequently spent much of his childhood with his grandparents on both sides of the family.

Bill's maternal grandfathers and his mother gave him little affection or attention, only seeing to his material needs. It was his father's mother who was the warmest and most loving influence in those early years. On many weekends, the young boy and his grandmother would spend time together, often going to the motion pictures, which they both loved.

Intelligent and perceptive, the lonely child understood very early that he was attracted to other males. His guilt about these feelings was sharpened by the example of the three sexually unfulfilled people with whom he lived. Bill says there was always an atmosphere of sexual dysfunction.

At the age of 12, after seeing a motion picture with his grandmother one Saturday afternoon, Bill began to cry uncontrollably while they were walking down the street. His grandmother was very concerned, and all he was able to explain to her was that he was sick and that he had to go to the doctor.

Bill's grandmother was concerned but had no real help to offer, nor did his mother. So young Bill sought out a therapist on his own. Understanding very little of medical jargon, he mistakenly made an appointment with a physical therapist who had an office near his home, thinking that perhaps he could be of help.

When the therapist asked how he could be of help, Bill told him, "I think I'm homosexual." In Toronto some 40 years ago this was pretty astonishing information from the lips of a young boy. The therapist, to his credit, was understanding and explained that his training didn't equip him to offer much help. He gave Bill the name of a doctor who might be able to deal with his emotional quandary. And so the therapy ball started rolling.

Throughout his teen years in Toronto, Bill met with a group for therapy sessions on a regular basis. The prevailing theory in psychotherapy at that time was that homosexuality was an emotional illness and attempts should be made to cure it. So the young patient was encouraged to date girls, go to dances, make as much physical contact as he could with the young women of his acquaintance. And Bill tried.

But as he was undergoing therapy and dating girls, he was also making his first exploration into homosexual encounters. This relatively frequent sexual experimentation continued and expanded once he went to college.

A talented artist even as a child, Bill continued to study art throughout his high school years and eventually entered an art school in Toronto. The more bohemian atmosphere of the art school facilitated his efforts to date girls, but it also gave him ample opportunity to explore male relationships more fully.

As a child of a single mother with a limited income, Bill lived at home throughout his college years. He was not freed into the raucous life of a college dormitory, but had to return home every evening to the repressive suburban world of his grandparents and mother.

By the time Bill finished his education, he was seriously dating a fellow female student. They moved into an apartment together once they received their diplomas.

Bill and his girlfriend enjoyed sex together regularly, and in fact, he remembers always being more enthusiastic about it than she was back then. After living together several years they married in their middle 20s. Both already held jobs they liked and led a busy social life together with other young couples.

When asked whether he ever had difficulty sleeping with someone who didn't excite him (women, for example), Bill offers an unusual reply: "The excitement is about imagining yourself making love to someone, so the other person isn't always that important."

Bill and his wife lived in Toronto for close to a decade after finishing college. For him, a turning point came the day he met the gay couple who resided directly across the street from his home. This attractive, youngish pair of men—whom Bill describes as "Frank and Fay Fabulous"—recognized Bill as someone who was yearning to learn more about the kind of life they lived. They encouraged him to drop in for visits by himself. Through his social encounters with them, he met their friends and attended their parties. He was then 28.

It's not easy to say whether Bill was becoming careless or whether he was consciously setting himself up to be discovered. Eventually, a female friend of his wife—another woman—happened upon him at one of the parties he was attending as a gay man. She telephoned Bill's wife to report, "I saw Bill at a party last night with his boyfriend." The fat was in the fire. Bill's wife demanded an explanation—and got it. Their marriage was over.

A good-looking, well-built, newly divorced man approaching 30, Bill Frampton lived alone, had affairs, and continued to see his therapist. Several years into this routine, Bill decided to see a different therapist. He chose one who also happened to be an Anglican priest. In their first session Bill carefully explained the problem he had with his sexuality. His therapist responded, "It sounds to me like you're gay. What's wrong with that?"

"It was though a huge curtain lifted upon my life when he said, 'What's wrong with that?'" Bill recalls. "No one had ever said that to me." Therapy had caught up with the 20th century in Toronto— homosexuality was no longer considered an illness.

Not long after that therapeutic epiphany, Bill visited Key West for the first time and found the warm weather and relaxed atmosphere very much to his taste. He began spending the winter months in Miami Beach and eventually bought an apartment there. He now lives a very open lifestyle, sharing his life with a lover in Toronto who is also the lover of a third man there. His lover visits Miami Beach in the winter months and sees Bill regularly when he is in residence in Toronto.

After a not-too-long hiatus, Bill has again become friendly with his ex-wife and her current boyfriend. Now in her early 50s, she is very enthusiastic about her married sex life, which Bill finds a little disconcerting. "She wasn't all that crazy about sex when I was married to her," he says.

Bill has not had any major confrontations with his family over being openly gay, mainly because he sees them infrequently and the topic is never discussed. For them, he is simply a gay man. He has introduced his lover to his sister, and at one point they all lived together. He says, "We used to compare nun stories."

Still attractive in his early 50s, Bill Frampton values the flexibility of having an undemanding, intermittent relationship with his lover. He continues to pursue sexual encounters when and where he can and finds his life satisfying on a personal level. He would not wish it to be otherwise, surrounded, as he is, by many friends and acquaintances in a busy career and social world.

Jesse Pulitzer:
THE LATE-BLOOMING PHARMACIST

How much can an interviewee be expected to tell? Is he telling all he really knows? Or is he telling only what he will admit to knowing? Jesse Pulitzer is one of those enigmatic persons who fits into the latter category.

A little less than average height and looking a good bit younger than his 53 years, Jerry was cheerful and composed when he arrived for his interview over lunch in Laguna Beach, impeccably attired in designer jeans and a well-cut shirt. He had been divorced three years before when he had fallen deeply in love with a young blond artist—a man. Yet during our telephone conversation before meeting for lunch, he had claimed that until he met that artist he'd had no inkling he could like men.

Jesse was raised in a family dominated by an aggressive, punishing father. A handsome but highly irrational man, Jesse's father met the young woman who became Jesse's mother shortly after World War II while sitting shivah, the traditional seven-day mourning period observed by some Jews after the death of a friend or family member. Eleven years older than the young girl he was to marry, Jesse's father had just been released from prison after serving 18 years for committing a robbery in the late 1920s. Upon his release he had found work as a rental agent and building supervisor.

Jesse's mother was an orphan who had been raised for the most part by her older sister, who had remained at home upon the death of Jesse's maternal grandmother and made a home for the large brood of younger brothers and sister left in her care. Only after they were all grown did she marry, at the age of 40. Never having children of her own, she mothered Jesse, which he now feels made it possible for him to survive the harshness of his childhood.

Jesse does not remember being attracted to boys or men. "I was always attracted to beautiful faces," he says. "I didn't fantasize that I wanted to go to bed with them. I just admired them—as one admires art."

When Jesse was 13, a local girl initiated him into sex in the back of a car. (He admits to having had a few masturbation experiences with another boy at 11, though.) At 16, Jesse first had sexual intercourse with another girl. He continued to feel no particular attraction to men, he claims, except to admire the handsomeness of some.

Jesse attended fashion school in San Francisco. Although he drew well, he had no ambition to become a designer. Instead, he wanted to pursue a career in the retail and marketing aspects of fashion.

Jesse began dating a young black woman, a fellow student, and that disturbed his family. Before finishing school, he fell in love with one of his sister's friends, a young woman he had known since she was 11. Jesse had also briefly dated her older sister.

Jesse declares he had a true love affair with his sister's friend, though she was already seriously involved with another man. But Jesse managed to woo her away and they were wed. At the ceremony, Jesse was spared the presence of his harsh and haunted father; the man had died when his son was 17. A much happier period was now about to begin.

At first the young couple remained in San Francisco but then moved north to Portland, Oregon, where Jesse had been given the opportunity to manage an upscale men's clothing store. His daughter was born while they lived there. At 25, Jesse decided he needed a more reliable income, and he and his family returned to San Francisco so that he could study to become a pharmacist. While he was in school for the next two years, Jesse and his wife both worked part-time to support their little family. After completing his studies at 27, he was ready to launch a new career.

Jesse's beloved aunt—his mother's maternal older sister—had moved south to Laguna Beach. Jesse and his wife liked the seaside town very much when they visited her there. They felt it offered better weather, better schools, and good work opportunities.

First working for other companies, Jesse was soon able to open his own pharmacy and drugstore. His business thrived, and so did his family life. A son was added to the family, and the young couple became extremely busy in various activities around town that eventually included parents' programs in their children's schools and a group that was creating a local film festival. "I'm a classic A-type personality and so is my wife," Jesse says. "We were always terribly busy with the children and what they were doing: their sports, their classes."

Despite this level of parental involvement, the children gave Jesse and his wife difficulties. His daughter became involved with a wild group of students that led her to neglect her studies and experiment with drugs. His son had problems with his studies, too, although he was extremely bright, and Jesse and his wife had to seek psychiatric treatment for him.

Jesse doesn't feel the children's problems can be directly attributed to any sexual conflict between him and his wife. At the time, he enjoyed sex with his wife very much. They made love daily, and their continued interest in each other sexually was in fact a source of comment among their friends.

"I always liked women's bodies—their curves and their tits," Jesse says. "My first homosexual experience was really disappointing. I began to think I had made a big mistake. It's a whole lot easier to get into a vagina, you know, than an asshole."

Returning to his troubled relationship with his children, Jesse adds, "My children probably saw me as an angry parent, and also suffered because their parents were too involved with each other to give them enough real attention, even though we were so involved with their activities."

When asked why he felt angry, Jesse says, "I feel as though at that time I was a kind of large ball or globe. On the surface I had some happiness and satisfaction, but down below in the core I was never happy. I wasn't doing what I had planned to do with my life. I hadn't wanted to be trapped in small-town living."

But when Jesse later came out and admitted his homosexual feelings to his wife, the weight lifted off the core of his being. "Finally, I felt free."

It took some doing and some time before Jerry—the superactive, responsible, if sometimes aloof parent and businessman—could get down to that core. "I hung out a lot with gay men here in Laguna Beach. As you know, there are many here—certainly in the business community and many of my customers, too. I would go to their bars, and later my wife would say, 'Don't you feel uneasy? Doesn't it make you feel uncomfortable?' And I would tell her, 'No.'"

Through some of his gay acquaintances, Jesse met a young artist who painted in a realist style. Among the subjects he liked to paint were male nudes. Jesse created a small display area for his artist friend in his pharmacy. One afternoon, while Jesse was looking at paintings at the artist's apartment, the two men suddenly fell into each other's arms and began to make love.

Jesse was then 50. The experience swept him off his feet. At first he imagined he would leave his wife and try to replicate some version of his married life with the good-looking young artist. However, this was not to be.

"Peter was a transitional person for me, a mix of female and male," Jesse observes. "He was small, blond, and beautiful. He had beautiful blue eyes and a fabulous mouth. For the first time, I was sexually attracted to another man. I wanted to kiss that mouth. I didn't want to suck his dick or anything like that."

But Peter didn't see them as a couple. Young and attractive, he liked his free lifestyle. "He was more seductive than sexual," Jesse adds. "But I was obsessed with him. We would go out together, and new gay friends would say to me, 'You're married to a woman?' They just couldn't believe it. I was discovering a new world." Not surprisingly, while having sex with his wife, Jesse began wishing he was with Peter.

Unable to discuss his situation with his wife, Jesse became very aloof and difficult, hoping that if he were disagreeable enough, she would ask for a divorce. This difficult period lasted for about two months. "At that time I decided that I was bisexual," Jerry reflects. "My feelings now are that if you're 80% drawn to men and 20% drawn to women, it is more of a label than a fact—a label some men prefer so they aren't identified as homosexual. I was also horrified at the idea of giving my wife AIDS. We went to a marriage counselor, but I just couldn't say, 'I want out of this marriage.'"

Jesse's once-cherished married life had become a real misery. "I came to dislike my life. One evening my wife asked, 'Do you love me?' I just couldn't bring myself to say, 'Yes.' And finally, after a very long silence, she said, 'Don't bother,' and stormed out of the house. I felt terrible but I was hoping for a divorce so I wouldn't have to come out to her." He adds, "Of course I'd been seeing an analyst for years but I never could discuss this."

Jesse was sitting alone watching television one evening when his wife came home, entered the room, and announced, "I've just been talking to your sister and she thinks it's very strange that you hang out so much with gay men."

Realizing that his life was on the brink, Jesse summoned all his courage, looked at her, and said, "I'm gay." His wife lost control, screaming and cursing. She tore off her wedding band and threw it across the room at him. Jesse and his wife spent the weekend sleeping in separate bedrooms. Their children were no longer living at home, so they were not aware of this new development. As the weekend wore on, Jesse kept thinking, *I'll have to kill myself. She'll tell everyone. My life is over.*

On Monday he discovered that his life wasn't over, but his financial security was. Except for his business, Jesse co-owned everything with his wife, and that morning she took everything, removing his name from all bank accounts and holdings. Now he was truly alone.

Slowly, Jesse pulled his life together. He moved in with some gay friends. He attended a coming-out group at the local gay and lesbian center. He was happy to discover that the group did not primarily attract "teen queens" but was in fact geared toward middle-aged gay men and bisexuals who had been or still were married.

A man Jesse met in this group asked him out for coffee. They found out they were quite compatible and became lovers, eventually moving in together. Looking back, Jesse feels they cared for each other because they shared so much in common. Both men were Jewish, both had been married, and both had children. Though these mutual concerns made them care deeply about each other, Jesse doesn't think what they felt was love. After a while they began to explore sexually—experimenting with threesomes, foursomes, and fivesomes. As the new century began, Jesse broke off his relationship with this man and is now seeing someone else.

Jesse continued to see a therapist after coming out, though not the one his wife and he had seen together. At their first session, Jesse asked, "Are you gay?"

"No," his new therapist replied, "Is that a problem?"

Jesse responded, "No. Is my being gay a problem?"

"No. I have many gay clients."

Therapy has proved helpful in Jesse's transition to becoming more comfortable with himself as a gay person, but he now feels he no longer needs this help.

Jesse's problems now center mostly on his former wife, who has cancer. They have once again become close, and Jesse tries to be as supportive as he can. And he admits he feels guilty about her becoming ill after he left her. In part, this has made him feel that a gay man or a lesbian should not enter into a committed relationship with a heterosexual person without being totally up front about sexuality from the start.

It troubles Jesse that his son, who lives on the other side of the country, remains estranged and contacts his father only infrequently. Fortunately, Jesse's daughter has been more understanding.

Jesse's summing-up of his coming-out experience strikes notes both of gladness and regret: "Something was wrong, and I finally figured it out. And that was that. Finally, I think I could say I'm happy, but it's sad that it takes 50 years to find yourself.

Robert Cloud:
THE BRAVEST MAN IN HIS FAMILY

Robert Cloud is a fine-featured, soft-spoken gentleman. For most of his life he was everything his parents wanted him to be, and he made every effort to be just that. But in his 40s, after a marriage and fathering a child, he began to emerge from his parents' heavy programming and become less of a WASP and much more of his own person.

The Cloud family has a traditional American past. They came to America as Quakers and after several generations had found their way to Indiana. There, Bob's father attended Indiana University, where Bob's grandfather taught physics. Both Bob's father and a young woman named Clara, who was to become the wife of Dr. Alfred Kinsey, were students of Grandfather Cloud. The professor liked to tell his son, "You should be more like Clara," who was his smartest student.

Bob's father went on to Harvard Medical School, where he met a very correct young lady who was also attending college in Boston. After he received his degree and completed his residency, they were married. The young couple settled in Englewood, New Jersey, and had two sons. Their first child, Bob's older brother, was the more athletic and outgoing of the two boys, but both were brought up to fulfill their parents' expectations.

Neither parent had come from the kind of East Coast upper-middle-class world in which they were now living, but the doctor's ample income made it possible to offer his sons a fine education and many economic advantages.

Young Bob attended a country day school in Englewood after 4th grade and then went on to Philips Exeter Academy for his secondary education. At this prestigious New Hampshire school he was much happier than he had been in grade school in a rigidly conventional New Jersey suburb. He was good at foreign languages and English, and his failure to do well in the sciences didn't hold him back from performing well scholastically. The fact that his older brother had come close to flunking out of Andover during his first year made Bob feel that he was holding up his end in accomplishing his parents' dreams.

During this period Bob was not aware of having any particular crushes or strong feelings for other boys. Reclusive and dreamy, he spent a lot of his spare time reading. Curiosity and an unnamed longing led him to explore Truman Capote, Paul Bowles, and Carson McCullers. It is easy to conjure up the small and rather delicate boy he must have been, attending the same school but not really living in the same world as many of the other boys.

From Exeter, where he graduated in 1954, Bob went on to Harvard, where he started dating a girl from Radcliffe College but did not sleep with her. Occasionally, they went to movies and dances and social functions together. After graduation, they drifted apart.

Bob was also beginning to be aware that he was gay—and that he wasn't the only homosexual in the world. By this time he had added Proust, Gide, and Oscar Wilde to his reading list. In a less exalted fashion, the men's room in the undergraduate library announced the same news: The graffiti in the toilet stalls signaled that he was not alone, as did the men who came on to him from time to time. But whenever they did, he always rejected them, thinking, "How can they tell?"

One has to remember the world of the 1950s: pre-pill, pre-female liberation, and pre-drugs. The values of the upper middle class held sway. Nice girls didn't sleep around. Homosexuality didn't exist for most people. Everything was nice in Bob's world, everything was comfortable, and nearly everyone conformed to a set standard of behavior. After graduating from Harvard with a degree in English, Bob went on to get an advanced degree in Anthropology, by his own admission because he wanted to do something that would help him break free from his inhibitions and that was more connected to the real world.

Getting even closer to the real world, Bob joined the National Guard after completing his advanced degree. Once he finished his basic training for the Guard, he returned home to live with his parents while he started a new job with a news agency in New York City. Back in his parent's home, Bob felt increasingly distant from his father, who by now regarded his younger son as a disappointing "also-ran." Bob hoped to become closer to his father by temporarily moving home. But this was not to happen.

A quiet undercurrent of tension developed between Bob and his father. "I wasn't the kind of person I had been brought up to be." Bob states. "I had feelings of shame, not guilt. In the WASP culture, if the people who matter in town don't know what you're doing, it doesn't matter."

Still living at home, Bob switched to working as a writer for a publisher of encyclopedias. He still had no thoughts of making any kind of sexual contact with another man, and his conscious effort to dissuade himself from acting on his desires was causing him some anxiety. Soon he met a young woman who also wrote for the encyclopedia company. They were not really in love but "two people who wanted a life and felt they could make it together."

Bob had never had sex before this relationship and at first was not too put off by heterosexual contact. "I was young and I was healthy, and just putting the two bodies together made it possible." Everything in his life had prepared him for marriage and a home and children. He still had no intention of doing otherwise.

Doctor Cloud started to put even more familial pressure on his second son. Bob's older brother was already a lawyer; he had married, and his wife had given birth to two daughters. At a family dinner the doctor said to his older son, "You have two lovely daughters. Now you must have a son."

"I have all the children I can afford," Bob's brother replied. "Talk to Bobby."

Bob soon left his parents' home and moved to the East Village, but the change of scene didn't really expand his horizons. "Of course I found the only boring middle-class street in the whole swinging East Village," he rues.

Bob married his coworker at the encyclopedia company, and the young couple then moved to the West Village. There, Bob's feelings toward men began to stir, though his marriage remained pleasant. "I enjoyed sex with my wife, but I also still found myself looking at men longingly. I could function well as a heterosexual, and with all the garbage dumped on me by psychoanalysts, it would have been impossible for me to act otherwise. But it wasn't as though I didn't have a kind of nervous interest in homosexuality."

Though Bob and his wife had a son, they divorced after five years of marriage. Strangely enough, the subject of Bob's latent homosexuality never came up during the divorce proceedings. His wife simply felt their relationship was over. Once the divorce was granted, Bob moved to Brooklyn, while his wife and son remained in the West Village brownstone.

Bob had secured very good visiting rights through the divorce agreement and was able to have his small son with him on Thursday evenings and every weekend. As a divorced father, Bob did not encounter discrimination against gay fathers—he hadn't come out yet—but discrimination against noncustodial parents. The parent who didn't retain primary custody of the child become invisible to the structure of society.

Bob's son completed his primary and secondary education in Manhattan and went on to a large Midwestern university. Now married, he has a successful career and lives with his family in a major metropolitan area in the Midwest. Bob's duties as a father are now largely over, and he can congratulate himself on having provided his own father with the grandson he so dearly wanted.

At the time his son entered college, Bob had a frank discussion about homosexuality with him. Quite wisely, Bob had decided to wait until this time, in case anything revealed in their conversation would turn out to be a problem. Since his son was no longer living at home and had become part of the structure of a university, Bob believed the full truth about him would be easier to handle. But it turned out that Bob's son had long understood his father's situation. Their relationship continues to be close to this day. "My son likes me as well as loves me," Bob proudly avers.

Finally, at 41, Bob had sex with another man. A close gay friend offered to initiate Bob in his first homosexual experience. "I said no, but fortunately he asked again," Bob says winkingly. Then, on election night in 1980, Bob met a man who, like him, was a gay father. This man was still married, lived out of town, and came to New York several days a month seeking encounters with gay men. Bob remembers that on the first night they spent together the other man kept awakening him—not for sex but to discuss being a gay father. "I think he was interested in me because we shared the same problem," he says.

Naturally, Bob felt this relationship would be ideal. "I could be straight 29 days a month and gay for two days." But it didn't last.

Bob then started attending the Gay Fathers Forum, an organization created for gay men with children. Founded in 1980, the Forum is still in existence. Meetings, which averaged about 50 attendees when Bob was introduced to the organization, remain relatively unstructured; attendees usually split into small groups to discuss a variety of subjects such as custody, visitation rights, and how to come out to your children.

At one meeting Bob got acquainted with another divorced gay father. They soon discovered a mutual attraction and many shared interests and eventually ended up in a six-year relationship. Though they talked about living together, they never overcame the difficulty of finding an apartment large enough to provide bedrooms for the various children who spent time with them each week.

Bob was very much in love with this man, but when the relationship failed to work out, he took a breather. "I decided I was driving myself crazy looking for someone and decided to relax."

That's not to say that Bob has shied away from continuing the coming-out process. He has since come out as openly gay to friends and family members and even announced it in his Exeter alumni newspaper and the class report for his 40th Harvard reunion. Recently, there have been more happy changes in Bob's life. At a July 4th party, he met a handsome lawyer who is now his partner. And this past winter his son and daughter-in-law made him a proud gay grandfather. Without narrowly adhering to his parents' rigid paradigm, Bob has continued their line after all.

Donald De Wolf:
THE DRAG QUEEN'S DREAM

Is Donald De Wolf even gay? Very likely, he would say he is not. Technically, he may not even belong in this book; he has never been married. He is, however, the father of two children by two different mothers. And he fancies drag queens. Sound fascinating? He is.

I met Donald De Wolf at a Gay Men's Chorus concert in Miami Beach. He was in line by himself to buy a ticket. He knew the friend who was accompanying me, so he sat with us for the performance. After the performance, we went to dinner together on nearby Lincoln Road.

Donald De Wolf resembles a fitter and sexier Carroll O'Connor from *All in the Family*. A neatly built man of medium height somewhere in his 50s, he has the air of a very solid citizen, with a faintly Irish charm. Leafy, affluent suburbs are full of nice, responsible, successful men exactly like Donald De Wolf. Except somewhere along the line he slipped off that track onto one of his own devising.

I had already met his brother, Mickey De Wolf, a more raffish man, and very openly gay. Mickey makes no bones about his predilection for black and Hispanic street boys, whom he likes to take home, sleep with, and then photograph. Guests to his home are shown thick albums of these photographs. He has pursued his hobby with great relish all over the world.

Donald is far more conservative. At our dinner together he told me that his two children, both in their early 20s, are in the northern city where he still spends part of each year. They were born only a year apart, although each has a different African-American mother. Though he was never in any kind of permanent liaison with either woman, Donald has never hesitated to assume his paternal responsibility. Every other weekend through the years the two children have joined Donald at his home, and he has always provided for their educational expenses. But after telling me all this, he asks enthusiastically, "Did you go to the Drag Queen evening at Score last Monday?"

I said that was not one of my big priorities, but Donald De Wolf waxed very enthusiastic. He said, "Oh, I always go, and I usually take someone home with me. I'm really into drag queens. Pre-op, of course. When you get down there you want to find a penis."

Donald De Wolf's taste for the theatrical has some sources in his background. His mother was a very successful dance teacher in several East Coast cities. She left high school to open her own dance studio and throughout her adult life always managed and taught in successful studios.

Still young and already successfully launched in her career, Donald's mother met a good-looking Ivy League graduate who was finishing his medical training, and eventually they got married. Donald's father served in the U.S. Navy during World War II, and it was during this period that Donald and his brother were born.

Only after the war, when the family was settled in a large city, did their home life deteriorate. The parents battled, and the boys took refuge in their mother's attention. A modern woman before her time, she always earned her own income and did not easily submit to her strong-willed husband.

She was particularly willing to spend money on her children's education and both boys received excellent schooling at Catholic schools and universities. But Donald at times resisted his mother's efforts at upward mobility; halfway through his college years he transferred to a university in the Midwest. "I was tired of the East Coast mentality—that everything had to be on the East Coast; that you had to be educated there, work there, and live there; that you had to be a doctor or a lawyer. The Midwest seemed friendlier and less competitive."

Donald is very clear about his attitude toward sex during his college years. "I had a girlfriend who attended a nearby school. She was very nice and we slept together, even though that wasn't so commonplace at that time. But I never had the urge to marry. I never got that point where I would say, 'Gee, I've got to get married.'

"I would look at other guys who were getting married and think, *Why don't I have their urgent desire to get married?* I don't think I had any gay tendency then. I don't think it was that. I never had any thoughts about having sex with men. I think I needed my freedom more than anything else. I grew up with a feeling for independence, growing up without a father. He was never really around."

As a student, Donald already was experimenting with other sides of his personality—rather bravely, in fact. There weren't many other students in his college who were going into the predominantly black neighborhoods to pick up women, many of them prostitutes. On one occasion he took a long-legged woman home from a pool hall only to realize looks can be deceiving. "She didn't really undress, and while we were fucking I realized that it was a man, but that didn't bother me. Afterward the police stopped us out on the street and insisted she give them identity. Her name was David- something, as I remember. They didn't do anything to us, but they just wanted to make sure I knew I had been with a man, not a woman."

After college Donald returned to the East Coast for graduate work in philosophy, but his enthusiasm for the Catholic Church was waning. "I was stalling," he says, "But I benefited from it."

He started to take on part-time teaching jobs and shared an apartment with two other men. There were many black students at one of the colleges where Donald taught, which set the stage for his beginning to date black women in a major way.

"It was sort of the peak of my career in dating. I was seeing eight women at one time. I was at my most prolific in making love. It almost became a burden, I had a real sense of obligation." There must have been something surprising and appealing about this self-effacing, soft-spoken ex-Catholic student, who was in fact a very eager beau and adept at making love.

Donald had some contact with homosexuals at the time—one of his roommates was bisexual. It was the late 1960s, and Donald and his friends had several discussions about what being gay was all about. Donald's strong liberal feelings led him to let his hair grow out, wear a bandanna, and move to San Francisco. But he quickly wore out that image. He cut off his hair, moved back to the East Coast, and decided to abandon education as a profession. Always the seeker and not afraid of changing course midstream, he was a true child of the '60s.

Donald made his first big career switch by answering an employment ad for laborers. In the dead of winter he found himself digging ditches—and digging it. From digging ditches he moved on to plumbing. Also, he began to invest in a modest way in inner-city real estate, buying old buildings and renovating them. Income from his family and money pooled with his brother helped fund the property investments.

Meanwhile, Donald was dating a number of women, one of whom became pregnant. At first, she made no claim that he was the father. About a year later another woman Donald was dating announced that he was the father of her daughter. A blood test subsequently proved her right. At this point, the first woman came forward and said, "My son is your son." Donald did not contest her claim. Donald's own mother at first had some difficulty accepting her half-black grandchildren, but now she is close to them, especially her grandson.

Over the years, Donald paid child support to both of the women and saw his children with great regularity. With the mother of his son, Donald has never had any kind of permanent relationship. He had begun a relationship with the mother of his daughter, though, only to break it off around the time she announced she was pregnant. As for love relationships with other women, Donald says he was very much in love with a black woman in his hometown not too long ago, and he counts perhaps five other such affairs.

Donald reports having only had a few gay sexual encounters, most of them quite fleeting. Once, while he was hanging around African-American bars, he was in a men's room when a large black man approached him and said, perhaps a little playfully. "Hey, Buddy, I'm going to have you tonight." Donald cleared out fast. On several occasions in San Francisco and elsewhere, Donald had been offered blow jobs and happily obliged, thinking, *Why not?*

Donald's sexual cruising has often occurred in less than safe locales. When asked about the element of danger, he says that only piqued his interest more. Recently, he has begun to study boxing to be able to better defend himself if he ever got into a fight.

About a decade ago, the block around the small apartment house where Donald lives became a rendezvous point for African-American drag queens. Despite his interest in some of the men, Donald has not gotten to know that many of them, let alone become involved in a relationship with one. He had in fact given a relationship with a drag queen as try, but he soon found that his partner's first and foremost commitment was to wigs and nails and gowns and and not a live-in man.

As for his sexuality now, Donald explains in a neat and analytical way that could certainly be called Jesuitical. "I think my interest is divided between a latent homosexual tendency and also a tendency to explore further. Certainly I'm beginning to appreciate guys as guys. In the last five years I have begun to admit that I am actually interested. The homosexual aspect has begun to assert itself as I have begun to get more excited."

But when it comes to men, Donald's tastes extend only to effeminate guys. "If I live to be 150, the beefy guys who look straight do nothing for me." Donald reports that good-looking young men who are not at all effeminate have tried to pick him up in bars, but he has always turned them down.

Recently, Donald has been sexually intimate with men who,

though they weren't in drag, were still overtly effeminate and dressed in a feminine way with tight pants and plunging shirt openings. Despite their feminine appearance, Donald says, "The fact they have a penis is definitely a turn-on."

It is quite evident to Donald that, except for providing for his two children, he has avoided commitment all his life. Yet he has no plans to change his lifestyle, or lessen his sense of responsibility for his two children. He will be a grandfather soon by his daughter.

At least for now, Donald sees no reason to call a halt to his life of sexual adventure. The mystery of where it will lead him is reason enough for him to continue his quest. So here he is, Donald De Wolf: a good-looking, well-to-do, middle-aged man with a definitely eclectic—and ever-expanding—set of sexual preferences.

Victor Valentino:
THE DOCTOR WHO GOT AWAY

Most of the men interviewed for this book felt great pressure to conceal their homosexual interests in order to achieve what they hoped for in life. Perhaps one of the most pressured was Victor Valentino. His emergence as an openly gay man is especially interesting to explore, given how much he had once wished to conform.

Victor was born near a large city in Pennsylvania. The community in which he grew up was almost entirely Italian, and all the families there were from the same region of southern Italy. His grandparents on both sides of his family had emigrated as children. At home, Victor's father spoke some Italian dialect with relatives and friends, but since Victor's mother had never learned Italian, it was never taught to the children.

Victor's world as a boy was similar to that of other middle-class American families, but beneath the cars and kitchen equipment and split-level houses, the Italian village life from which people in the neighborhood had come still remained. If they even knew such a thing as homosexuality existed, it was regarded as something to be avoided, and it was certainly never discussed.

Victor was brought up to share the goals of this community. "I was in love with the idea of being married to a beautiful wife and having beautiful children and a nice home. I wanted to be popular in the community where I lived. My only plan was to live the ideal life. I didn't even imagine any other possibilities.

"But I never understood passion. As a teenager I read D.H. Lawrence and I never understood the passion they were always talking about.

"I played around sexually with my cousins when I was young but I never interpreted that as being attracted to men. And as for women, I always wanted to be married, as it felt safe and protected. Being passionately attracted to someone was something I really knew nothing about."

Victor's family enthusiastically supported his plan to go to medical school to become a doctor. He went to an undergraduate college and then medical school not far from his own hometown. Rather than broadening his perspective, going to medical school reinforced the intense first-generation immigrant programming he'd already received.

"When I was interviewed for medical school, one of the first questions asked was if I had a girlfriend. Then, when did I expect to get married?" The interviewer counseled Victor that getting married between junior and senior years was generally a good idea and what many students did. Not surprisingly, this male-dominated school had only a handful of female students at that time.

The admissions counselor also queried Victor about what sort of role he planned to play in the community where he would eventually work. "It was quite obvious that only heterosexuals were going to be admitted to that medical school," Victor notes. "And this really didn't bother me at the time, as what they wanted was what I wanted."

Victor's wife was a local girl who had gone to high school with him. He had dated her sister, but they became involved when she attended the same undergraduate school that he did.

In remembering this period, Victor adds that in medical school in 1968 he had studied homosexuality as a disease—but drew no comparisons to himself. "There was definitely a homophobic atmosphere when I went to college," he says.

Victor's first homosexual encounter took place the day before his wedding. A friend had come to his apartment to drive with him to the wedding the following day. They shared a bed, and during the night they had sex. "My friend lived in an apartment with two other men," Victor recalls. "They were all in their mid 20s and none of them dated. No one put it together. When I look back on it, it's funny. I got married the year of Stonewall. And I got divorced around when the AIDS epidemic started. I was married for 11 years."

Despite his sexual run-in on the eve of his marriage, Victor did very little to follow through on any needs arising from it. He was in the military for several years and then completed his residency in the same city where he had gotten his medical degree.

Although he was not sexually active with anyone but his wife, Victor believes that she'd always suspected he was attracted to men, even when they were still having sex every day. Quite the possessive sort, Victor's wife consistently stood in the way of her husband spending time with other men, even to the point of keeping him from going fishing with his friends.

While in the Army, Victor became very friendly with an attractive sergeant, who dropped in every day at Victor's office to visit him. They were together so much that they became the objects of neighborhood jokes. But they kept their relationship very much on a friendship level.

After Victor left the army, his sergeant wrote him every day and, upon his own discharge, came to visit Victor at home. Victor's wife became very hostile and unfriendly, and the sergeant withdrew to the guest room to cry on several occasions.

A woman friend of Victor's wife aggravated the situation. The woman had long been engaged to a man who had moved to San Francisco because of his work. When the woman went to visit her fiancé there, she discovered that he was living with another man in what was clearly a homosexual relationship. She reported all this to Victor's wife, adding that she was sure that the visiting sergeant was trying to lure Victor into a similar gay relationship. Although Victor now admits that he had entertained thoughts of breaking off his marriage at the time of the sergeant's visit, he had decided he couldn't leave his wife since they were raising a 4-year-old child.

Victor's sexual interest in other men became overwhelmingly clear to him once he and his small family had moved to Texas for a very promising work opportunity. In the basement of the house they bought, Victor came upon a cache of male porn magazines. He had never seen gay pornography, and suddenly all the images and sensations that had been drifting on the edges of his consciousness were fully formed before his eyes in the magazine photographs.

"I hid them away, and constantly I kept saying to myself, 'They're down there'—and kept going down to the basement to look some more." But by this time Victor and his wife had another child. For Victor, the idea of changing his life became more and more distant and, after all, he had accomplished his original goals. He had a beautiful home and an attractive wife and family, and he was a force in his local community. Slowly, though, he began to piece together what was missing.

Some major pieces fell into place at a wedding in San Francisco. The woman who had blown the whistle on Victor to his wife finally married her longtime fiancé, even though she was well aware that he'd had a ten-year relationship with another man.

The wedding dinner was on a Friday evening and almost everyone in the wedding party became very drunk. Only Victor and one other man—the same man he had slept with the night before his own wedding—were left upright. After everyone else had left or retired to their beds, Victor and this man went for a walk. The apartment of the bride and groom was very near the Castro district. Rounding a corner, Victor and his friend espied two men in tuxedos, one seated on a fire hydrant, the other bending over him for a passionate kiss. Victor said, "There is something here we need to investigate."

Oddly enough, later on at the time of the divorce, Victor's wife recalled yet another incident involving Victor at her friend's wedding party. "And that was a terrible time in San Francisco when I caught you with Kenny," she accused.

"Kenny who?" Victor replied. At first he had no memory of anyone named Kenny even being at the wedding. Then, slowly, he remembered that after the wedding all the guests had returned to the bride and groom's apartment, even drunker than the night before. Victor was lying on the living room floor in his tuxedo, and another guest named Kenny, whom he knew only slightly, was lying on the couch. Kenny said, "Let me help you out of those clothes." He had already begun to do so when Victor's wife entered the room.

At the time Victor's wife said nothing to her husband and they continued to have sex. And their family would soon expand: It was that same weekend, or shortly thereafter, that she became pregnant with their second child. In retrospect Victor sees the timing of their second child's birth as quite intentional.

Two and half years later, Victor's medical practice was firmly established in Houston. Thanks to the city's large and visible GLBT community, he gradually was becoming more exposed to alternative lifestyles. His wife's brother, a young man in his early 20s, also moved to Houston—and revealed to his sister's family that he was gay. Soon, Victor became acquainted with all of his young brother-in-law's gay friends.

A turnabout took place in Dallas, when Victor was attending a medical conference there. He went out one evening and allowed himself to be taken home by a man he picked up. The next morning Victor was standing naked in the man's apartment and looking out a window, when the man came up behind him and took him in his arms. *Now I understood those Victorian novels,* Victor thought. *Now I know what they meant by passion.*

Victor went home and told his wife he had to have two weeks by himself to think things through. She refused to let him leave. "You cross that threshold," she warned, "and you'll have a divorce faster than you think." He did cross that threshold, and his wife did divorce him. Within 21 days of her ultimatum, Victor embarked on life as a single gay man. It was almost 1980.

Victor says, "Once I was divorced, of course everyone said, 'We always knew!' That was a really boring part of coming out. But the worst part was feeling old and undesirable at 35. Everyone was coming out at that time and there was much more gay activity than ever before. Of course, the gates closed in 1981 when people began to wake up to AIDS."

He remained near his family, taking a little apartment and seeing the children every other day, and having them spend every other weekend with him. But then his wife decided to move back to the East Coast. Though Victor hadn't lost any friends in Houston because of the divorce and his coming out, he felt that it was time for a complete change.

Victor was offered an opportunity to go to an Arab country and supervise a clinic there flooded with patients in much need of his expertise. He remembers landing in a small plane in the desert and thinking upon his arrival, *I'm not giving up on being gay.*

No sooner had the thought crossed Victor's mind than a blond man—another employee of the social service organization that ran the clinic—came out on the tarmac. This man was to become Victor's lover for the next eight years. Upon meeting Victor he suggested they share a house, so Victor moved in with him. Immediately, the new roommate began having "rapid heartbeat crises." Victor then explained he was gay. Though it seemed obvious to Victor, his roommate was almost totally unaware of his own gayness, even though in his office there hung a large travel poster featuring a well-endowed cowboy squeezed into tight jeans. For two years Victor and his lover remained in the Near East before returning to the States, where they lived together in Cincinnati and Victor resumed his medical practice.

After eight years their relationship ended. "I was never in love with him," Victor claims. "He was cute and he loved me. But he was definitely not the love of my life, and I wanted that. I liked Cincinnati and wanted to stay there, but I felt I needed to live in a bigger city. I wanted to move to Atlanta, and I did. He came with me, but our relationship was over. We weren't sleeping together, and I was definitely ready for something more meaningful before I got any older."

Something meaningful soon hovered into view in the form of

Dave, a patient who came into Victor's office for an examination. Dave was 29 to Victor's 40. Although he was very attracted to Dave, Victor at first dismissed the possibility of something developing between them. Nevertheless, Victor admits, "I couldn't get him out of my mind," Victor says.

Victor then asked his nurse to pull Dave's chart, thinking he might call him on some pretext. Just as he made the request she said, "I have mail for you," and handed him a letter from Dave. In the letter Dave said he'd like to know Victor better. The two men then began to correspond with each other, exchanging about a dozen letters before they saw each other again, even though they lived in the same city.

Dave was just about to move to the West Coast when Victor made him this proposition: "Let's pretend we're lovers for two weeks and see how it works." They have not separated since. After more than ten years, they are still together.

Victor's relationship with his ex-wife has never improved. She has married three times since their divorce and still is not happy. However, Victor's children have become much more a part of his life. His son, now in his early 20s, has moved to Atlanta with his girlfriend to be near his father, with whom he spends a lot of quality time. Recently, Victor's son asked his father, "Dad, how do you know when you're gay?" Victor explained that you never have to ask yourself that question if you are. In response Victor's son said he didn't really feel any attraction for men but added, "Gay relationships seem so easy, compared to men and women, who have so many problems." Victor is happy that his life appears so problem-free to his son. And Victor's life is beautiful now. He enjoys close sustained relationships with his children and Dave. After all the obstacles he has overcome, Victor now has the kind of marriage and family he has always truly wanted.

Bill Clark:

A MAN OF EXTREMES

Bill Clark is a take-charge kind of guy: orderly but genial. It's easy to see why he has had both career and personal success—which makes it all the more difficult to comprehend the extremes he has lived through in his 50-some years.

Wearing a vivid yellow sports shirt that echoes the sunny expression on his face, Bill was smiling and looked very much at ease the day of his interview. He was born in Santa Rosa, California, in 1947. His parents were energetic, intelligent people who had been teenagers during the Great Depression and were determined to clamber out of the poverty of that time. They married just before World War II, had one child during the war, and Bill was born shortly afterward.

Educated in the Santa Rosa public schools, Bill had an unremarkable postwar childhood. His parents were happily married and relatively affluent, and his home life at times evoked an idyllic TV sitcom.

After first attending junior college in Santa Rosa, Bill finished his undergraduate studies at Chico State, taking degrees in accounting and psychology. Although his real scholastic talent was in mathematics, Bill pursued a degree in accounting because of the job opportunities it would open up. As for his other college major, he notes, "Psychology was my passion."

Bill's first job was with a large accounting firm in San Francisco now called KPMG. While working there he became fully accredited as a C.P.A., which further improved his qualifications in his field.

In San Francisco Bill began to have a very different life than he'd led in college, where he had been president of his fraternity and enjoyed a busy social life that had included dating and sex with a number of coeds. But in the big city, Bill found it hard to make friends. He began to feel very much alone. Eventually, he started making jaunts home to Santa Rosa to relieve his sense of isolation

On one such short trip, Bill got involved in a pickup football game and made several new friends. They were energetic and out-going—and all members of the Assemblies of God, a denomination that practices a form of Pentecostal religion. Very fervid believers, they were deeply involved in the life of their church.

Feeling himself adrift, Bill perceived a "can-do"sense of purpose in this circle of friends and was strongly attracted to it. Soon after meeting them, he moved back to Santa Rosa and started to share a house with several members of the local Assembly of God church, which he soon joined. It is significant that Bill's religious conversion happened during the Vietnam War. Like many in his generation, Bill was vastly disturbed by the war. His newfound religious faith, despite of its many drawbacks, helped him nurture the kind of focus he feared he had lost. His life with the Assemblies of God was to go on for eight years.

The church isolated its members as much as possible from temptation by keeping them preoccupied with church activities almost every weekday evening. Likewise, weekends were full of things to do with other church members. Another church policy was a form of discipleship; a member of stronger faith would mentor a recent and often younger member, who might need help in avoiding the temptations of the outside world. Besides participation in the life of the church to the exclusion of other spare-time activities, all members were expected to tithe and contribute at least 10% of their income to the church. Yet despite these demands, Bill saw little reason to complain. "I was naïvely happy," he notes.

Soon after Bill began sharing his life with the Assemblies of God, he was directed to marry Linda, who had been one of the members Bill had met that first day playing football on the lawn. Linda had then been engaged to a man born on the same day and almost the same hour as Bill—and only ten miles from where Bill was born. This man, however, left the church soon after his initial conversion. Shortly after his departure church members started urging Bill to marry Linda. Again, Bill had little problem meeting the church's request, despite an apparent rush bordering on implausibility. After all, he still considered himself a heterosexual and a Pentecostal Christian.

Even today Bill still has a somewhat biblical manner of speaking. "I always found men attractive," he reflects, "but I had never tasted that pleasure. Until I came out I had always been satisfied with the companionship of women." Similarly, when asked whether he had been in love with his wife, he replies, "We were reverently in love."

Bill and Linda had a son not long after they married. But then a turning point came almost out of the blue. "I came out at a religious retreat for men, Assembly of God members from many different churches around California," Bill recounts. "At the retreat one of the men said to me, 'Let's forget about religion. I'm really attracted to you. Let's see where it goes.' It was my first orgasm with a man. It was pretty powerful, and I realized I had gotten into something very serious. In retrospect our sexual encounter was nothing much at all, but it shook me. I went home and told my wife."

At home Bill and his wife prayed fervently. After a few days, Linda told him, "God says if I have another child, it proves you're not homosexual." She was soon pregnant.

Bill was not only working as a C.P.A. at this time but also as a bookkeeper for his church. Because of his bookkeeping responsibilities, he became close to the elders of the church Linda and he attended. Bill and his wife asked the elders to pray for them, without specifying the reason, which was a permissible church practice. After some time the elders called Bill before them and asked what they were praying for. He demurred, explaining that first he had to consult his wife.

Linda instructed, "You should tell them." And Bill did.

The elders then called Bill to a meeting and stated, "We feel you are possessed. We want to call in an exorcist."

Bill told them, "I love my wife and my family. If you can take this away I want you to."

A difficult and traumatic experience, the exorcism went on for at least eight hours. At the end he was told, "You're healed." Bill is still reluctant to say much about the exorcism ritual in detail, although he observes, "It was so emotionally wrenching. I was in another space. I felt a weight drop off my shoulders when it was over ,and I truly believed I had been healed. Now I think it was a kind of crash regression analysis."

Only 24 hours later Bill saw a man whom he found him attractive. He caught himself—*Uh-oh*. Already it was becoming apparent that he had gone through the exorcism trauma for nothing. He was still the same person he had been before.

Members of Bill's church then began to throw themselves into helping him with his "problem." He was kept in round-the-clock contact with several members and began to attend a therapy group in San Francisco called Love in Action, in which men were supposed to try to rid themselves of any homosexual feelings.

Love in Action was chiefly an inpatient treatment program, but Bill could only attend it some evenings, when he would commute from Santa Rosa. The program equated homosexuality with alcoholism and was based loosely on the Alcoholics Anonymous model of working steps toward some degree of recovery. Though designed to help men overcome homosexual feelings, the program proved more successful at being a clearinghouse for men with unresolved gay issues, as well as providing a sex and dating pool. Bill observes, "I learned more about gay sex and had more gay sex there with other attendees than I've ever had since in the same kind of time frame. These were men who also felt they were falling away from God. We would go for coffee to discuss our falling-away problem, then promptly go somewhere and go to bed together."

Officially, the program recommended abstinence. But even following official treatment policy could yield surprising results. Bill remembers, "We would be in a car discussing abstinence and then find ourselves in the backseat making love."

Bill returned home and took a six-month sabbatical from his job and the church. And he had good reason to; his hands were full, even without taking into account dealing with his sexual orientation. He was overseeing the construction of a new home for his family, and Linda was undergoing a difficult pregnancy.

Somehow during this period Bill found the time to slip away to the nearby Russian River area so that he could connect with gay and bisexual men. "This was my problem," Bill reflects. "I was gay and had deeper feelings about it at the time than I did about the church. But I loved my wife, and I wanted to make our marriage work." But he couldn't

The Assemblies of God advised Bill's wife to leave him. They told Linda, "He's demon-possessed and you should get out of there." Even now, years later, Linda believes that her ex-husband remains demon-possessed.

Coincidentally, Linda's former fiancé returned at this time to the church—and her personal life. Within a few months, she had divorced Bill, remarried her old flame, and started planning to move to the state of Washington with Bill's two sons. Bill had to place a restraining order upon her to keep the children in California until he had been granted appropriate visitation rights. He was granted monthly visits, and the children were to spend their summer vacation with him.

"The Church thought I was going to roll over and play dead," Bill says, "but I had no intention of doing that. My children hated me because the church and their parents had told them I was evil. But my love for them was constant and unwavering.

"They didn't want to visit me. On my visits to them I would arrive loaded with presents and would have to stay at motels. They were living in a very rural part of Washington. There was nothing to do and nowhere to go. They didn't want to spend summers with me because there were summer sports programs for them at home.

"My parents did come with me once, which was a big gesture on their part, since they had so thoroughly failed to understand the changes in my life and clearly had not wanted them to happen. When I first told my parents about being gay, my father knocked me down and tried to beat me up. So they're coming with me to visit their grandchildren was a pretty major thing."

When Bill's children were 8 and 10, Linda wife called out of the blue to say that the family was leaving in two weeks for Romania to serve as missionaries. "I called a lawyer," Bill says, "and told him. 'I need the best family lawyer in Washington State.' And I got him."

A second restraining order was put in place, and Linda's family, which by then included two children she'd had by her second husband, was forbidden to leave the country or the state. They perceived the restraining order as Bill's interference with God's will for their lives, which only made Bill's relationship with his children more difficult. Another result of the order was that Bill had to assume a considerable financial burden: "I had to support Linda, her husband, my two kids, and her two kids for two years. They claimed that I had taken her husband's job away from him."

At this time a court-appointed psychologist was given the job of interviewing Bill and Linda and their children as well as Linda's children by her subsequent marriage. Bill recalls the psychologist's conclusions quite clearly: " 'These kids need to see their father a lot more. There is nothing in Mr. Clark's history that suggests he's not a fit father. I'm going to recommend the children spend their whole summer with him, and these kids should go to public school and be out of the home schooling.' " Until this time the children had been schooled at home to keep them from contact with a contaminating ideas from the outside world.

Bill's older son has since become a successful journalist, and his younger son is now finishing college. Their feelings for their father have completely turned around since they have become adults. In fact, they have become influential in enabling their half-siblings to move into a less Pentecostal environment.

As an openly gay man, Bill never embraced a promiscuous

lifestyle. Instead, he has had "several serial monogamy relationships," adding, "I have never been to a bathhouse or a bookstore for sex. My connection to men has always been emotional as well as sexual."

Bill's first partner was Jim, whose regular use of marijuana threatened Bill's visitation rights with his children. Marijuana was difficult to keep in the house when the children were visiting—let alone Jim lighting up a joint in front of the children. The relationship soon ended. In hindsight, Bill also notes that when he was with Jim he may not really have been ready for a live-in partner. "We broke up perhaps because of my own emotional naïveté."

Wes, Bill's second long-term lover, was African-American. "He was a man I could say I was truly in love with after a year of dating," Bill says. "He pursued me, and when I finally got over my racism and prejudice and was prepared to live with him, he couldn't commit to the relationship."

Bill's next partner, Darin, was HIV-positive and up front about it. When they met in San Francisco in 1988, the long-term prognosis for AIDS patients was grim. Perhaps understandably, Darin's attitude toward was often fatalistic. Bill recalls: "Darin had a lot of trouble dealing with his situation and started to party, do drugs, and crash a lot. He would come home loaded when the kids were in the house, and I had to tell him that he just had to stay away until he came down. He ended up living with a dealer. It was tough on all of us—the kids especially, because they liked him." But Darin has since managed to turn his life around. Today Bill and he are friends, and his health has stabilized.

While Darin and he were together, Bill left his C.P.A. partnership and took over a mail-order sex toy company that originally was aimed at the heterosexual market. His partner was a heterosexual lawyer who thought the company had excellent potential. Called Xandria, the company was originally owned by Roy Raymond, who had founded Victoria's Secret. Xandria had been the brainchild of Roy's wife, Gaye. Because of her work in physical therapy, she knew that her more challenged clients needed some way to receive sexual pleasure they were unable to receive otherwise. With

Xandria, Gaye and Roy created a sex toy business that acquired the same positive image as Victoria's Secret. By the time Bill assumed control of Xandria, it was hugely successful.

Bill redesigned Xandria, which had been focusing on men's magazines like *GQ* and *Esquire,* and redirected its advertising toward women. After meeting with several magazine editors, he began to place ads in such publications as *Cosmopolitan* and *MS.* Soon Xandria's public relations campaign was effective in communicating a new positive mystique about improving one's sex life through toys and other devices.

Bill then set up a professional advisory board of therapists and doctors to support the company's position that it was serving a social need. This campaign led the media to take Xandria seriously, and the company expanded rapidly. Next, drawing upon the Tupperware sales strategy, Bill launched a spin-off company based on the concept of Pleasure Parties. Today, Xandria's spin-off has grown from 25 sales representatives and distributors to more than 900.

Since coming out, Bill has been deeply involved in socially responsible activities. He has been a founding director of both the Horizon Foundation, which raises funds to support various gay and lesbian causes, as well as the Bay Area Physicians for Human Rights (BAPHR), for which he also served on the board to oversee their accounting and tax procedures. Bill has also served on the board of directors for Continuum, a nonprofit adult health care service for late-stage HIV patients. This organization was created to care for people who have used up their financial resources and has proved to be a crucial safety-net agency in the Bay Area.

Somehow, Bill has made time to cochair the National AIDS Memorial Grove, a section of Golden Gate Park that commemorates people whose lives have been touched by AIDS. Benches, plaques, and various other memorials grace seven acres of greenery that had once been an overgrown brier patch.

Bill now lives with his life partner, personal trainer Jeff Stanfield, who is pursuing a career as a model in San Francisco. They have been together for four years and recently filed papers of domestic partnership in San Francisco. Bill's sons feel particularly close to Jeff.

After many years of reluctantly accepting his life, Bill's parents now say he is "the apple of their eye." They are proud of his achievements and have a much greater understanding of his life and the lives of other nontraditional people—a vantage point that Bill had once thought would be impossible for them.

Bill Clark has transited through a range of life experiences few other people have had. Now he has the successful, socially responsible, and personally fulfilling life he had always hoped for.

Jay Pagano:
THE FORTHRIGHT ROMANTIC

Tall and dashing and very much at ease with his gay identity, Jay Pagano is a familiar face on the Miami Beach social scene together with his equally attractive partner, Mark Fortier. A recently retired lawyer who had practiced in Washington, D.C., Jay now divides his time between New York and Florida.

Jay has a particularly direct approach to his own life story. A tough-minded man, he is able to talk in great detail about his own sexual history and has clearly thought it out. He doesn't dissemble when it comes to revealing things that do not reflect well upon him but should be told.

Thanks to the Stonewall rebellion, Jay believes his life has been less difficult than it might have been. That same year, 1969, he came out. "I didn't even know about Stonewall myself in that year, but it focused the world on the situation of homosexuals in society, and there was a great deal more acceptance and openness from that date on."

Born in Baltimore in 1945, Jay comes from a sturdy working-class family that had no pretensions of being anything else and little wish to achieve anything more. However, one of his grand-mothers, who had a love for fine cooking, was influential. Besides her inspiring example, it was solely Jay's own drive that led him to go from Baltimore public schools to a small college in Pennsylvania, where he originally had plans to become a history professor.

During his college years Jay was a civil rights worker in several Southern states, which included spending a summer in Vicksburg, Mississippi. While still a student, he met his future wife and upon graduation shifted his sights toward a law degree and marriage.

At 22, Jay got married before starting his legal studies at George Washington University. He had lived with his fiancée for three years before they wed; they were subsequently together for five years, then separated for two years before they divorced. Both Jay and his wife pursued advanced degrees after getting married. Though still in graduate school, they were already enjoying a gracious lifestyle. They were able to afford two cars and had purchased a home in a desirable suburb—a house Jay loved that was a major step up from the kind of homes he had known as a child.

Financially, Jay underwrote his studies and standard of living by working for a research company. "I spent a lot of late hours taking the census in very poor neighborhoods. They were not particularly surprised to find a researcher showing up at 11 o'clock at night. That's how I piled up the hours to earn a good living at the same time that I was attending school."

After receiving his degree Jay worked in the Baltimore area for three years and then moved back to Washington. He first was a specialist in employee discrimination cases and then worked for a variety of federal agencies, including a stint as a civil rights administrator. Long active in Washington civic life, Jay has been involved in many gay organizations and worked for a while with the National AIDS Fund.

Jay is hesitant to consider his early sexual exploration as a teenager part of his sexual history as a gay man. "For whatever reason, they never led to orgasm, and I don't really consider that true sexual activity. I fooled around with some boys, and when I was about 15, I was involved with a young neighborhood married man about ten years older than myself. We would go out for rides in a car, park in an empty field, and fondle each other. I can't explain why things never went any further, but they never did."

Around this time Jay was actively pursuing girls and taking real enjoyment from the sex he had with them. "I'd already had sex with women well before I had real sex with men. I didn't have sexual contact of any kind with other men after the age of 15 because I was aware that it was taboo and unacceptable. The most sexually active time of my life with women was before my marriage. I had a lot of sex at that time."

Jay recalls first having a truly sexual experience with another man the month before he was married. "I was earning some extra money as a house painter. While I was up on the ladder, I noticed the married man of the house was looking up my leg from the foot of the ladder. And I came down the ladder. It was only a sexual contact that we had, nothing more."

Of his marriage so soon after this encounter, Jay observes, "My recollection of my marriage is that certainly I was in love. But it also was a part of moving up and forward. And in retrospect it was a way of repressing, because I made my life so full. I finished law school in two and a half years. Eighteen months into law school, I had a nice home. By the time I finished we had two cars. My wife was getting her Ph.D., and I was very focused on having the things that went with a nice middle-class life."

Jay's parents did not encourage his climb. In fact, while he was in law school, he discovered that his mother was telling her friends he was in teacher's college (she was embarrassed to claim more than that to her friends). Even if there had been parental support, Jay had always had a strong desire to put distance between himself and his background.

"I think that's the gay part," he says. "Being aware that there is a better life somewhere. The big half-million-dollar salary, the famous name—that didn't matter to me. I wanted the trappings, the pretty surroundings. What you eat and where you eat it both were important to me."

In 1969, Jay found himself with a daughter and an attractive, professional wife. He was already in the process of buying a second home in the country. He had made it, materially speaking, though now he views his success as a form of compensation for a lack of passion. "Now I think my ambition was a way of sublimating energy that could have—should have—been directed towards having the kind of sex I wanted to have."

Once Jay fully recognized the kind of sex life he wanted to have, he started to pursue it. "By 1970, I was out sexually. I now wanted some kind of fantasy life where I would have a house with a white picket fence and a doctor boyfriend." Always the social climber, Jay began by pursuing men who were socially and economically better off than he was. His first real affair was with Gale, a Harvard-educated lawyer.

"I thought gay life was great," Jay recalls. "I had access to a lifestyle where I was associating with doctors and lawyers and antique dealers." Jay became part of the more affluent and professional gay life of Washington. "This was part of what seduced me to make the break from the security of my marriage and fulfill my sexual needs."

Jay came out to his wife before anyone else. She did not take the news well. "She was bitter. I was a big part of her life, and she didn't like losing me. I was her hero." They divorced because she wished to remarry. She married a psychologist, whom she divorced not long ago after 25 years of marriage. Despite the divorce, Jay has remained close to his daughter and played an active role in her life. She now has two children of her own. Being a father has been an important part of his identity.

After Gale, Jay next began a serious relationship with a good-looking medical student from an aristocratic Southern background. Jay feels this coupling was ill-fated from the start. "This was never a successful relationship. For me, a successful relationship is passionate—there is love but also harmony. This was an attraction of opposites."

In the eight years this relationship lasted, Jay and his lover lived together for only 18 months. The breakup proved to be quite painful for Jay. "My history is to never be alone. I have to have somewhere to go emotionally before I can leave. I have no fear of someone leaving me. I just find it very difficult to end a relationship."

As for beginning a new relationship, Jay observes, "There are two things that draw me to people: first, the potential for a nice life and the world that goes with it. And, second, I'm attracted to the role of Guardian Angel. I think there is a part of me that is truly altruistic and I want to play that role in someone's life."

Jay's new lover, Jerre, who grew up in Alabama, was the man to experience this "Guardian Angel" treatment. "Jerre was floundering," Jay recalls. "He worked part-time at this and that. He had no real occupation. He was pretty and charming—and fun. He was from a working-class family also."

Jay remained with Jerre for eight years. "Finally, I saw that Jerre had difficulty developing a career. He was just hanging about, unhappy with his life and career in Washington. I said to myself, *Oh, my God—what about my dreams for a richer, grander life? It's not happening.*"

Adding to Jay's increasing frustration with the relationship was the looming presence of AIDS. "I have always had sex outside any primary relationship that I have had," Jay confesses. But Jerre was afraid of the epidemic and refused to be tested. "This became an issue between us and played a role in the breakup."

At this point Gale, Jay's first longtime lover, returned to live with him—not as a lover, but because he was now sick with AIDS and had nowhere to go. He lived with Jay the last year of his life and died in Jay's home.

A year later Jay's second lover, Jerre, died of AIDS, too. He died while living with a male model who had also become ill with an HIV-related disease. For Jay, Jerre's death greatly traumatic. "I felt very guilty. I felt I had failed him."

After that, Jay had a series of relationships that were short-lived and purely sexual. "Some of these men may have thought of me as their lover." he says, "But I never thought of them in that way. These relationships were not romantic for me." Jay simply saw his sexual interludes as pleasant diversions that did not get in the way of his career or buying a new house and acquiring other material trappings of the good life. He was not in the market for a new long-term relationship.

After "playing the field" for a bit, Jay found himself embarking on another long-term relationship, one that would last a number of years and combine his penchant for fine living and personal altruism. "I was trying to fix everything that had been wrong in my second relationship," Jay says.

A successful, socially prominent lawyer, Jay's new lover had a terrific sense of humor. While the initial attraction was sexual, Jay soon recognized his new lover as a well-rounded person with whom he shared many interests and goals. The couple began to enjoy a life of dinner parties and other Washington activities.

With this relationship Jay made a new rule for himself. Previously, he had allowed himself to become close to the men he slept with outside his relationship. In one case Jay had been having sex regularly with a man who was both his closest friend and his lover's. Jay found this stressful and in this, his third major relationship, he determined he would not seek an emotional connection outside his committed relationship. Despite his efforts in this regard, Jay's third relationship eventually foundered, too.

Now Jay is determined to make a go of his relationship with his present partner Mark. They recently entered into a civil union in Vermont. Jay says, "I don't want to repeat patterns," and so far has been successful in staying committed to Mark.

Brian O'Banion:
THE BRAVE BATTLE THROUGH

Brian, or Barry as he is known to most people, was the James Dean of the small city in Maine where he was born and raised. "I even had the red nylon jacket," he quips.

A descendant of Irish workers who had come to Maine in the early 19th century for employment as fishers, Brian was raised in an atmosphere characterized both by affluence and parental neglect. His father had been the first of his generation to leave the traditional family employment in the fishing industry to become the head of a small department-store chain.

The senior O'Banion was not particularly affectionate, nor was he indulgent. When Barry was 10 years old, he asked his father for an allowance, only to receive this reply: "You have a unique opportunity. You can work." And work he did in the family business, which gave him more than enough money to spend.

As a teenager clad in T-shirts and blue jeans—not so common a school uniform then—Barry was known for driving the family car about town, hell-bent for trouble. He became part of a disaffected group of students at his school. To an extent his parents put up with his behavior. "But my mother would never let me wear my hair in a D.A. [a duck's ass haircut, with a pompadour and swept-back sides meeting in the back]. However, I did come down one morning with silver hair, which set her back quite a bit."

There was probably a Barry O'Banion in many towns during the

'50s and early '60s—the sort of "bad boys" and "bad girls" recaptured later in the musical *Grease*. Barry remembers, "No one did well scholastically." Everyone in his crowd was sure to have intercourse so as to set themselves well apart from the "nice" girls and boys in their school.

Besides his introduction to sex with some of the "bad" girls from his school, Barry O'Banion was having sex regularly with boys, too. But this was his secret.

After his anti-establishment period in high school, Barry went to a junior college for a year in Boston. He was ejected from the college when the proctor of his dormitory walked in and found him having intercourse with a girl from his hometown, who was also going to school in Boston.

Barry had been very much in love with another hometown girl when he had left for Boston, and upon being thrown out of college, he rushed home to find solace in her arms. Unfortunately, when he got there, he found she was pregnant by another local young man. When asked whether he would have married her anyway, his answer is enthusiastic: "Oh, God, yes!" He did propose to her, but she refused him and announced that she was going to marry the father of her child, for whom she had no love. This union would prove to be a terrible mistake, bringing much unhappiness to the young woman he loved so much.

Barry's immediate reaction to his sweetheart's rebuff was to take his father's new Cadillac, drive to a nearby roadhouse, down 24 whiskey sours, and completely wreck the new car on the way back into town.

True to his insurrectionist mindset, Barry joined the Army as a reservist. After six months of active duty, he was in the Maine State Reserve for another five years, thereby managing to avoid overseas duty in Vietnam. During this time he continued to live at home and work for his father in the department store. Barry is not without admiration for his parents' patience with him. "To their credit they never mentioned my many failures to me."

He then went to work in Boston—"my play city," as he calls it.

He was sleeping with both men and women then—more often women than men, because they were more readily available. For the most part, his encounters with men were still limited to the same partners he'd had in high school. For Barry, gay sex remained something unspeakable. "My huge, huge secret. I refused to even think about the gay side of my persona."

While in Boston, Barry met a nice girl from Washington, D.C., and when she became pregnant by him, he decided it was time to settle down. At 23, he married her, and they returned as newlyweds to his hometown, where he again worked in the family business. Despite his rebellious youth, Barry's stoic Catholic upbringing had made some impression on him: He did not for a moment contemplate *not* marrying the woman whose child he had fathered, even though his bride was not Catholic.

For the next decade, Barry was swept into the many challenges of raising and supporting a young family. After their first child, he and his wife had two more children, giving them a total of two boys and a girl. But their marriage was at best uneasy. When asked whether his wife and he had ever been happy together, Barry replies, "Not really."

Success with the department-store chain allowed Barry to provide his family with a large house, expensive cars, good schools, and stylish clothes. Flush with funds, Barry grew to admire several local wealthy men who threw their money around, lived wild and dissolute lives, and "shitted on their wives." Without much careful consideration, he modeled his behavior after the example of these men. He told himself that drinking heavily and chasing women—and occasionally a man—amounted to nothing more than having a good time. It was the sort of life captured deftly by American writers like F. Scott Fitzgerald, John P. Marquand, John Updike, and John Cheever.

But Barry did make some attempts to be socially responsible at the community level. He once led a fight to save a local kindergarten. Thanks in part to his effort, the school was saved. But trouble loomed at home. The night the election returns came in, Barry's neglected wife chose to sleep with the local tennis pro to make a statement of her own—a statement that sounded the death knell of their marriage.

The bell had been tolling some time in the background. A stylish young woman named Sally, whom Barry describes as "local royalty," and her husband had become Barry's neighbors. Younger than Barry—he hadn't known her in his school years—she was beautiful and hard-drinking. Sally and Barry immediately clicked in a way neither had ever experienced with their spouses.

Barry's wife's indiscretion led him to file for divorce. Next door, Sally soon followed suit. And as quickly as they could, Barry and Sally got married. The two had a total of seven children by their first marriages. Their union did not produce any more children.

On the surface, Barry's life seemed stable enough, even after the divorce and second marriage. But gaping rifts were occasionally perceptible through this veneer of security, giving Barry the sense that the earth was never steady beneath his feet.

Barry's father was one of the chief instigators of this insecurity. Having spent so much time working in his father's business, Barry had expected to inherit it. By chance one day, he ran across a letter at the company office, in which he discovered that his father was planning to sell the business. The terms proposed by the senior O'Banion would have bound Barry to work for five years in the business after the sale—a scenario worthy of Arthur Miller.

Barry acted decisively and rapidly. He organized the financial resources to buy out his father and forced him to sell by refusing to honor any contract wherein he was required to work for five years for the new buyer. Because Barry was vitally important to the management of the company by this time, his father was unable to sell the company without his cooperation and assent.

Once he bought out his father, Barry truly had a new life. In the following decade, he headed a department store chain that rapidly expanded from a handful of locations in Maine to well over two dozen stores in New England. He was living with his very compatible new wife and her children in one of the most splendid houses in his hometown.

Though Barry's ex-wife had gone South to live near her parents and siblings, she continued to receive a great deal of attention from him. She developed cancer, and in her final years Barry was constantly fulfilling her wish to travel. "There I was in Acapulco in a hotel with both wives and all seven children," he recalls almost jokingly. "I asked myself, 'Is this a vacation?'" There was another en masse trip to England in an attempt to satisfy his ex-wife's wanderlust before she died.

Barry passed from his mid 30s into his mid 40s, still leading this hard-living, hard-drinking, constantly busy life. His stepchildren and oldest son by his first marriage were attending the same Catholic school where he had been educated. Many of their teachers told them what a hell-raiser Barry had been. Still ambitious, Barry continued to expand the department-store chain, which required some overextension of credit, though the stores continued to thrive and overall his finances remained in the black.

Thirteen-odd years ago it all came to an abrupt halt. Sally's youngest son, then in his mid-teens, killed himself. It was the fifth and last in a rash of teen suicides in their small city. Barry says, "It stopped everybody's clock."

Barry and Sally struggled on for a few years. The other children had all left home for college. His despairing wife could not remain in their hometown any longer. Barry says, "I would lie awake in the night and hear her weeping in her sleep. I would have done anything for her."

They moved to Palm Beach, planning to run the department stores from there. This did not prove feasible, so Barry began the process of trying to sell his business. In a meeting with his lawyers and the buyer's lawyers he heard himself say, perhaps absentmindedly, "That would be suicide." He was unable to continue the meeting—or attend any further ones. Plans for selling stores were put on hold. "We had money for the children to go to college," Barry says, "but the party was over for Sally and me."

Barry made a last-ditch attempt to salvage his business by returning to Maine, but bankruptcy was unavoidable. Barry and his family returned to Palm Beach almost by default. There was no reason to go anywhere else.

While weathering these trials Barry never looked into therapy as a way to work through his problems. He states very directly (one of his winning qualities), "No. I was never honest with myself. My primary activity was alcohol consumption. And my wife was right there with me, smoking pot every day starting at 10 in the morning."

In the early '90s, Barry's second marriage finally capsized. "We went to Key West for a long holiday weekend. I'm not sure why. Actually, I probably know why, but it didn't seem evident then. Our first evening there, I got very drunk and disappeared with some guy. When I got back, my wife and I had words, and then I proceeded to get very drunk again the next day and disappear with another guy. At that time in my life, when I was very drunk I actually thought I was invisible. I thought no one saw me doing these things. When I got back the second morning, my wife had taken off with the car. I had to rent a car and drive home. I was in a suicidal mood."

Barry admits his behavior in Key West was no longer that shocking to Sally. "I had been caught red-handed several times by my wife. We were in Los Angeles once and had hired a car and chauffeur to go out on the town. We were drinking heavily and took the chauffeur home with us. She wandered out of the bedroom in our suite. When she came back she caught the chauffeur sucking my dick. That time I assured her I was bisexual."

The drive back to Palm Beach was miserable. "I was hurting as much as I've ever hurt in my life," Barry recalls. "I thought, *I've got to stop drinking*. And immediately I thought, *I can't*. And then I started planning my suicide."

His plan was much in the style of F. Scott Fitzgerald. He was going to go home and collect some clothes, fly to New York, and check in at the deluxe Plaza Athenée hotel. There he was going to indulge himself thoroughly with professional sex partners (male) and then swallow 100 Percodans with champagne, leaving a note: "The Prozac made me do it." He hoped his family could then sue the manufacturer for a fortune.

Luckily, Sally intervened when he got back to Palm Beach, and he went into a clinic for alcoholics instead. He was there 28 days, and came out clean, which he has remained. He says of his return to Palm Beach after the clinic, "I was awake for the first time in my life."

Misfortune continued to plague Barry, however. In a nearby town he bought a business that made blankets and equipment for horses. While attending the college graduation of one his children, he received news that someone had broken into his factory and stolen everything: stock, equipment, sewing machines—the works. He was out of business. With little remaining enthusiasm, he got involved in a series of other business ventures.

At the personal level, though, things were finally beginning to gel. Especially important were the men Barry was meeting in the recovery groups he was attending. For the first time in his life, he was getting to know openly gay men who led satisfying, openly gay lives. Despite the high-flying life Barry had known, he had never had much contact with gay men who were comfortable with their sexuality. He found them fascinating and listened eagerly to any tidbits they dropped about gay life. Barry spent many sleepless nights before he could bring himself to say, "Yes, I am gay." He adds, "What a revelation that was. I realized there was a life out there that could work."

Finally, Barry told wife, "Sit down, Sally, we have to talk." Then came the news, which shouldn't have been that much of a surprise to her: "I'm gay." But it was. Sally's immediate reaction was that he should go to a clinic in Tucson to be deprogrammed. In no uncertain terms, Barry said he didn't wish to do this.

Sally shot back, "I've already got a brother who is gay. I don't need another one."

Barry responded, "And I've got a sister. I don't need another one."

Barry moved out immediately. He lived near his wife for a year, but she was very hurt and decided to leave for the West Coast. Today they have an amicable relationship, but the emotional wounds they both suffered have taken some time to heal.

After his confession to his wife, Barry hastened to explain himself to his children. Thankfully, he had more success with them. "I had a great feeling of release when I talked to my kids. It was like getting a huge rock off my head. It wasn't just that it had been terribly heavy, but that it had to be balanced. I couldn't let it slip. Now I didn't have to do that anymore."

Fortunately, Barry soon befriended a gay man his age who'd had similar experiences to his. With his guidance Barry was introduced to the life possible for a middle-aged gay man in South Florida. He had a few casual relationships with other men and for a while frequented bathhouses and pickup bars—he freely admits, "I was very promiscuous." Because of his age Barry had to work through very real fears of rejection, but with his friend's help he trod all the highways and byways possible until he was at ease in his new life.

Now sober and well-advanced into middle age, Brian O'Banion remains quite attractive. His demeanor is sociable and direct, if more reserved than in his drinking days. Most important, he is completely comfortable in his new life. He enjoys a mutually satisfying relationship with a handsome, amiable lover who has a successful career in the construction industry. And his lover enjoys going to the get-togethers Barry's large Irish-American family still holds. "For the little ones," says Barry's partner, "I'm just like their grandmother. It works fine."

But current good fortune notwithstanding, there remains a slight guardedness in Barry's eyes that is particularly evident when he meets someone new—a guardedness that reflects the tough road he has traveled to find himself.

Otis:

THE ONE WHO WAS ALWAYS A LITTLE DIFFERENT

That is what Otis says of himself: "I was the one who was always a little different, preferring to live my life on the creative fringe of reality." As he came from a conservative, well-mannered Southern family, this little difference always made a big difference to Otis's relatives. It made them uneasy. He tried to keep them from feeling uneasy, but he finally had to give up.

Otis was born in a small town in the center of Mississippi. His childhood revolved around a number of similar small towns in Mississippi and Louisiana, towns where his parents came from and towns where his father worked. In a scenario typical of many men Otis's age—in their 50s—he had a father who served in World War II and who after the war had a job that required him to relocate regularly. Otis's parents were childhood sweethearts from a tiny Louisiana community where his maternal grandfather was doctor, dentist, pharmacist, and town father all in one. On his maternal grandfather's side, Otis has connections to the oldest families in the region, which is important in Louisiana and Mississippi—particularly if you are from an old, Catholic family.

He attended a Catholic grade school—unusual, he points out, for the rural Mississippi area where he was born. He then attended public schools and went on to Louisiana State University.

Otis was something of a whiz kid. He followed up his undergraduate degree in business from LSU with an MBA. He moved to New

Orleans without a job and was promptly hired to be a member of the think tank being created by the Economic Development Council for the Chamber of Commerce of New Orleans. That city had fallen upon difficult economic times at the time Otis left school, and in a very forward-thinking way it hired for its think tank a trio of brilliant recent college graduates: Otis, a woman, and a gay Hispanic man. Otis was 22, the others perhaps a year or two older. They created a program of development for the city that Otis eventually directed. He supervised a team of 50 people devoted to improving business in New Orleans, which they very successfully accomplished in the 1970s.

Otis did this for ten years, and in the same decade his private life developed equally rapidly and successfully, certainly in his own and his family's eyes. When he moved to New Orleans he rented an apartment from a young woman whose husband had been tragically killed in an automobile accident shortly after their marriage. Both Otis and the young woman had a strong interest in the real estate of New Orleans and wanted very much to restore the beautiful old homes in the heart of the city to their former glory. This shared interest brought them closer until they decided to be married.

"At this time I was not conscious that I was interested in developing emotional relationships with other men," Otis says. "As a young kid, from about 10 to 13, I had experimented with other boys my age, which I believe is very common. I dated in high school. In college I almost got married twice. In the most long-lasting of these relationships we came close to tying the knot, but we never got as far as sex. That just wasn't part of my fiancée's world. However, I did have a wild fling with a New Orleans woman in this same period. So I didn't have any reason to think I wasn't sexually attracted to women. The mysterious but intriguing fantasy of same-sex relationships was something that I didn't rule out of the realm of possibility in the future."

During college in the 1960s, he says, "I do remember going to a pop music festival, as we called them, a kind of Woodstock, in Mansura where guys were nude off and on for the whole week. And I was aroused by the naked men around me and had difficulty controlling it. But I think I repressed all of that strange, unknown sexual desire."

Otis's marriage was highly successful in many people's eyes. He had two beautiful little daughters, a beautifully decorated Victorian home, and a very gratifying job. His business life was reported on regularly in the local media. Of this period in his life, he says, "I think it was very important to me and I really wanted to create this kind of enviable life, but I didn't realize how much I was compelled to do it until later."

But despite his success, restlessness gnawed at Otis. Part of it grew out of the relentless pressure of his job. His work often required him to organize major events—like playing host and tour guide to dozens of businessmen on a trip to Paris, where they wined and dined top French business and government officials at places like the Crillon Hotel. His work required constant travel, which took a toll on his health. He soon learned he was diabetic. He also says, "I was probably drinking, smoking, and eating and stressing too much.

"At work I was bitter and difficult with my coworkers. At home I was aloof and removed from my wife, who also thought I wasn't spending enough time with my children. I was very unhappy with myself but I didn't know why."

This situation might have continued indefinitely had Otis's wife not sued for divorce. The divorce was very acrimonious, with the process going on for two years, and left Otis with no assets, living in a small apartment near his former home. He agreed to surrender his home and almost everything he had to his wife. He also left his job with the Chamber of Commerce, whose decision-makers couldn't handle the bad press associated with Otis's divorce.

Otis started working for a small weekly local newspaper as a freelance writer. To cover his child support bills he also began work as a consultant in the real estate business, at which he was immediately successful. Many of the contacts he had made in his work with the Chamber of Commerce sought him out immediately. He also immediately began seeking relationships with other men.

When asked how it was that he stepped so rapidly and neatly from a heterosexual life to a homosexual life, Otis explains that during his days with the New Orleans Chamber of Commerce, the public relations firm it employed was in New York, where Otis frequently went. There were gay staff members in this company, and on nights out they sometimes took Otis to gay bars. "I found myself wanting to participate," he says. "I was comfortable in this environment."

After having initial exploratory affairs with other men and some playing the field, Otis met a young man named Clay who was to become a great affair of his heart. He at first moved in with him, and then they moved to an old mansion to house-sit while it was being sold. This was the early 1980s. At this time Otis was developing a condominium property with his father, who had recently retired from his career in the oil business.

Otis's family strongly disapproved of his relationship with Clay—to the point that it came down to "It's him or us." Otis chose Clay.

When asked whether he felt the real struggle in his life was choosing between the code of behavior that his family so strongly believed in and the newfound life he was living, Otis replies, "I was always different. When I was very young I was a preppy little model for a local manufacturer of boys' clothing. Later, in school, I went to a wedding with a pregnant girlfriend and everyone said, 'That's Otis.' In college someone did a cartoon of me saying, 'I can't even spell psychedelic, but I am.' And finally my family didn't approve of my wife, because she was pregnant before we married. They found her very difficult but then reversed themselves because of my overwhelmingly charming children. And then I divorced and I ended up with a man. I really gave them a lot to put up with.

"My relationship with my parents and one brother has never recovered, but my other brother and my sister and I stay in touch. I also discovered I had a gay cousin. That was an eye-opener. He was fully accepted as long as he lived with another man in a house with two bedrooms. It was clear to me where I was going."

Clay and Otis split after about five years, an event that was the most difficult emotional experience of Otis's life. "I've never felt so strongly about anyone and I never will again," Otis says. "I couldn't even work for about a year after he left me." The situation was made more difficult by the fact that his children and Clay had become best friends. "I had to excommunicate him from my life in order to survive," Otis says. "I don't even know where he is."

Since then Otis has had several relationships with younger men that lasted long enough to qualify them as more than casual affairs. But Otis broke off the last one, with a man who took Otis as his first male lover, because, he says, "I just didn't feel comfortable in it any longer."

His work as a real estate consultant has continued to flourish, and he has developed a secondary career as a talented photographer. Many of his photographs are of the young men he knows.

When talking about his life Otis is very straightforward and calm. When queried about this, he says, "I'm not an openly emotional being. I don't easily or quickly express love." When prompted to recall his dramatic love affair with Clay, he qualifies his statement by saying, "I'm a very emotional and very sexual person, but I'm discreet and reserved in the overt display of my inner feelings."

Otis is a tall, slender, somewhat formal man with a refined manner and speech. His deep hesitation about revealing his feelings only makes him more appealing. When asked what his life plan is, he says, "I wish I had a plan. My children are grown and living on the West Coast. One is married. The other is engaged to be married. I guess, for myself, I'd like a mature relationship with someone mature, perhaps near my own age. I think I'd like to do that."

Since Otis was interviewed he has become involved in an intimate friendship with a neighbor, Brad, who has lived across the street for some ten years. He reports that 30-something Brad is a "free soul" and adds, "I have been very happy and excited to pursue this friendship, which seems to just 'click' without any effort or future expectations. It's real comfortable living in the moment, hanging out with a soul mate, going with the flow. I'm being very objective about the situation and using my past experiences to build a mature friendship, openly expressing how I feel and respecting the same from my friend. What happens, happens."

Brad Appel:
THE DOCTOR WHO IS HEALING HIMSELF

Brad Appel is a dashing guy. With his powerfully muscled body and wrestler's stance, he attracts quite a few admirers at the gym he frequents. Few of them know he has passed the 50-year mark, or that he is a successful urologist.

From both his parents Brad inherited natural ability as an athlete as well as the determination to excel academically. He was born in Miami in 1946, shortly after his father had been separated from the United States Army. Before World War II, his father had been a second-string quarterback at the University of Miami. Brad's mother, whose family had come to Florida from Cleveland, did not complete her education until after getting married and giving birth to several children.

While still a youth, Brad was much occupied in caring for his younger twin brothers, once his mother had returned to school. She finished high school, then completed an undergraduate college degree and went on for her doctorate. In light of his responsibility for his brothers, Brad recalls not surprisingly, "I didn't have much time to play as a child."

At 18, Brad left home to attend Western Reserve University in Cleveland before going on to the University of Rochester Medical School. Brad spent two years as a resident in general surgery at Yale-New Haven Hospital and then served another two years as a physician in the Air Force at Eglin Air Force Base in Valparaiso,

Florida. And completing his stint in the military, he returned to Miami to train in urology at the University of Miami.

By this time Brad had already been wed nearly six years, having married his high school girlfriend during his second year of medical school. They were both in their early 20s then. Originally, Brad's new bride had been dating his best friend in high school. When the friend had to leave for military service, he had asked Brad to keep an eye on her. The young woman and Brad soon became very close.

After three years of rigorous training, Brad was able to open his own urologist's office in Miami. (Many specialists are not ready to set up a private practice in such a short time frame, let alone be successful at it.) Brad feels fortunate that his practice developed very quickly. Soon he could afford a three-bedroom house in an attractive neighborhood in southwest Miami for his family, which now included two young daughters. The first was born while he was still in general surgery in New Haven, the second while he was finishing urology training.

After 11 years, Brad's marriage unraveled when his wife discovered he was having a long-distance affair with another man. He explains, "I had been to Kansas City for urology boards, and I had met an attorney there and spent the night with him. He started writing me letters at my office. My wife was working as my secretary at the time, and she opened my mail as part of her job. I had been at the hospital, and when I walked in the office, I saw that she was in tears. That was when I actually came out to her."

Brad had already discovered that he was attracted to other men when he was in junior high school. He and a boy of his own age would go to a pool at a nearby hotel, where they would flash their genitalia underwater and fondle each other. The boy also came over to Brad's house when his parents weren't home. "There was no penetration or oral sex," Brad notes, almost wonderingly.

Brad's next relationship was with a man he met his second week in college. They remained together for four years. "We joined the same fraternity, and we often went out on double dates and then went home and had sex." Brad was the quarterback for the fraternity football team and active in campus politics. At the time Brad had thought the relationship was pretty discreet, though he now muses, "I wasn't aware of people suspecting anything about our relationship, but people must have."

After Brad and his friend graduated, the relationship was over. "We separated after college, when I went to medical school and he went to law school. But curiously, his life has mirrored my own life exactly, only one year behind me. He married one year after I did, then had two daughters one year exactly after each of mine was born, and divorced one year after my divorce went through."

While still a married man, Brad started going to the baths every couple of weeks, more out of a need for release than anything else. "I would be on call from the hospital. I'd fuck my brains out for four hours and get it out of my system. That would last for about two weeks."

Nevertheless, Brad insists that he loved his wife and valued his marriage. "I *did* love Ally, but it was very much about my wanting the life. I wanted to be a successful doctor with a nice wife, a beautiful house, and the children. I wanted the whole package. I liked sex with my wife for about four years. Then I began to have premature ejaculations. I began then to have fantasies about men in order to ejaculate. It just got worse and worse."

Being so closeted, Brad did not look much beyond carnal pleasures when it came to gay life. "My attitude then was that my gay life was all about raw sex. I never allowed myself to get close to somebody, no matter what, no matter how good the sex was.

"Then I met my first love at the baths after I was divorced. We ended up talking for three hours at the pool after we had sex. He had a house, a very settled lifestyle. Here was this man: kind, compassionate, a person who had friends who came over to dinner. Wow, it was so strange to me. After his friends left, we would hug. I wasn't like that at all. My mother always stiffened when you hugged her goodbye."

Brad remained closeted after his divorce, even though he was already sharing his new life with Carl, the lover he met at the baths. Brad underwent intensive therapy for a year after his wife had left with the children for Texas when she remarried. The separation from his children was particularly painful. "I sat in the backyard and cried and cried, telling myself, 'I've really fucked up. What have I done? I'm all alone.'"

After three years with Carl, Brad bought a house with him. Their property included a second dwelling so that Brad could easily explain Carl's presence. Brad was still firmly closeted, especially when it came to his professional acquaintances. "I was afraid all the time that if it got out that I was gay, I'd stop getting referrals. That other doctors wouldn't send patients to me. My lover and I started having major issues about my not being out.

"We were in a bar called the Double R one evening. A male nurse I knew from a local hospital came in the door, and I ducked under the bar. I kept pulling at Carl's pants saying, 'Tell me when he's gone!' Carl looked down and said, 'What do you think you're doing?' And I said, 'That guy is going to recognize me!' Carl thought it was crazy."

Five years into this relationship, Brad had still had little experience with the gay world, so Carl allowed him to sally forth and have experiences outside their relationship—which may have been for the best. "He was an alcoholic who had a desk job he hated," Brad notes wryly about Carl. They eventually separated. By the time Brad was in his late 30s, he was living alone.

Brad's next lover, a very good-looking man from Georgia, proved to be more than a handful. "He moved in and stayed for three years. It was a disaster." During this period, pressures to come out to at least his parents began to mount. "I just couldn't come out to my parents. Finally, one day I called them and said, 'I went to meet you at your house at 3 o'clock.' I went loaded with ammunition: my marriage's failure, my being gay—I blamed them for everything. My father was a loving, affectionate man, but I never got that side of him. My mother dominated the marriage." Brad's parents were shocked and hurt by the confrontation and for some six months they kept their distance. But then they called to see how he was and there was reconciliation.

As he approached 50, Brad's life started going into a slow tail-spin. He was then in another relationship that would end after five years when he reached 52. When he was 48, Brad and his partner had started using drugs. "I believe I have an addictive character. In sex I have addictive behavior. I have to watch constantly so it doesn't get out of control," Brad observes. "My boyfriend came back from a business trip with crystal when I was in my late 40s. We began using it one night a week, then two nights a week. Then weekends began to start on Thursday night running through Sunday. We broke up. My drug use escalated. I was using drugs every night, having sex all night and still managing to work."

This wild period came to a halt when Brad was arrested. "I was arrested on Meridian Avenue at 4 A.M., driving 15 miles over the speed limit with my lights off while wearing only my under-pants and sneakers. The police found a vial of Special-K in the tire well of the trunk. And they also found my identification. One guy said, 'Hey, this guy is a doctor.' I'd been on my way to see a trick at Second and Washington, but I never got there. They took me in and charged me with reckless driving and possession. I spent three hours there, and then they took me downtown, where I was pho-tographed and fingerprinted. They threw me in a cell with 15 other guys. All I had to eat while I was there was a ham sandwich, which they brought me. I was in jail something like 16 hours. I had to call my secretary, and she went to the bank and drew out $15,000 to bail me out.

"The reckless driving charge got reduced to careless driving, but I got one year's probation on the drug charge. I joined PRN, Physicians Recovery Network and I signed a five-year contract [to stay clean]. There are meetings every Tuesday night at a hospital. You have to call in every day. You have a urinalysis twice a month. That was two years ago."

Just as he was coming out of his drug period, Brad broke off with yet another lover. While they never did drugs, they separated because of what Brad calls "intimacy issues"—the feeling they could not get close to each other.

By chance Brad recently ran into a man who had always interested him. They have since started dating, and Brad hopes their relationship will be monogamous. "My goal is a long-term intimate relationship." Brad has taken a new interest in spirituality and recently began attending services at the Unity Church, a religious organization devoted to New Age spiritualism. Armed with an emerging spiritual understanding, Brad Appel has taken a philosophical stance on the difficulties of the past few years. "I believe it has all been my destiny. My leaving my wife, even my drug use, has all been part of a greater path that we are all taking."

John Welsh
A WORK IN PROGRESS

John Welsh's story is particularly interesting. He remains married, and although his wife is aware that he is homosexual, she does not want a divorce. They have been married for many years, and their annual trips to Europe and other places are a source of pleasure to her. And she enjoys her husband's company. John says that although his wife is not entirely happy about the diversions he pursues when he travels alone—which he often does—she is willing to rise above her displeasure.

John is perhaps less pleased with the situation, as he is less interested in casual encounters or short-lived romantic affairs and would like to have a long-term relationship with another man. On the other hand, he is reluctant to leave his wife to live a life by herself. A life, that would, strangely enough, duplicate the one his divorced mother had.

John is in his middle 50s, an attractive dark-haired man with a very easy social manner. Born in 1946 in Missouri, he grew up in a family steeped deeply in small-town life. His parents met in his father's hometown, where his mother was teaching in a one-room schoolhouse. They met shortly before World War II, which interrupted their married life. They were married for eight years before John was born. He is the elder of two brothers.

His father was a graduate of the University of Missouri and planned to become a lawyer. His mother had started her studies at

Maryville College in Tennessee but had to leave college so her father could afford to educate her two brothers. She always resented this, John says.

During the war his father worked as a dental technician in the U.S. Army but was never sent abroad. After the war his father became the last administrator of a Confederate soldiers' home in Kansas City. John was born in Kansas City, Missouri, and remained there until the age of 4. At that time the home his father supervised was closed, and shortly thereafter the family moved to the remote small town of Rolla, Missouri.

In Rolla, while John was still a small child, a friend of the family noticed that John frequently stumbled into things. His eyesight was checked, and it turned out that one eye contained a tumor. The eye had to be removed when John was 3. John says that he received a lot of attention because of his disability, but unfortunately he was never able to play sports.

His father took the loss of John's eye very much for granted and never favored him because of it. In school, however, John was treated as something of an outcast. He had little upper-body strength, and he lived much more in the world of the mind than in the world inhabited by rowdier boys his age.

By the time he was in sixth grade his family was living in Jefferson City, Missouri, and there he met the young girl who was later to become his wife. He claims that to this day he remembers exactly where she was sitting in the classroom. When he first saw her he thought, *I will marry that woman.* Evidently there was a great affinity between them at first sight, although John says they were never passionately in love.

John reports that in high school he was "Mr. Good Boy." His school was very large, and he was involved in numerous social activities and managed to get good grades. He worked on the school yearbook and newspaper and was the president of the concert and marching bands. He was given the all-school service award for his contributions to the school's extracurricular activities. "I was very active," he recalls. "It distracted me from myself."

When he was in third grade he realized he had an interest in boys and men. He was particularly captivated when he caught a glimpse of his swimming instructor undressing. When he was 10 years old he was drawn to his best friend's 12-year-old brother. On one occasion the other boy's father took them all swimming and declared, "We're not going to wear swimsuits today." John found that exciting, but he never had any sexual encounters with the boys he knew, not even close friends.

In his high school boys did not wear swimsuits in the pool. John says these encounters were the closest to anything he could call "sexual" at this period of his life. "I was very innocent," he says.

Not so innocent that he didn't notice several boys in the school who were "softer around the edges." One became a pianist. Another was a boy whom his wife-to-be dated in high school and who later became a very distinguished banker.

Of his early sex, life John says that he did not masturbate until he went to college, although he does remember having wet dreams about boys. A product of thorough religious training, he had strong feelings of guilt about interest in other boys.

Before marriage he had a good many relationships with girls who were merely friends. He began dating his wife seriously when he was a junior in college. He had previously dated another girl, but he says, "It never went so far as heavy petting."

He thinks his wife has something of a taste for gay men: One of her summer romances was with a man who turned out to be gay and who became an Episcopal priest. John adds that he and his wife, even after their marriage, never "pushed the sexual envelope."

His wife's father encouraged her marriage to John, which took place after John graduated from college with a degree in business administration. He later added two master's degrees to his vita— one in public health and a second in business and finance.

Before he started his first job, he and his wife took a long trip through Europe, after which he was employed by a consulting firm in Chicago. He was the firm's first employee with a master's degree and also the first who was hired directly from university without practical experience in the field.

His wife taught fourth grade in the suburb of Lake Forest. They eventually found a home in the northern suburb of Highland Park. In 1973 he became an executive director of recruiting for his company, and the family moved to Chicago's western suburbs, first Hinsdale and then Oak Brook.

John and his wife have three children. His son was born in 1971, followed by a daughter in 1975. Their youngest, also a daughter, was born in 1982 and is presently attending Indiana University.

John's work involved a lot of traveling, and he found himself going to nude beaches when they were close to the cities he traveled to. He had always had an interest in nudity—which he calls "a theme of my life."

He began going to nude beaches in 1978 and had what he calls "jack-off" experiences. But in 1983 in Charleston, South Carolina, a young man on the beach invited himself back to John's hotel, where "he brought out oil and condoms and we went the whole nine yards. And I didn't feel any guilt." John adds that it was the first time he experienced that kind of ecstasy, even though now he doesn't even remember the man's name.

He continued to have encounters on beaches through 1987, and he says he felt those beaches were a kind of "safe haven." By 1986 he realized that he didn't know for sure where his life was heading. He was entitled to a sabbatical from work, and he decided to take his family on a trip around the world for three months. He says, "It was the first time that I had had a chance to think about what I wanted from life." He warns that a sabbatical will always change your life, which he emphasizes to everyone who suggests they'd like to take one.

He had trained a younger woman to succeed him as CEO of his company so that he could move on, but discovered upon his return from his sabbatical that she was leaving. He was not able to go into any kind of semiretirement or alternate activity but had to return as CEO. He finally rid himself of the responsibility by merging with another company so his firm could have a younger man as its chief operating officer.

His life felt increasingly confining. On his trip around the world he had written a gay novel that was autobiographical in the sense of "this is the way my life could be." He says his behavior was almost deliberately crazy; he hoped to get caught, which would force him to change his life. But this was not to be. Finally, in 1998, he thought, *This charade is over.* He decided he had to tell his wife, which he did. John says, "You think this is the biggest midlife crisis in history, and when you tell your wife, she only answers, 'Yes, I've known that for several years.'" The crisis was over, but nothing really changed.

John felt the need for camaraderie and thought about joining the Chicago Gay Men's Chorus during Gay Pride Week in the spring of 1999. He had sung with his church choir of 40 men but felt that didn't fill the bill. He hoped the Gay Men's Chorus would.

It was also three years ago that he went to talk to a Methodist minister who had been forced out of the church for marrying a gay couple. This man told him he should talk to Terry Normand, a minister who had left a wife and three children to have a relationship with a 17-year-old. Normand had written a book about his experiences and was now counseling men like John. Normand was from John's hometown of Jefferson City and not only counseled him but gave him the news that he had taken the post held by John's wife's father. He also told John that his wife's father had been gay.

John frequently went to see Terry and his young lover, Jeff, in Fort Lauderdale, Florida. He was dismayed when the younger man committed suicide while in the middle of counseling. John says that despite this, and though he knows there are many problems in the gay world, "I like it. It's a world."

As John faced the year 2002, his therapist asked him what he planned for the coming year. John told him:

1. I'm going to tell my wife we can't continue like this. I'm gay and I have to lead a gay man's life.
2. I have to tell my children.

John had already told his brother—whose sexuality John had questioned, but who turned out not to be gay. John also told a close friend who was gay but did not suspect that John was. Now he fulfilled his promise to himself and told his wife, his son, and his two daughters at the same time.

He did not sing with the Gay Men's Chorus in Chicago, nor did he tell his wife's gay friends.

He says, "In the gay world I'm an anomaly. I'm a gay man who is out to his wife and children but not out to many of the gay men in the world around him. A lot of gay men I know and meet don't know how to relate to me."

John is a gay man whose coming out is in full transition. He talks about his mother, who divorced his father after John was married and went on to forge a successful career working for Hallmark Cards. For him, she was always a strong leadership figure, and she always strongly espoused feminism. He says, "I believe that she is a latent lesbian, and she gives me faith that I can start totally new. And have the life I want."

He says firmly and in a very touching way, "I so long to have the freedom to have a new life."

He wants to become a full-time professional writer, and to that end has written several published articles and three books as yet unpublished. He would like to write a screenplay and hopes to sing and perform in some way, too.

What keeps him from doing this? Perhaps most of his long history as a "good boy" and his great wish to not hurt those who are close to him. Will he achieve his desires and goals? We must now wait and see.

John Welsh left his wife in 2003 and now has a younger male lover.

Wade Firestone:
MY GREATEST FEAR: BEING HOMOSEXUAL

Wade Firestone is dynamic, even audacious. He is an inspired teacher whose students adore him. Wade is a very well-known author. He is an inveterate cyclist with the body of a much younger man. And he would be the first to admit that he is not as self-assured as he seems.

His first confession to his interviewer was that at 17 he refused to have his handwriting analyzed en route to a Boy Scout Jamboree in the Philippines with a group of boys for fear that it would reveal that he was homosexual.

One year later, on entering college, his English literature class was asked to write an essay on "Your Greatest Fear." His essay stated that he was afraid of being homosexual. At first his teacher asked, "Is this a joke?" When Wade said no, the teacher referred him to a psychiatrist who told him, "You're not queer. You need to fuck girls." Wade says, "It was the best $45 I ever spent." And he proceeded with his life, reassured for the time being.

Wade is from the South. Not the deepest South, but South enough. His parents met while they were in college at neighboring schools. His father was a short, handsome dandy connected to the local gentry. His bride was from a poorer, farming branch of a merchant family. Wade is very heritage-conscious.

His parents created a stressful atmosphere for the family they were raising in a small Southern town. Wade's handsome father was a textile designer at a nearby mill, an elegantly dressed man who was also an alcoholic. Wade believes that, with his taste for fine clothes and design talent, his father may well have been gay. His mother was a woman of high intelligence who taught school most of her life under duress because her husband's income was insufficient for a family that finally was to have three sons. Wade was the middle one.

Although his mother never discussed her marriage with Wade, she told her grandchildren that she was unhappy in her marriage in its early years but was financially unable to leave and was also afraid to do so.

An essential element in Wade's upbringing was that his paternal grandmother was of very aristocratic stock by Southern standards, and though she had married beneath her station for some reason (Wade says his grandfather was handsome in a very striking way) the family was always very aware of this heritage. Wade says, "Firestone was not a local aristocratic name. My first name, Wade, was from my grandmother's family and indicated to fellow Southerners that I had some good connections." Although he has lived most of his life far from that childhood world, it is clear that the standards of that world still matter very much to him.

Wade attended a local grade school and high school and then attended college in a nearby town—a college with an excellent reputation in his part of the country.

"My high school was thoroughly undemocratic," he says. "There were the kids from the local gentry who held all the class offices and made the good grades. There were the mill workers' children and then the farm kids. When I attended our 25th class reunion someone asked that all those with ancestors in the Civil War raise their hands. The only ones who did were the upper-class group. I thought I was an obvious sissy, but this passed unremarked upon by the gentry students, among whom I counted myself. At the reunion one of the men who had a farm background said to me, 'Wade, I can still see you now, swishing down the hall.' I was curiously bi-polarized. I knew I was homosexual, but at the same time

I thought I wasn't." Being able to distance himself within his special social group must have helped him to ignore his real nature.

After he received a college degree in history, Wade decided to spend a year in Europe. He studied German, worked in volunteer work camps (he adds, "I wanted to do volunteer work, to do good—all that bullshit stuff"), and wound up his grand tour with a two-month stint in a German machine factory.

"I was adventuresome and puritanical at the same time," he says. "I went to the Oktoberfest, and didn't drink a drop of beer. That was my mother's influence. She had a deadly fear of drinking." Wade's family was staunchly religious, and he remains very devout.

He talks a bit about his mother and grandmother. He reports that his mother was extremely straitlaced and strict with her children, yet her mother, when she became a widow at 38, married a man 17 years her junior. She was not averse to a bit of swearing, and when her grandchildren overheard her, she made them promise they would not tell their mother, her daughter. He adds that his mother was also very parsimonious and at 83 was still saving her money carefully—a characteristic completely at odds with her own freewheeling mother.

After returning from Europe, Wade found a slot in the Army Reserves and avoided being drafted into the regular Army in the Vietnam years.

Of his sex life up to this point, Wade says, "I fooled around with the a neighbor boy when I was 14. And with my best friend, who was a year younger. I had no ideas at all that sex with a man was romantic. It was strictly fooling around. And I was afraid of sex, quite frankly. Not just homosexual sex, but any sex. I found sex terrifying. I had a great fear of losing control.

"My masturbation fantasies were bondage fantasies. I had been captured somewhere by natives. If you didn't have sex with a native woman, you would be boiled in oil. However, I stopped having any kind of heterosexual fantasies by the age of 20." Wade notes, "I enjoyed being in the sack with women. But my fantasies are completely gay."

In college. he says, "I guess I had a crush on my roommate my senior year. He was a handsome, muscular athlete. And *he* asked *me* to room with him." He remembers that the music students in his college made a kind of quasi-gay underground, but very little sexual activity took place. He has remained in touch with them and knows that one man has had the same male partner for 35 years and that another is single and has never slept with a woman.

After completing his military duty, Wade enrolled in graduate school and earned an advanced degree in history. He was involved with two women during this period, and he asked both of them to marry him. One accepted and became his wife.

In the same period he was acquainted with a gay Anglican priest who was attending the same school who said to him once, in a very leading way, "What about those salacious remarks you made at the party last night?"

Wade could only reply, "Who, me?" He says again, "I was living in two worlds. I was two different me's."

He now believes that one of the two roommates he had while he attended graduate school was gay. Though there was no mention of it then. Later this man was to die of AIDS.

Wade married in 1969, while still in graduate school. His wife was a woman he had known since his high school years, although she had attended a private school in his area. She was a beautiful woman of impeccable family background, raised in something of an unhappy household. She and Wade had started dating in 1962. They broke things off when she had demanded, "I want to know what your intentions are." Wade fled from her life, but they started seeing each other again while he was in graduate school. She visited him at school and they spent an entire weekend in bed together. "I discovered that I loved her," Wade says. "It wasn't just the sex. I loved her. Her persistence was very moving to me."

Of himself in this relationship, he says, "I loved her but I didn't always treat her very well. But she was the woman I wanted to have my children with. She is a woman of enormous integrity, never whiny. And I enjoyed her company. She always laughed at my jokes. She respected me. And I think I made her complete."

Once married, they immediately began having children— three in the ensuing four years. Soon after their marriage Wade had a crisis, hinging very much on his sexual identity. He remembers thinking, *I like to look at men.* He even shared this with his wife.

About the time Wade began an affair with a teaching colleague, he also visited his first gay club with an old chum from college. "It helped and didn't help," he says. "Looking around at all those men, I thought, *Wow, all these guys are in here and they aren't wearing pink tutus. They look like absolutely normal people. This is what I should be doing.* But I didn't. It was over 15 years before I entered a gay club again."

Soon afterward, the family moved to the Southern city where Wade has taught at the state university for the past 30 years. He says, "I hate change."

He became very manic—biking, running, gardening, and working at the library. He reports this only because his wife recently discussed it with him. She had doubts that their marriage could last— she wasn't sure he had the energy or the will to stay married. Their marriage survived this period, though Wade claims he has no memory of this troubled time in his life.

What he does remember is that his inner conflicts came to a critical juncture in 1974. He says, "I bought my first *After Dark* magazine. I had got along with *International Male* catalogs until that point. It was a big thing for me to buy a pseudo-porn magazine. Looking at it, I made a conscious decision that I wanted to have sex with a man."

Wade accomplished this by deliberately seducing a colleague. An older, single man with a very self-consciously masculine demeanor, he had misread Wade's signals because he couldn't believe that a married man was coming on to him. This man had not had sex with another man until he was 39 years old. Wade remained ambivalent about his own sexuality. Of his feelings, he recalls, "Part of it was just horniness, and part of it was my own denial and then acceptance, which kept ricocheting back and forth.

"I always had to initiate sex with my wife; she never initiated it. My feeling that I always had to approach her was matched with her own fear of rejection. It builds up enormous pressure. I wouldn't come on to her unless I thought she wanted to fuck. She told me later that she felt ugly and rejected, but she never brought it up at the time. We went through three years sleeping in the same bed every night and never having sex."

In 1983 things came to a head. Wade went away for a summer of advanced study on a grant. There he responded to a sex ad for the first time, although nothing happened.

Meanwhile, back at home his wife fell into the arms of a close friend—another married woman—and had her first lesbian experience. When he returned she told him how wonderful it had been. Her lover was a woman with preteen children—and she was now mothering his wife, too.

Wade, who had been experimenting with other men, now found himself married to a woman who was doing something similar on her own side of the fence. He was shocked and blown apart by this news. He stayed in his marriage because of the children, he says, adding, "And frankly I could not imagine any other life, especially a gay one." At this time he threw himself into writing a major biography of a Southern writer.

He lost himself in this work which, combined with his teaching responsibilities, sometimes kept him occupied seven days a week. He found that the emotions and experiences of his life and his wife's affected the content and the process of writing his book, which was finished in 1991. Once the book was finished he had to face the reality of his life, resolve his interest in other men, and deal with his wife's attachment to another woman.

"I just couldn't go on crying myself to sleep every night," he says. "My wife was involved with that other woman; I felt I couldn't handle it anymore. I'm standing in the shower crying and crying one morning, and finally I said to myself, *I don't know what's best for me, but I know what I can't tolerate anymore.* So I went to my wife and said, 'We can't go on.' And like a true gentleman, she said, 'I will leave, of course.' I kept the children and the house. We didn't get divorced. We're still married. But we don't live together anymore."

As soon as his wife and he were no longer a couple, Wade started engaging in pickup bathroom sex. It was 1991, and AIDS was rampant. Wade was 49. He says, "It was really scary. Marriage had been like a condom. It had kept me straight, in many senses of the word. I had wanted to stay married, but that was all over. I was getting sex, but I was greener than a 15-year-old and was feeling guilty about what I didn't know about gay sex."

At exactly this time his biography was published to glowing reviews that made Wade was a literary star. He went on book tours—for two years he did a lot of overnight living on the road.

Now his life was changing. Of the period, he says, "I had never even gone out with another man up to that time. For me, homosexuality wasn't being gay, it was just sex." Then in 1993, Wade fell head over heels in love with one of his students. In his mind he says he told himself, "Maybe I wasn't homosexual. Maybe I was a gay guy. That was a big difference for me. I asked this man to marry me; he had been flirting with me for two years but I just had been too myopic to get it."

He never succeeded in forming a relationship with the student, but seven years later he fell into his first live-in affair. He has just terminated this relationship with his 23-year-old partner. They lived together for a year, but Wade very recently asked him to move out. He says, "I couldn't live in two worlds. I felt schizophrenic between my boyfriend and my family."

Wade's offspring are grown, with the last child just finishing college. He describes them as "eccentric and peculiar, as my wife and I are." Although there are no children at home, it is quite clear that he still has not shed his identity as a father and husband, despite an effort to have a permanent liaison with another man. He remains devoted to them and even to his wife he insists.

Very recently Wade has written another biography, this time about a notable homosexual artist. "My first book established me as a writer," he says. "This book, I believe, establishes me as a gay writer. It was a real coming-out for me."

As for his personal life, Wade says he has returned to "bonking my original academic friend, whom I still love. And I must say, I do like cruising. I love fishing, trolling to see what I can find."

He concludes, "I don't know that everybody needs a marriage. Satisfying your sexual appetites without matrimony can be not too difficult, and for some of us it not only works, but it's superior.

"I was married all those years; I love my independence now. I think about the possibility of a permanent partner. But not very often. I like my life the way it is."

The Out and About Generation: 40 to 50

The younger the men I interviewed, the younger they seemed to have been when they shifted gears from being a husband and sometimes a father to becoming a gay guy—and pretty much an "out there" gay guy.

Perhaps the statement above is self-evident, or perhaps there is something more to it. Many of the men in the older age groups had not confronted their homosexuality until their children were grown and they themselves were firmly in middle age. By contrast, most of the men in the 40-to-50 category have been openly gay for half or most of their adult lives. As soon as it became clear to them that they preferred men, most of 40-something interviewees immediately struck out to create lives for themselves as members of the gay community.

Evident, too, is that the men in this group, after having been formally married and then coming out, still valued being part of a couple. Used to domesticity, they seemed to feel more comfortable in this situation and saw it as a desirable goal. Even though many have had a series of partners—and have joined their partners in sexual activities with outsiders—their relationships have hardly differed from many heterosexual ones, where serial monogamy and occasional sexual adventurism stir the appetites of committed partners.

A marked characteristic of this age group is that they now have little interest in keeping a low profile about their homosexuality. They make no attempt even at partial closeting, making it clear in their professional and social worlds who they are and whom they love. This is a group who has reached out to other gay men, involving themselves in AIDS causes, paying attention to the plight of gay teenagers, and bonding purposefully with lesbian activists.

Men in this group were quite young when AIDS was first identified. They saw their friends dying in horrible ways, and many became engaged in the efforts to fight the disease when it was totally ignored by their government. They have seen how their own actions brought results and realize that gays and lesbians cannot hope to drift unseen and unnoted through a dominant heterosexual culture and still have the kind of life and rights they deserve.

Whether or not they have had close relationships with women, men in this age group have often forged lasting friendships and political alliances with lesbians, transgendered individuals, and straight women. It has been largely through the efforts of this generation that gay characters are now common in movies and television. It is also to their credit that many public figures have become brave enough to announce their own homosexuality and that gay couples have advanced toward marital legal rights and have begun to raise families of their own. People in this age group have worked hard so that gay lifestyles can be seen as healthy and nonthreatening.

Randy Fizer:
THE MAN WHO LET LOVE LEAD HIM

You would like Randy Fizer. Somewhere in his 40s, he has hung onto his looks and his body. And despite his repressive redneck blue-collar background, he is irrepressibly ready to talk about his life journey from an early marriage to his high school sweetheart to being the partner of the successful male proprietor of a Key West gay bookstore.

Randy has a rollicking way about him. He smiles readily and his eyes beam in a friendly way from behind his glasses. And when he tells you about what has been a difficult life, there is no trace of self-pity, more a tone of very adult amusement.

Quite significantly, Randy Fizer was one of the first interviewees for this book, and he immediately assented to the use of his real name; many other interviewees have not. His honest character shines forth, and his willingness to tell his story is part of that honesty.

Born and brought up in West Virginia, Randy from his earliest days knew he was sexually attracted to men. He also knew that being attracted to men was completely taboo in his part of the world. On his way home from school one day when he was a young boy, he walked past a burned car wreck with KILL THE QUEERS spray-painted on its side. The taunts and gibes of classmates, who accused him of effeminacy, didn't make him feel any better. More of an outsider than effeminate, he was the kid in the class who just didn't fit in.

Randy experimented early with sex, but it was of the "fooling around" variety with other boys. In high school he dated girls and became comfortable with heavy necking and petting.

His college was in his hometown, and he lived at home through his undergraduate years since finances were always tight in his family. He acquired a steady girlfriend and they began regular love-making, borrowing college friends' dormitory rooms and apartments for their sexual encounters.

Randy had sexual run-ins with men during this same period, too, but says, "All the guys I'd fooled around with as a teenager were growing up and getting married, so I assumed that I'd grow out of it, too."

At the beginning of their senior year in college, Randy and his girlfriend very privately got married—in blue jeans. Only seven friends attended the ceremony. His new bride's subsequent pregnancy during senior year caused her parents a flurry of dismay, but that was quickly dispelled by her marriage to Randy.

Although Randy's new wife's first pregnancy ended in miscarriage, she was heavily pregnant again at graduation time. The young couple soon moved to Washington, D.C., where Randy found work and their daughter was born.

The young couple embarked upon a fairly conventional life for a young college-educated couple in the early 1980s. Randy worked, and his wife only stayed home six weeks after the baby was born. They made good money and soon moved to a better apartment. They made many friends and often went out to movies and clubs.

When Randy was 28, his life took a dramatic turn, for which he was completely unprepared. A young neighbor couple suggested that Randy and his wife accompany them to a transvestite bar as a wild way to spend an evening. There was a mix of people in the bar, and at a nearby table Randy noticed a man whom he describes as "the man of my dreams." When the young man got up to get a drink at the bar, Randy excused himself on the pretext of going to the bathroom and followed him. He struck up a conversation at the bar with the attractive stranger—and got his telephone number.

Evidently, this sort of behavior was not too much of an anomaly for Randy. During his marriage he had continued to have rendezvous with men he met in the streets, bars, and restaurants of Washington. His extra job as a sign painter often required him to work erratic hours and travel long distances in the Washington area; consequently, these forays into occasional casual sex with other men went unsuspected by his wife. Randy believed at the time that this was to be the structure of his life. He loved his home life and his growing daughter, and his sex with his wife was regular and enjoyable. To relieve any pressure that his other sexual interests might generate, he would let off steam with strangers. This was how he saw his future.

But the new man in Randy's life was to prove different. The man didn't return Randy's first two calls but responded to his third. They quickly made plans to spend a weekend together driving along the Blue Ridge Parkway in Virginia. Telling his wife he had a distant weekend job, Randy departed to be with his new love for a few days—and what an experience it was "This was totally different. He made love to me in ways I had never been made love to before," Randy remembers. "When we left to go back to Washington, I knew my marriage was over. I went home to say my goodbyes."

Randy avoided the immediate revelation of the new path his life was to take. He just told his wife that he wanted out of the marriage and would be sharing an apartment with a coworker who was an old friend. His new lover also went home and broke the news to the man with whom he was living. And the two new lovers began to spend their nights together.

Because Randy offered his wife no real explanation for his departure from their marriage, she was profoundly shocked and distressed. She had no inkling of his interest in men and was in no way prepared for the end of her marriage.

Visitation rights were arranged so that Randy could spend time with his much-loved daughter, who seems to have weathered the storm of her father's departure with a certain amount of equanimity.

The ruse of Randy sharing an apartment with a coworker while he was actually pretty much living with his new lover did not last for long. Among his friends and fellow workers the word got out, and his wife's fury escalated greatly. She had no problem telling everyone they knew—both in Washington and their hometown—that the man she had married was now a "faggot." Within three months the lovers had moved to Key West to avoid the hostile atmosphere. Randy found work there in a government office.

Randy's romance was highly charged sexually, but his lover had a wandering eye. Soon Randy learned he was not to be trusted. After several years of his lover finding it impossible not to stray with other men, Randy decided that they had to split up.

Then followed a period of living a gay bachelor's life. Randy enjoyed this freedom for a time, but when he met a stable and attractive guy while visiting Washington, he began a new relationship. The new lover was of a far steadier character and had no desire for extracurricular activities. This kind of private life suited them both very well. His new lover joined Randy in Key West but was never happy there. He eventually moved back to Washington with plans for Randy to follow in a year.

Again Randy was on his own. Soon, though, his daughter relieved his singleness when she decided to come to Key West to live with him, with her boyfriend in tow. Randy has always remained very close to his daughter, who once before had opted to live with him for two years. But she was still a teenager then and didn't know what she really wanted to do. She attended school in Key West but after one year felt that she would be more at home back in Washington, where she now had a half-brother and sister. Now that she had finished high school, she returned to Key West, where Randy had the opportunity to be a full-time father to her and the boyfriend she brought along.

At this time Randy discussed his sexual orientation with his mother, who was supportive and loving and had no problem with his new way of living. But she suggested he not discuss it with his father right away.

Eventually, Randy's daughter and her boyfriend returned to the Washington area to marry and start a family. Again, Randy felt the need to restabilize his life. He had never followed his lover back to Washington—his lover liked his work in the capitol—and they decided to part. At a party he met Paul Haus, a good-looking young man who was living an adventurous shoestring-budget life in Key West and held a half-interest in a bookstore.

Randy was immediately taken with Paul, but the dashing bookstore owner was already involved. Three months later he was again single, so Randy began to call him. He was busy the first two times Randy called and tried to make a date, but he finally found time to go out for dinner. Randy's luck was on the third try, much like his experience with his first lover. After dinner they retired to Randy's home, where Paul spent the night. They have not been apart since.

Paul opened a new bookstore in in Key West called Flaming Maggie's. Devoted to gay and lesbian books and other materials, it has not only been successful but has become something of a rallying spot and meeting place for the gay community.

The two men plan to have a commitment ceremony in the near future. In preparation for the ceremony, Randy, whose mother has died, recently had a discussion with his now aged and ailing father. Randy was somewhat surprised to find that the elder Fizer only wanted him to be happy. His father was not outraged and said he had understood the situation for some time and only wanted what Randy wanted. Randy's daughter, who has made him a grandfather twice, has always been very supportive and comes for regular visits with her husband and children.

Only Randy's sister has been unhappy about his open gayness— she requested that he not bring Paul to a family get-together. Randy says, "I guess she thought Paul was going to show up in a dress or something since he's my life partner." She has become more accommodating, after having met the charming Mr. Haus, so Randy no longer feels at all estranged from her.

Randy is very highly regarded at the government office, where has advanced to an upper managerial position. He has what any person of any race, creed or sexual orientation seeks: a happy home and a job he enjoys—and a person he loves with whom to share those blessings.

Don Ferguson:
THE MISSIONARY'S SON

Of all the men interviewed for this book, Don Ferguson had the most exotic place of birth. He was born in Ruanguba—the hill of lightning—in Zaire.

The missionary station that was his childhood home was built on three hills with a view of dead volcanoes across a valley through which wild storms flung themselves, rain pouring down and lightning and thunder zinging and crashing. And the drama continues in the life he has lived since then.

The child of conservative Baptist missionaries, he was the second oldest of four children. His mother was a second-generation missionary, having been born in Africa but educated at the University of California in Los Angeles, where she received a nursing degree.

His father had come from a farming family in the northeastern United States and had a calling to do mission work. He met his wife in Africa, where he supervised the Bible schools established by his church's missionaries.

When asked whether his parents had been in love, Don says, "I believe my parents were more in love than any straight couple I've ever seen. They were very committed to their work. And certainly they enjoyed each other's company. In their marriage of 52 years, I never witnessed an argument."

The Ferguson family visited the United States every four or five years on sabbatical. During their sojourns, they toured the country speaking to church groups about their work in Africa.

In the early 1960s when Don was still small, Zaire became an independent country. The two civil wars that followed interrupted much missionary work. "We had to leave, then return. We had to evacuate six times," Don recalls. "We went to Rwanda and Kenya until things blew over. Once we went to the United States for a year, to Orange County in California. When we finally had to leave for good, it tore the hearts out of all of us."

From this exotic African world Don went to college at the University of California at Irvine, leaving behind a community of friends who spoke English, French, and Swahili—friends both black and white whom he had known all his life. "I spoke Swahili before I spoke English," Don says. "Even though we didn't share the same school with African students, they were my friends and they were the children I played with."

But now his life would become entirely American and entirely modern. Fascinated with technology, Don majored in computer science. Although the science-fiction aspect of his studies appealed to him greatly, the artwork he did to support himself in college became his career.

Don had studied art as a child in Africa in a limited way and soon found that he had a natural skill for painting African subjects. Drawing upon his years in Zaire, he painted wildlife and foliage in a highly original way and quickly found an eager market for his work. Of an analytical mind, Don says, "For years I had studied the technique of paintings that I had seen in museums and galleries and then I would go home and practice." He has since developed an international reputation for his work and has had a number of shows on several continents. In the world of wildlife painting, his name is famous.

Still in the early years of his college studies, Don met the girl who was to become he wife. She accompanied him when he transferred to the United States International University's Nairobi campus, and they were married in Kenya.

When asked whether his family was disappointed about his not continuing their missionary work, Don says, "No. As Baptists, they believe that you have to have a calling to become a missionary. And even though none of their children ever had that calling, I never heard them express any disappointment at this."

His Baptist missionary background notwithstanding, Don has plenty to say about his sex life prior to his marriage. "I was always fascinated by strong and attractive men, but I didn't know what it meant to be gay. I had always had a girlfriend in high school, I was on the rugby team, girls liked me. But I was just so ignorant I didn't know anything about being gay.

"Earlier, as a preadolescent, I had fooled around with boys but forgot the fact that we had fucked each other. The whole concept of being gay was completely foreign to me. When I read about gays in San Francisco, it didn't seem real to me.

"In college I did have girlfriends and we had sex. I thought it was interesting and exciting, but somehow it wasn't fulfilling. The mechanics were doable, but it left me unfulfilled. And, yes, in college men were attracted to me, but I just didn't put it together. I didn't know what it meant."

Certainly, men had every reason to be attracted to Don. He had already started lifting weights in Africa, using equipment that had been brought to the missionary station. And he also was not unaware of his older brother's physique magazines. Blond and blue-eyed with a very well-developed body, Don would not have easily escaped the interest of both women and men in his college years.

Don was 28 and still living in Nairobi when one evening, as he ate alone in a restaurant while his wife was out of town, he ran into a Dutch flight attendant. The other man came over to his table and spoke to him. "I knew instantly what he wanted. And I wanted it, too," Don recalls. "When I had sex with a man it was satisfying. It was fulfilling. And I knew this was what I was supposed to be doing."

Once awakened to this new aspect of his sexuality, Don found himself feeling deeply disturbed. *I have a responsibility here to my wife,* he kept telling himself. So no immediate action was taken, although he continued to see the Dutch man whenever he came to Nairobi.

The decision was soon taken out of Don's hands when his wife discovered a letter to him, written by his Dutch lover. "She asked me about it, and I said, 'Yes, this is what it appears to be and the feelings are mutual.' She was devastated. We loved each other. I don't know if we were in love when we married, but I loved her very much as a person and felt responsible for her. The only guilt I felt was because of this.

"We continued to live together for six months, but it was a big problem for her. She was a religious person and what I was doing was evil to her. It wasn't against her—she didn't take it personally. It was just something very wrong. Which finally allowed her to feel vindicated and slightly superior when we divorced."

Afterward Don returned to the United States with the plan that his Dutch lover would follow and they would live together there. But he admits, "It was only an exciting idea. He never really planned to move, and he never did. I was on my own, living with my brother in Orange County."

Don's parents, who were also living not far away, knew that he had divorced and soon discerned the reason why when his ex-wife also moved to Orange County and told them. There is something very kindly and forbearing about Don's retelling of these events. He only tells the facts; he doesn't comment on what could be interpreted as other people's spitefulness.

Don never discussed his homosexuality with his parents. He is especially saddened that he never discussed his sexuality with his father, who passed away not long ago. His mother, he says, knows about his life and accepts it, but they do not talk about it. His sister, however, has been completely supportive, as has his younger brother, who had the situation explained to him by his sister.

In 1981 Don Ferguson moved to West Hollywood to manage a gym. He was 30. Of this departure from his painting career he says, "My uncle had brought exercise equipment out to Africa and I always enjoyed the physical exertion—just for the sheer pleasure of it. The repetition and the focus is a kind of meditation for me, and it's been very much part of my life." He adds, "Also, what you paint reveals what is in your mind. My paintings were dark and not nearly as good as those I had painted earlier. So I took a break for a year."

Don met a preacher's son who worked in construction, and they both moved to a community just outside San Diego. They were together for seven years, during which Don resumed his painting career very successfully.

But this didn't last. They then drifted apart, after each met someone new and fell in love. Don subsequently moved to Laguna Beach and bought a house there. By now his work had been accepted at a prestigious art gallery in Chicago and was earning him an excellent living. His new lover was a successful chef in Laguna Beach. They enjoyed six years together before his partner met someone and wanted to add him to their living situation.

Don balked at this. "I wasn't getting all the attention. It was as simple as that," he says.

He then had a job offer in San Francisco that he found irresistible: He was to co-manage and co-own an adult video company.

Don remains strikingly handsome with a magnificent physique. He has starred in two recent video offerings, sharing the screen with his current lover. He is unsure whether he will continue in this highly successful venture, despite the pride he takes in the high quality of the company's filmmaking. He has recently had another opportunity to invest in a small energy company in the north of California. He views his transition from missionary's son to porn star with great equanimity and calmly regards other possible novelties that await him.

Hector Castile:
THE GAY REPEATER

Sometimes when interviewing a man for this book, I couldn't help but feel that there was more to the story than I was being told. It was not that I was being deceived or that parts of the story were being omitted, but more that although the interviewee was telling all he knew, there was something more in the depths of his life— almost as though some kind of destiny was relentlessly forging a plot that was impossible to avoid.

Or, in the case of Hector Castile, perhaps the hand of destiny is because he is Cuban. A handsome man in his 40s, Hector has already lived a life that could fill an endless number of episodes in a daytime soap opera. Much of his history is improbable, but it is all undeniably true.

Hector was born in Cuba before Castro came to power. Hector's father was an employee of the Ford Motor Company in Havana. When it became quite clear at the time of the revolution that it would be wise to leave Cuba, Hector's father was able to send his wife and children to Miami to live with relatives. His own departure was not that simple. It was many months before he could emigrate and join his family, eventually settling them in Dallas, where his company found sales work for him.

Hector's father spoke English fluently because of his work, but Hector credits his own fluent bilingualism to having been educated as a child in Dallas. He enjoyed his schooling there and was glad to be away from the Catholic school where he had studied in Havana. There he had been prey to a priest who fondled him sexually during private conferences.

Hector was never able to reveal this to his parents, and was beaten by his father when he occasionally skipped school, in part to avoid the priest's advances. Hector's father not only beat him—he went so far as to take his son to school and pull down his pants in front of his classmates to show them the strap marks on the Hector's buttocks.

Hector is really only one generation removed from his Spanish heritage. Both his parents immigrated to Cuba from Spain and met while studying at the University of Havana. Both parents were also bilingual in Spanish and English, which made their transition to life in the United States easier than it has been for most Cubans.

Even as a schoolboy, Hector was already quite sexually aware. "I knew I was a gay person." His early experience with the priest had both frightened and excited him. But Hector was also aware that his mother greatly feared having a son who might be a *maricon*, one of the most insulting of all epithets in Spanish. Despite their educated upbringing, his parents and their friends often made disparaging remarks about gays in Hector's presence during his years of puberty.

At about the time of the onset of puberty, Hector used to create beehive hairdos out of soapsuds when he shampooed, artfully placing decorative pendants in the suds on his head. To his horror, his mother once walked in on him when he was so decorated. Afterward he wrote her a note pleading with her not to tell his father and promising never to do it again.

Despite the "soapsuds beehive" run-in with his mother, Hector was exploring sexually with another youth when he was 11. At this time he also encountered a slightly older boy at the school swimming pool. In the shower room Hector couldn't help but notice that the boy had a large penis. The boy saw Hector looking at him, so he taunted, "Why don't you play with it?" Hector didn't—but went home and in bed that night played with himself, discovering masturbation.

However, the shower-room incident left Hector feeling ashamed. He avoided any possibilities for similar encounters at school throughout his teen years. In junior high school Hector developed a great crush on Robert Wagner, who starred in the television series *To Catch a Thief*. Frequently, Hector retired to his room to masturbate after watching the show. He also had a crush on the actor Jan Michael Vincent. Hector laughingly admits that whenever he watched television as a teenager his gaze was invariably drawn to the actors' crotches.

By this time Hector's family had moved back to Miami. Though still in junior high school, Hector already sensed his family had some kind of tendency to be gay—which later turned out to be true. Of his 23 first cousins, 13 are gay. In a similar vein, Hector's great-grandmother had a twin sister who never married. Hector believes she was a lesbian. Because he correctly perceived that some of his relatives were gay, Hector felt a special pressure to be straight. "I felt I needed to try not to be gay."

Hector had no close friends who showed any tendency to be gay, so his isolation was complete. And his situation was aggravated by the fact that, rather atypically for a Cuban-American, he was living in western Miami, which is very much part of the "Anglo" world of that metropolis. As many as 90% of Hector's fellow students were not Spanish-speaking; only about 8% were Hispanic.

Hector's closest friend in his junior high and high school world was Gustavo, a larger and stronger boy who defended Hector when he was picked on by other students. Sometimes Gustavo even fought Hector's fights for him, warning him beforehand, "Run home now." Along with a third friend, Jorge, they were inseparable pals. Later, after both Hector and Gustavo were in heterosexual marriages, the two men and their wives frequently socialized together.

Hector began his college studies in Miami. In one of his laboratory courses, he met two young men who were already great friends, having both graduated from the same high school. One of these friends became Hector's lab partner. When they were doing research one day, the young man started to play footsie with Hector under the lab table. "Instead of taking the opportunity to have my first gay friend," Hector says with some regret, "I rejected him when he came out to me. I told him I didn't feel that way about other men."

But Hector soon contradicted his lie to his lab partner. The two young men went out on a double date soon afterward, taking the lab partner's car. Incidentally, the young woman Hector took on that date was Annie, who was to become his wife some time later. After the date was over and the men dropped off their dates, they got a bite to eat together. Then they started to drive back to Hector's car. While they were waiting a stoplight, Hector was seized with the desire to give his new friend a blow job, which he did. From there they drove to the darkened beaches of Key Biscayne and made love.

Hector proceeded to have an affair for eight months with his fellow student, while also becoming engaged to his new girlfriend Annie. As his affair with the young man continued, Hector realized that his engagement was a mistake. He explained he was gay to Annie, and their relationship ended—though only temporarily, as it turned out. Hector was beginning his pattern of repeating himself.

Hector's male lover was now working weekends in an office, where Hector often stopped to visit him on Sundays. Once while Hector was there, his lover's close friend from high school and college called and was told, "Hector is here." The close friend immediately rushed over and started beating up on Hector—who only then realized the two men had been lovers when he first met them.

But Hector was no longer the shy high school kid being beaten up by bullies. He had a new macho image—and was more than able to live up to it. In the ensuing fistfight he drew blood on the enraged lover's face. The man they were fighting over managed to break it up, but it was the end of romantic entanglements for everyone concerned. Hector's lover later married and had children, but the man who had felt himself betrayed was never to marry.

Hector left Miami at this point to spend a year studying in Germany. While there he had sexual encounters with other men, but he also enjoyed a flamboyant affair with a girl from Georgia named Tiffany, who taught him a thing or two about heterosexual sex. Those experiences emboldened him when he returned to Miami after his studies abroad.

Traveling the disco circuit in Miami, Hector met several women and slept with several of them. He also ran into Annie, his former fiancée. He had slept with her during their engagement, but very infrequently. "She was frigid and never easy to have sex with," Hector confides, though he adds a note of self-critique. "I closed the closet door with myself inside."

Now in his 20s, Hector didn't close the closet door all that firmly. He was temporarily not attending college and met a man at the office where he was working. Quite bravely, Hector had a talk with his parents and told them, "I'm in love with someone and his name is Rolando."

This attempt to clarify his sexual orientation met with great resistance from his parents. First, he was sent to a psychiatrist, who told his family and him that he was a latent homosexual and eventually he would want to orient this way. Hector's parents found this unacceptable and then placed him in the care of a hypnotist, who tried to get him to regress to his childhood and uncover the reason for his condition. The hypnotist told Hector, "You can make yourself be straight, if that is your great desire."

That was certainly Hector's parents' great desire, so their son made an effort to be heterosexual. Annie was in love with him, so he decided to marry her. He asked her to marry him one evening at a local restaurant. Hector claims that he did seriously want to have children—as well as to please his parents. The honeymoon in Bermuda was successful, but on their last morning before returning to Miami, Annie began crying at breakfast and said, "I just feel when we go back to Miami this will all be over."

She wasn't far off. Once the domestic pattern set in, Hector found he was married to a control freak. His wife's tendency may have been aggravated by her concerns about what he might do if she did not precisely monitor his whereabouts and his activities. After six months Hector had to have out. Annie and he were divorced.

To escape the scene of so much drama in his life, Hector went back to school, this time in New York City. Here he abandoned any attempt to straddle the sexual fence and started living an openly gay lifestyle. Annie, meanwhile, became a flight attendant. Her flights brought her frequently to New York, and after about six months she called Hector—"Just to say hello," she said.

During spring term Annie called Hector again, saying she had a layover and thought she might come over and "visit him." Although Hector told her he had plans, Annie decided that she would like to come over and stay overnight anyway.

Hector's plans included going out with a particularly attractive blond man, so he left Annie in his apartment alone. Coincidentally, he also left his diary out where Annie could browse through it— though, as with so much in Hector's life, one wonders how much is by chance and how much is the product of emotional and psychological undertow.

The diary detailed Hector's gay sexual encounters. His therapist in New York had asked him to keep it. The therapist, who at the time was in a heterosexual marriage, soon revealed that he, too, was gay and also had a gay son. As if that wasn't enough, the therapist professed his love for Hector. He told Hector that his wife tolerated his being gay and that he was married merely "to give him his face."

Annie found the diary, read it, and found everything in it very distressing. She was crying when Hector returned from his date, but found the wherewithal to put on a black lace teddy before climbing into bed with Hector, who proceeded to have intercourse with her out of a sense of duty.

Annie disappeared the next morning, only to reappear in Hector's life some four month later. She called, saying she was feeling very unwell, throwing up on her flights and not at all herself. Hector was concerned for her health and demanded she see a doctor. She called back to say she was pregnant. Hector knew that Annie had a regular boyfriend and demanded to know how she could be sure the child was his. Annie replied, "I never have sex with my boyfriend. The only person I've had sex with is you."

Hector says this was the most stressful period in his life. His gay therapist had fallen in love with him, and his ex-wife claimed to be pregnant by him. What to do? After some consultation with his parents, who were thrilled to be prospective grandparents, Hector decided to fulfill parental and marital obligations and re-marry Annie. He moved back to Miami in midsummer to be with Annie during her pregnancy. When the baby was born, Hector was overcome with joy and parental love for his baby son. "He gave me the strength to move forward."

Following the pattern of new parents, Hector and Annie bought a home and moved in with their son. But all the problems that beset their first attempt at marriage remained in evidence.

Shortly after the baby's birth, Hector began an affair with a young man who worked with him in the same office. He stopped by the man's house each weekday morning to take him to work. But Hector liked to come inside first and make love to the man. Then they would drive to work together.

Unhappy with the relationship, the young man left Miami and returned to his home in Minneapolis. Hector started jogging miles every day to deaden himself with fatigue and to keep himself from thinking about his predicament. Finally, he got on a plane and went to Minneapolis. Hector was ready to announce to his lover that for the sake of their relationship he was ready to leave his wife and child. But the younger man said, "I want you to go back. This isn't the answer for you." Hector went back to Miami, and his young lover later married a woman.

Hector returned home and stayed with Annie another 11 years, taking no male lovers during that time. Married life was beginning to look good. Annie soon presented Hector with a second son. They began to socialize with other young couples they knew who had small children. They had a beautiful home and enjoyed family vacations together. Of that time Hector remembers, "A small part of me could love her when we were traveling."

By this time, Hector had finished his legal studies and taken a position at a successful law office. But Hector had higher ambitions. Along with another young lawyer from the same office, Hector left to open his own law firm, which soon acquired a number of Hispanic clients, many from Latin America. After returning from a business trip that had taken his partner and him to Mexico for five days, Hector suddenly had to face unrest on the home front. Annie refused to speak to him and made him sleep in the guest room. The situation became more intense when one of Annie's friends phoned and said she believed Annie was having an affair with the manager of her office. Hector went to the office and confronted the man but became convinced there was nothing to the rumor.

After two weeks in the guest room, Hector went out cruising. In front of a popular club, he saw a good-looking young man, so he pulled over and parked along the curb. The young man looked into the car at the very handsome Hector and said, "Oh, my God." This young man was Jerry. In his state of need, Hector says, he believed he was in love with Jerry and began to see him every night. Though he was still living with Annie and the children, he'd say to himself, *This is my coming-out party. I'm not going back to a heterosexual life.*

Life wasn't easy with Jerry either. One night, after they'd had a fight, Jerry called him at home. Annie answered and handed the phone over to Hector. "What's the matter? Afraid your wife will find out you're a faggot?" Jerry said. Annie was listening on an extension and confronted Hector, who was able to convince her that it was a casual acquaintance trying to organize a drug deal.

Hector continued to see Jerry every night, getting home the next morning in time to see the children off to school. But he was able to keep up this arrangement for only a few months before things collapsed and he found himself living with Jerry.

Annie called Hector's parents and told them everything. They counseled him to try to keep his marriage intact for appearance's sake and to have his gay love affairs on the side. Hector was unwilling to do this. Now that he was thoroughly immersed in a gay lifestyle, he no longer wanted to straddle the fence.

Hector was with hard-drinking, hard-drugging Jerry for two years. They separated, but Jerry begged to come back, swearing he was off drugs and booze. Hector took him back, but when he saw Jerry surreptitiously pouring vodka into a bottle of 7-Up, he knew the situation was hopeless.

On a trip to Atlanta Hector met Edwin, a divorced gay father of two. He fell head over heels in love with Edwin, and very rapidly it was decided that Edwin would move to Miami. Jerry proved difficult to dislodge and finally had to be told, "Edwin is on a plane coming to Miami to live with me. You must move out." Jerry's solution was to rent the apartment next door, where he remained throughout the eight years Edwin and Hector were together. He frequently told them he listened through the wall with a glass and overheard their conversations in detail.

Although others recognized them as a gay couple, Hector and Edwin had separate bedrooms where they stayed when their children visited, which was very frequently—usually every other weekend. Toward the end of their relationship, Hector began to feel Edwin was cheating on him—though he admits that he was also cheating on Edwin. One evening after dinner with friends, they decided to drop in at a gay bar. Hector was reluctant and said to his partner, "I want you to behave."

Edwin answered, "If I have to be walking on eggshells around you, maybe you should go home." Hector did, and Edwin never came home that night. Furious, Hector set out to look for him. As dawn was breaking, he found himself in front of an apartment complex not far from where he lived with Edwin. Hector says a voice said to him, "Go there." He discovered an old lady feeding cats . She proved to be the manager of the building and agreed to show him an apartment. "You can move in today," she told him.

Hector called an upholsterer friend who had a truck and a helper. By 9:30 that morning, Hector was moving out of the apartment he shared with Edwin. He was almost finished, leaving only the bedroom furniture in Edwin's room, when his lover showed up and unconcernedly went directly to the building's pool. Shortly afterward, Hector went over to Edwin where he lay by the pool and said, "As we speak, I'm moving out—and moving out of your life." Edwin was left dumbstruck as Hector drove away furiously.

Hector and Edwin were in fact only separated for a week before they were reconciled, but Hector didn't move back in. He stopped at his old home for coffee each morning on his way to work, and in a pattern he evidently had come to enjoy, made love to Edwin before they both proceeded to their jobs. But this lasted only for about a year. Edwin was always surrounded by a coterie of younger men at the pool, where he spent a lot of time. A mutual friend tipped Hector off that Edwin was having an affair with one of his poolside admirers.

Hector immediately called Edwin, who vehemently denied the allegation. But Hector rushed over to the apartment and found Edwin naked with an erection and his friend darting unclothed into the kitchen. That did it.

Miserable, Hector went back to his apartment. Soon afterward, though, Hector bought an apartment that was not only in the same building where both Edwin's and Jerry's apartments side by side but also on the same floor.

Next up in Hector's love sweepstakes was Don—a young man who fell madly in love with Hector but who lied to him about his HIV status. When Hector found out, he broke off the relationship. Don tried to commit suicide, and the affair ended messily with Don's family having to come from New York to take him home.

Hector's tumultuous private life then focused on Bruno, a young Australian man who was living with one of Hector's friends in the building. Hector and Bruno began to have an affair—behind the friend's back. Bruno soon moved in with Hector, but they maintained the pretense that he was merely staying with Hector while working things out with their mutual friend. Hector kept a pillow and comforter ready on the couch so that whenever the friend dropped in, Bruno could hurl himself down there and feign that this was where he always slept.

The friend caught on soon enough and was outraged. No longer needing to put up a front, Hector and Bruno became a live-in couple. After a year Hector and Bruno moved to a house in an up-and-coming Miami neighborhood. For five years they lived there while Bruno attended Miami-Dade Community College. His immigration status as a student meanwhile remained in question and was a constant source of tension between them—as was Bruno's habit of letting the $500 he earned every week as a part-time bartender slip through his fingers while Hector paid all the bills. Hector put Bruno on a budget, taking his money and giving him a sum for spending money. This worked well, and their relationship was still relatively smooth by the time they celebrated their fifth anniversary in the spring of 1999. But Bruno's situation as a resident alien finally could no longer be avoided. He was forced to return to Australia, which left Hector feeling brokenhearted but "with a certain sense of relief."

Now Hector is alone again. His sons are now young men, and his relationship with them is good. He is dating someone new and his dark good looks show little wear and tear, despite the emotional turbulence of his adult years. He believes lasting love can be found and is still looking.

Jerry Kenna:
THE MAN WHO HAS NO REGRETS

I met good-looking Jerry Kenna at a book party in Atlanta while on tour. Friends in Chicago had suggested I call him for this book, and he was willing to see me. Because time was tight I suggested that he come to the signing and afterward we could have dinner together.

I correctly guessed Jerry to be the dark-haired man of medium height who was hanging back a bit while I signed books. At dinner I was surprised to learn that Jerry is in his 40s, since he looks a decade younger, and that his two sons are in their late teens.

Born in New York, Jerry was raised in Pennsylvania and has had the life of many other youngish, attractive American men: marrying early, fathering several children, and always successful as a business representative for a manufacturer of household furnishings. His life followed this path until only very recently.

Although Jerry's life has been conventional on the surface, there were unusual energies at play in his background. His parents met at a military facility in New York, where they were both working and, oddly enough, were introduced by Jerry's maternal grandmother. This energetic and high-spirited lady had been the first to meet Jerry's father and, although she was long married, thought his romantic interest was in her. She was not at all pleased to find that the new young man in her life fancied her daughter. She was so adamantly opposed to their dating that Jerry's future parents had to elope so they could get married. The bride's mother took a long time to reconcile herself to her daughter's marrying a man she thought had been interested in her.

Without any prompting, Jerry offered the possibility that his own father had gay interests. Jerry was the least athletically gifted of the sons in the family and his father frequently called him "faggot." Later in life, when Jerry told his father he had decided against accepting a sales position because he didn't want to lose certain insurance and medical benefits, his father replied bitterly, "Only real men have management positions and you have been effeminate all your life." This anger, Jerry now feels, betrayed his father's fear that his own interests in men might be revealed in his son. Jerry discussed the possibility of his father being gay or bisexual with his mother, who then told him that she and his father only had sex when she initiated it.

During his teen years Jerry was particularly interested in boys and men. He becomes very animated when talking about how he fell in love with the girl who was to become his wife. "It was at her aunt's 25th wedding anniversary party. In Philadelphia. I had met her before, and we were dancing and the band was playing a song I'll always remember, and it happened. Wham! I was just very, very much in love with her. And that was it."

They became engaged and soon married. And it was only when a new job assignment brought them to the Atlanta area that Jerry began to feel that his life wasn't moving in the right direction for him.

Interestingly, he did not divorce because he became interested in another man. He divorced because he no longer wanted to continue living with his wife. He says, "We had come close to divorce several times before, but I really left her over a green Toyota. Ever since our first child she had become more and more controlling. We had few friends because when I invited people over she was civil but made it quite clear she wasn't interested in knowing them. I just found her mean-spirited.

"When our oldest son totaled our car, we had to buy a new one and she specifically wanted a green Toyota. We went to the dealer, and they had one left. It was what we wanted, and I asked her to write out a check. Our insurance money hadn't cleared yet, but we had the money in our joint account. She froze up. She refused to write a check. I asked the salesman if he could put in a proviso that we could return the car if for some reason our insurance didn't come through. He agreed he could. She still wouldn't write the check, and when I reached for her purse she went ballistic. I told the salesman the sale was off and we left. In our broken-down old second-hand car that wasn't even going to make it through the week I told her our marriage was over. 'I just can't do it anymore,' I said."

Reflecting further on this period, Jerry says, "You know when you're 15 and you're driving down the street and you notice a workman on a building and you shouldn't look, but you do look. Well, that was as far as I had ever gone. But now that I was out of my marriage, I said to myself, 'I've had all these feelings all my life—let's see if they're real or not.' So I went out and found somebody and made love to another man for the first time.

"And you know, I expected to feel terrible, feel guilty, feel ashamed, but I didn't feel any of those things. For about a day and half afterward, I just couldn't wipe the smile off my face. I realized that this was what I should have been doing all along and I just should have started sooner."

Jerry's wife had been Catholic when he married her but had absented herself from practicing her religion since then. Because of his wife's Catholic background, Jerry wanted to try to get an annulment of their marriage to give her the freedom to marry again. He consulted a priest and was told that an annulment was out of the question, as they had been married over 20 years. Jerry then challenged, "What if I tell you I'm gay?" The priest then agreed an annulment was possible and proceeded to apply for one.

Jerry told his wife he was getting an annulment for her but did not explain the reason. She demanded to know how he had arranged it, and he continued to refuse to tell her. But it was clear that eventually there would have to be a confrontation. To prepare the ground he told each of his sons separately. He took the older one to dinner and explained there was something he had to discuss. His son replied, "I know you feel you have to tell me, but before you do I want you to know that I don't care." There was little more to say after this.

His second and younger son received the news in shock. It continues to be difficult for him to handle.

He chose to tell his former wife at a basketball game in which one of their sons was playing. Seated near one another among friends she began nagging him to know how he had gotten the annulment. She said, "Oh, I know what it is. You've been a bad boy, haven't you?"

He didn't know what she was referring to, but he replied, "You're getting an annulment because I'm gay." She became hysterical, and his friends' mouths dropped open. His wife ran from the basketball court, and he followed her to calm her down. She ran out to her car, then returned, only to continue behaving hysterically in front of their friends.

Jerry said to her, "You're behaving like an ass, why don't you just go home." Then he took her to her car. From her car window she screamed "faggot" at him. He replied, "Just don't try to run over me as you're leaving the parking lot."

He passed his son, who had finished his game, as he was heading for his own car. His son said, "You told her, didn't you? Looks like I'm going to have a real bad ride home." Jerry replied, "I'm afraid so."

There is some theatricality in Jerry's accounts of these encounters. As traumatic as the breakup was, one easily suspects that both Jerry and his wife have extracted the maximum amount of drama out of retelling their side of the story.

Jerry's former wife now has a boyfriend and is beginning to weave a kind of life for herself, but she is haunted by the possibility that other men around her may also be gay. Prior to her marriage to Jerry, she'd had a boyfriend who broke off with her because he was gay. So it was not surprising that she demanded of her current boyfriend, "Are you gay?"

He replied, "No, but my brother is. Does it matter?"

Jerry's youngest son seems to have suffered the most from the dissolution of his parents' marriage and has had to seek psychological help. Jerry feels that his wife's continual references to him around the house as "the faggot" and "that damned faggot" hasn't helped his son's state of mind.

Jerry Kenna's private life now includes a lover whom he met some 18 months ago. The lover was bartending at a club that Jerry frequented. Although the man was attractive, he struck people as withdrawn and had a depressed air. Jerry's friends explained that the man had lost a lover to brain cancer a few months earlier. So Jerry decided to steer clear.

However, Jerry kept coming to the bar from time to time. One evening, the bartender asked him to step into the next room for a minute. When he did so, the man picked him up and gave him what Jerry calls "the best kiss I ever had in my whole life."

Jerry and his lover have been together for a year and a half, and they have lived together for the past year. When asked about his new life, Jerry says, "I have a lot of friends now—friends I know I can count on, friends who will come through in a pinch. I never had that before."

John Rowe:
THE SENSIBLE MAN

John Rowe is a very sensible man from the Middle West who looks a good deal younger than his 40-odd years. Tall and slender, he also looks a good deal sportier and more relaxed than you would expect from a man who heads a division of a medical device company. He oversees the firm's Latin American business, with over 100 people reporting to him.

Surely, beneath John's calm demeanor more emotions are charging around than are easily perceived. Even so, he displays great poise while describing his transformation from a young, heterosexual, married Midwesterner to the urbane gay lover of a good-looking Puerto Rican. "I never even entered a gay bar until after I was married," John confides. "But when I did, I said to myself, 'There's something here I need to explore.' "

Brought up in the suburbs of a small city in southern Michigan, John had a sensible upbringing by sensible parents. One of four children, he views his father's frequent work-related international travel as the only somewhat out-of-the-ordinary factor at play in his childhood. His father's frequent trips abroad seemed exciting and interesting and predisposed John to contemplate a similarly paced career for himself.

Around the turn of the 19th and 20th centuries, one of John's grandfathers had traveled through Europe east into Russia as a representative for an American manufacturer. This, too, made the idea of an international lifestyle welcome.

Other than his father's globe-trotting, John's formative years were relatively stable. Surrounded by parents and siblings who loved him, he enjoyed a secure start on life's road. He had every reason to think his life would more or less follow the same course as the lives of the people he grew up around. He attended a college in Michigan, dated a nice girl there, and, after they drifted apart for awhile, resumed his relationship with her and planned to be married. His training in international business prepared him for a life very much like his father's; he did not think of rebelling against this ideal or living in any other way. He felt very close to his wife and found sexual intercourse with her completely satisfactory.

On the other hand, John had been sleeping with other boys for a good bit of his young life. During the inevitable sleepovers, there had always been fooling around, and once John joined the Boy Scouts, sex with other boys became a regular thing. He now thinks that his scout leader was homosexual—he spent an undue amount of time with his assistant whenever the scouts were camping out or on overnight hikes.

John notes that same-sex sexual experimentation was so common among boys he knew when he was a teenager that he felt no guilt about engaging in it himself. All the boys he knew were involved, and he just assumed this was something everyone did but eventually would outgrow.

He does remember that it was something that you didn't discuss openly because adults wouldn't approve of it. As quite a small boy, John was already wrestling with pals on his parents' lawn and getting into sexual positions while at play. At such times he would hear someone rapping on a window and look up to see his mother wagging a disapproving finger. He also remembers how looking at hairy chests on adult men began to excite him when he was this age. At a summer cottage his family went to each year, there was a neighbor's son, an older boy with a hairy chest, who was very friendly and may well have been interested in John—if John had only followed up on getting to know him better.

In addition to his scouting outings, John also engaged in regular sexual play with his college roommate, who, like John, had been the president of his high school senior class. But still, this did not make John think that his life would be anything but normal—until he went to France to study. There he had experiences that would begin to make him rethink his life.

John first stayed with a young couple and their child who lived in a city in central France. The father was quite good-looking and told John he had worked briefly as a male model. Without making any real overtures, he made it clear that he was open to some romantic activity. John remained aloof, making no attempts take up his host on his thinly veiled invitation.

Some months later John's training program transferred him to the largest city in the Massif Central, the highlands in the middle of France, where he was at first placed with a highly emotional and hard-drinking young couple on a farm. Their extremely dramatic lifestyle made it impossible for him to concentrate on his studies, and he asked to be transferred to another home-living situation.

While abroad John had been writing home regularly. Some months later he learned that his father, disturbed that his son was forced to live with half-crazed alcoholics, had also contacted his education program and demanded that they find him alternative accommodations.

He was then placed in a situation that was not alcohol-driven but only marginally less crazy. An aristocratic and eccentric French woman in reduced circumstances had opened her town house apartment to student boarders. The huge antique furniture in her small town house suggested that she had come to her new home from a much larger chateau in the countryside. She selected her student boarders from photographs presented to her, and she had a handsome young American already in residence. Evidently, John had been considered also, but he believes the other young man had been chosen because he was more handsome. The French landlady claimed she'd gotten a better "feeling" about the other young man from his application photograph.

A second room was to be available in the landlady's overstuffed household a month later, when a female student would be departing. In the interim John was to move in and share a room with the attractive young man already in residence. John recounts this story, which hovers somewhere between a French farce and a hyper-realistic French movie, with a very straight face and a restrained manner. Only when mentioning that the other young man and he immediately fell into a sexual relationship does he explain that they also had to share the same bed.

After John moved to a different bedroom, he continued having sex with the other young man, who dropped in every morning as the day was getting started. It was at this time that John started to realize he was as capable of having an affectionate and loving relationship with a man as with a woman. Upon finishing their studies, John and his new young lover traveled around Europe together. "Up until that time," John observes, "I just assumed that sleeping with other guys was something that many men did when they were young and that you grew out of it. I never saw it as anything but sexual activity. Then it began to dawn on me that you could love another man. But I shied away from really understanding and accepting this at this time."

John finishes talking about this chapter in his life by speculating that his French landlady was a lesbian, since she always had female acquaintances visiting her in what appeared to be intimate circumstances. But she also seemed to develop strong crushes on the male students who lived in her home and added John to her list of passions before he escaped. Interestingly, John confides this in a manner that suggests he found the situation unusual but not distressing.

By the time John returned to the United States, he had been exposed to the sort of sophisticated experiences that many college students only dream or read about. As for the other young man, he already had a lover in the Middle West, to whom he returned once his sojourn in Europe with John was over. They did not keep in touch, and John has no idea where he is now.

Not long after finishing college, John and his longtime girlfriend made marriage plans. "I liked women," John insists. "The thing with men was just on the side. I was definitely in love with my wife. We'd been together a long time, and it all kind of made sense. All our friends were doing it and it seemed like the right time to do it ourselves. So we did."

But after marriage John realized that he still felt an attraction for other men. His new job with an international firm required much travel. "I was fooling around when traveling. Not a lot, but a little bit." Travel certainly broadened John's opportunities for meeting other men. "I felt as though it was fate that put me in certain situations. I was working in Hawaii and in Waikiki I saw a lot of guys walking into a bar, so I went in. Once inside I said to myself, 'This is a gay bar. Oh, my God.' I found it intriguing and frightening at the same time."

It was during this first visit to a gay bar that John met an attractive Polynesian man, whom he would see on subsequent visits to Hawaii. John and he developed a long-distance relationship over the course of a year. On one visit, though, John learned that his Polynesian friend was in the hospital—and dying of AIDS. John was in shock and didn't even recognize his friend in the hospital room. It was the mid '80s, the early years of the AIDS crisis before effective treatments had been developed. Little could be done for the Polynesian man, which elicited mixed feelings of concern and fear for John. His friend passed away only a few months after the hospital visit. John was devastated by the news but dealt with the ordeal mostly alone, confiding only in a close friend.

"After this experience in Hawaii, I started thinking seriously about my situation," John says. "I didn't want to lead a double life. It's not fair to the other person to be in this situation. You have to realize that all this began to happen when I had only been married about six months.

"I wanted to think about it a lot. Should I be free to explore this? Can I be married and do this? There was certainly the temptation to stay married, be with men on the side. I wanted to explore and see if there was really something there for me or not. I didn't want to divorce until I knew where I was going."

John Rowe remained married for four years and then was separated from his wife for two more before he finally divorced her. "Had I waited another year to get married, I probably wouldn't have gotten married. Certainly getting married and having children was not a priority for me."

During this time John still slept regularly with his wife whenever he was home, and they both enjoyed the sex they had. He was reluctant to divorce his wife, since she had been the child of divorced parents and had been very unhappy because of that. He didn't want to subject her to more unhappiness, but finally he told her that he found himself attracted to both women and men and felt they should separate. John believes his wife hoped they would reconcile during their trial separation, and she was very unhappy about his final decision to divorce. She has subsequently remarried and now has children.

At the time of his divorce, John had only told his parents that things weren't working out between him and his wife. He later told them of his interest in other men, which they have since accepted. However, John notes how a barrier that had not existed before soon developed in his relationship with his parents. His experience in coming out to them makes him wonder whether revealing one's homosexuality to one's parents is always a good idea.

At this point in his interview, John discusses a brother who is some 11 years older and also gay. This brother had never been very present in John's life, having left home when John was still very young. He was as surprised as John's parents to hear that his younger brother planned to leave his wife to explore his interest in other men. Apparently, the older brother had suspected nothing. John and his older brother now see each other regularly, but his brother's experiences had no impact on John's decision to come out.

During his two-year separation from his wife John met a man at a bar in nearby Chicago and decided to move to that city to live with him. He felt he loved this man and believed he could have an ongoing relationship with him based upon more than physical attraction.

John then returned to college for an advanced degree during this time. Upon finishing his degree he resumed work in his chosen field, which again required a certain amount of travel, both national and international.

Work responsibilities also required that John's lover spend much time outside of Chicago. For most of the years John and his lover were a couple, they were only intermittently in the same place at the same time. John feels this repeated separation finally took its toll.

On one spring weekend, John had traveled to Los Angeles to meet up with his lover. Upon arriving John learned that his lover would be delayed on a business trip. While waiting, mutual friends introduced John to a neighbor, a handsome young man of Puerto Rican descent. John fell in love with him. They now live together in Miami.

Of all the younger interviewees, John is the only one who clearly expressed that there may be something to be said for keeping one's sexuality a secret from family and certain friends. "I've seen both sides," he says. "I lived a long time not having everyone know. Now they do and I'm not sure it's the best solution. I have a close relationship with my brother. With the rest of my family it's not as comfortable."

John Rowe feels he has made the right decisions in his life, but he regrets that they may have been at the cost of true closeness to his parents, his siblings, and their families. In a few years, John hopes to be financially secure enough to leave his present career and start a new and more creative one. He is very interested in landscape photography and sees this as a potential direction. Meanwhile, he hopes that with time acceptance from his family will grow and his lifestyle will no longer be an issue for anyone.

Wood Kinnard:
The Good Son

Poised and charming in the Florida sun, Wood Kinnard is quite an eyeful. His glittering smile, bright blue eyes, and trim physique in no way suggest that he is in his late 40s. Self-assured and well-spoken, behind the wheel of his zippy sports car, he is the epitome of a great catch.

Nothing in Wood's calm demeanor betrays the many personal struggles he has faced and overcome. The son of a Midwestern Presbyterian minister and his wife, Wood as a young man was a married, upwardly mobile lawyer, the father of two children who are as bright and charming as he is. Wood's children are still very much a part of his life, even as they evolve into adults themselves. But Wood now lives with a handsome male lover from Costa Rica in West Palm Beach, Florida.

Wood was born in Quincy, Illinois, to parents who had met at Bethel College, a small Bible college they both attended in Tennessee. They were married after his father graduated and his mother had finished her freshman year. After a stint in Florida, they went to Quincy, where they remained until Wood was in his mid teens.

In 1963 Wood's father accepted a ministerial posting to St. Louis and moved there with his family. And there, in 1967, Wood's father committed suicide. The reason? His son believes it was a combination of worry over debts, which may or may not have been realistic, feelings of failure, overall depression, and guilt over his hidden sins. The loss of his father was to have a powerful effect on 15-year-old Wood.

After finishing high school in St. Louis, Wood went to Westminster College, a small all-male school in Missouri. He majored in political science and business. Despite his athletic build he did not play sports. Wood liked Westminster, which had only 800 students. In the Middle West it had an excellent reputation, and he says, "Most important, I could afford it with scholarships and grants." An excellent student, he graduated third in his class.

Wood went on to law school at the University of Missouri in Kansas City, interrupting his studies to work as an assistant in a statewide election for governor. His candidate won and is now a United States senator. As a result of working on this campaign Wood went to the Ford White House and was on staff there for a year. He made many useful contacts there and after his year was completed returned to Kansas City to finish law school.

Wood met his wife when he appeared as a talk show participant on a local TV station, where she was the public service director. Young, beautiful, and a native of Kansas City, she fell in love with Wood. They got married one semester before he obtained his law degree. Wood still insists, "I was in love and determined to be straight."

Upon Wood's graduation from law school, the trajectory of his life continued upward in accordance with all his plans. He took a position with a small law firm in Joplin, Missouri. One of the firm's two partners was straight, while the other was a highly closeted single gay man. Wood never became close to the gay partner in the years he worked for the firm.

Six months into their marriage the Kinnards discovered they were also three months into a pregnancy. Wood's son arrived on the scene not long after their arrival in Joplin. Despite having the baby, Wood's wife continued to work, finding the same kind of position with a local television station that she had held in Kansas City. In Joplin, the young Kinnard family lived in a beautiful restored house built around 1900. Not long after having their first child, Wood's wife gave birth to a daughter. Wood's upper-middle-class heterosexual life was on schedule and very much the one he had planned for and hoped for.

Wood notes that he had felt comfortable in Joplin and did not want to work in Kansas City. In part this was because before his marriage he had not been able to entirely resist the gay temptations of Kansas City. He had felt it best to keep a safe distance from them.

Wood's sexual life with men had involved little direct activity until he had attended law school in Kansas City. As a small child he had admired men in the underwear section of the Sears catalog. He also used to search for information about homosexuality in his father's ample library. As a Presbyterian minister, his father was often called upon to counsel members of his flock and for that reason kept a number of books on psychology and sexuality, which Wood perused. Wood suspects that his father's own problems, quite apart from any pastoral counseling needs, may have prompted him to include these books in his personal library. Besides the psychology texts, the library held several physique magazines, ostensibly because Wood's older brother was interested in bodybuilding.

Wood had dated girls in high school and college, but once he was attending law school in Kansas City he began to visit bathhouses, albeit with some trepidation. During the year he worked in Washington, he had sex with a famous photographer at the YMCA. The photographer was a familiar face at the White House and in the Ford household. Wood recalls, "When Jack Ford and this photographer went out for the evening and didn't ask me to go along, I figured they thought I was just some provincial kid and I was jealous. Later it occurred to me that they may have been going to gay bars and didn't want me to know."

Just before they got married, Wood confessed his sexual ambiguity to his wife. He vowed that he would sincerely try to avoid sexually tempting situations. She accepted his confession and believed that he would remain faithful to her—although that would later lead to Wood concealing his occasional lapses from her.

It was at a television convention Wood attended with his wife in

San Francisco that he met a gay man who had divorced after having two children. Wood had sex with the man, who quickly became a kind of role model for him.

During this same trip to San Francisco, Wood slipped away to see *Making Love,* a film about a married man who falls in love with another man. "I sat in that theater and cried and cried," Wood recalls. "That was in May. By December I was divorced."

Neither Wood nor his wife felt much passion for each other by this time. "I wasn't able to meet my wife's needs—and I don't mean sexually. I couldn't give emotionally," Wood says. "I couldn't reward her as a beautiful woman. You can't give what you don't have. She deserved better. She had started an affair with a married man during the last year of our marriage. She's now married to that man."

Upon his return to Joplin, Wood firmly resolved to himself, *Let's deal with this.* Two years earlier he had seen a local psychiatrist, whose technique had been to simply try to get Wood to stop seeing other men. That treatment had proved patently ineffective.

A new therapist was more helpful, guiding Wood through a divorce and setting himself up in an apartment near his former home. Wood still saw his children very regularly; according to the settlement the children spent their school week with him.

At the age of 30, Wood came out to his mother. She in turn revealed to him that his father was bisexual. She told him that back in Quincy his father would go to a nearby park in the evening and have sex with other men. Upon returning home, he always confessed to his wife. As a clergyman's spouse, she believed it was her duty to be forbearing in order to keep their marriage intact.

At the time of the divorce, Wood's wife received a large bouquet of black roses bearing a ribbon with the inscription, "My condolences on the death of your marriage." Understandably outraged, she felt outraged and phone Wood immediately. Though Wood denied any knowledge of the flowers, they both realized that his mother had sent them. Wood's mother had never fully approved of her daughter-in-law, who she believed had "failed" her son. According to Wood's mother, a woman's duty was to remain in her marriage, despite the circumstances.

The news of his father's bisexuality caused Wood to return to Quincy later and talk with a man who used to attend an all-male "Gentlemen's Dinner" that Wood's father had also attended. The man denied ever having sexual encounters with Wood's father, though he did admit, "I never did anything with him, but we all thought he was quite a catch."

A year after his divorce, Wood moved to Kansas City, a two-hour drive from Joplin and his children. This was 1984. He went there to work for Sprint, which was just then beginning to expand. There were 24 employees when he first reported to work. Wood remained with Sprint for 11 years. During that time his children spent three of every four weekends with him in Kansas City, as well as their summer vacations and holidays.

Wood's first venture into romance in Kansas City was with Chris, who lived with him off and on for the next five years. Wood still says he was very definitely in love with Chris, who has remained his CPA and closest friend.

Besides Chris, there were the three men Wood's son calls "The Big Three": Doug, Jerry, and Peter. Doug was a therapist, who eventually left Wood because their relationship was marred by Wood's inability to get over Chris. In therapy Wood has recently uncovered what he feels was another reason for the breakup: the abandonment he had felt when his father died.

Wood's next lover, Mark, was about ten years his junior. Their two years together amounted to what Wood calls a "caretaker relationship." Wood adds that he was not in love with Mark.

But he was very much in love with Jerry, an artist and designer for the Hallmark, whom Wood felt was an ideal companion. They had similar interests in the arts and decorated a beautiful house they bought together. Jerry was very much a close friend to Wood's children, also. But after three years, Jerry left, a devastating event for Wood. Now Wood sees that he had been too controlling—again because of his fear of desertion and abandonment.

In this same period Wood brought his aging mother to Kansas City and rented an apartment for her near his home. She had few friends but did not seem unhappy, although when she later turned 78 Wood felt she had become too old to care for herself and her apartment. He arranged for her to be admitted to a Presbyterian retirement home, which she vigorously resisted. He recalls, "In her best Bette Davis manner, she said, 'I will never go live in that little dump. I will die first.'" Wood says the home was anything but a 'little dump.' But true to her word, after an enormous row with her son, Wood's mother went to her apartment on the evening in 1994 before she was to go to the home and died there overnight. Wood says the causes appeared to have been natural but inexplicable. She must have been a fearsome woman.

Wood's new lover, Peter, helped him through this traumatic and trying period. Of Peter, Wood says, "He attached himself and I let him be attached."

About a year after his mother died, Wood took a very high-pressure job: He was to oversee opening an office for the Human Personnel/Decision International Resources firm in Chicago. Although successful at this venture, he found himself tiring in the unending round of travel, meetings, and long hours. On a visit to a doctor for a general checkup in 1996, he discovered he was HIV-positive. Three weeks later, Wood went on a relatively generous disability plan. The plan was reevaluated by his former employers and terminated in 1999.

The first autumn that he was no longer working, Wood met Hugh on a gay-organized vacation. Soon afterward, he moved to West Palm Beach to live with Hugh, a fund-raiser for the local police benevolent association. Wood was happy with Hugh. They bought a home together, but after three years their relationship deteriorated.

Wood then met José, his current lover. With José, Wood feels he has earnestly tried to overcome personality flaws that contributed to the demise of his other gay relationships. Now Wood finds himself reconsidering where life take him. José and he have a beautiful home in West Palm Beach where they live together contentedly. Though he is on the National Board of Governors of the Human

Rights Campaign, Wood is no longer as affluent as he was before. He pieces his income together by helping out at society functions, about which he admits, "Let's face it, it's being a waiter." But he's quick to qualify that remark: "I made a lot more money when I was an assistant prosecuting attorney, was married, and had a subterranean sex life. I had a good life, but I wasn't satisfied with myself."

Wood has no regrets about his ongoing relationship with his children. His son is out of college and successfully pursuing a career in Chicago, and his daughter is now midway through college. "The best role I've had in my life has been a father. I feel most successful at one thing and that is being a father."

Laura White:
IT'S NOT THE WOMAN, IT'S THE WARDROBE

On almost any weekend evening in Miami Beach, you will see Laura White walking on Lincoln Road Mall. Her tall figure will be wearing a tight miniskirt, and her red hair will be flowing in the trade winds from the Atlantic Ocean nearby. Often her pal, Lori, long blond locks blowing, will be at her side. All eyes turn as these two tall dames pass by wearing very high heels.

It is pretty commonly known that Lori's regular job is being a male police officer in nearby Key Largo. What Laura White does for a living remains a mystery to most.

The truth is even more startling than one might suppose. Laura is the married father of two children now in their 20s. Her wife and children live very comfortably in the Midwest. Laura is also the cofounder of a successful business with branches in several states. No one in Laura's family or among her business partners knows how she spends her weekends: strutting her stuff, decked out in cutting-edge couture among the beautiful people in South Beach.

People in art circles recognize Laura as a favorite model for Wulf Treu, Germany's answer to Andy Warhol. Wulf, who is currently working on a photo book called *Naked Trailer,* has done pictures of Laura cavorting in white lace panties and bra around an ancient dilapidated trailer. He is using the trailer as a setting for many nude and near-nude portraits of interesting people in the Miami area. He has also done a number of videos of Laura White that detail her fictitious life in which she must work as a stripper to support herself and her none-too-bright son, played by Wulf himself. In his gallery shows in Vienna, Wulf has shown his photographs and videos of Laura and she is on the verge of becoming an art celebrity in Europe.

For Laura, though, it has been a long and difficult passage from being an ambitious young man in the Middle West to a tall, vivacious redhead in one of the sex and beauty capitals of the world.

Laura's parents are both immigrants from Central Europe. They met in the United States, after having entered the country separately. Laura's father, born in Europe during the World War I, came over with other family members who found work in steel mills near Chicago. Laura's mother came to the U.S. as a girl of 15, the only member of her family to emigrate. She was never to see any of her relatives again. First working as a cleaning woman in New York City, she later came to the center of the country, where she met Laura's father through friends. The young couple was married just as World War II was about to start. Laura's father was a tank driver during the war, and afterward found work as a test driver for a company that manufactured tanks. Laura always found it incongruous that her gentle, kindhearted father earned his living in this brutal, mechanical environment.

At the close of the Korean War, the demand for tanks fell off and Laura's father held a number of jobs before finally landing a job working for the city in which he lived. Though Laura has several siblings, she remembers that her mother always held down a job while they all were growing up, in addition to managing her home and being an excellent cook. Laura still sees her parents as ideally matched: "They are perfect for each other. My father loves to eat; my mother loves to cook."

As immigrants, Laura's father and mother brought up their children to achieve, and their son certainly fulfilled their expectations. Laura went to the state university right after high school graduation. After receiving her undergraduate degree, Laura found her first job: managing the assembly line at a truck manufacturing company. Most of the men on the assembly line were older and tougher than their manager, and it is a tribute to Laura's skills that she was so effective in this job. Meanwhile, Laura began to pursue an advanced degree at a nearby university. After five years of attending evening classes, she received her MBA.

By this time, Laura had already married her high school sweetheart, who had received a teaching degree from the same university Laura had attended. Musically gifted, Laura's bride bore a marked resemblance to the film star Ali MacGraw. They were married in 1970, when they both received their undergraduate college degrees. A daughter was born to the young couple after half a dozen years, and a son came a few years later. Laura remains quite fond of her children. "My children are my passion. My parents, even though of modest means, gave us everything they could. I have always wanted to do the same thing."

Moving to another job with a manufacturer of heavy equipment, Laura proceeded up the corporate ladder at a relatively rapid pace, finally becoming an upper-level manager at the company's headquarters in Chicago. The young executive had arrived. Everything appeared to be in place: an excellent job, an educated wife with her own career, two bright children. But there was another passion that was slowly beginning to take shape: the persona who would become Laura White.

Laura recalls that as early as when she was 3 or 4 some of her family members were fond of dressing Laura's sister, one year her junior, in Laura's little boy clothes—and putting Laura into her sister's dress. "That feeling of pulling on that silk dress has stayed with me to this day." Laura says.

Later, while taking baths when she was 8 or 9, Laura would revel in the smell and feel of her mother's undergarments that were hanging up to dry over the tub after hand-washing. At about this time Laura and another little boy, who was a neighbor, began to play "dress up." Laura had found an old dress in the attic. They started to experiment with dressing up at the playmate's house, using face powder and makeup found in the bathroom cabinet there. Once, Laura was careless about removing the face powder before going home. "I saw nothing wrong with it and didn't really try to remove it. We were just playing." But when Laura got home and her dad saw her, he made it very clear that this was not the right kind of play for little boys. A sound beating drove the message home.

"That experience made a very lasting impression upon me," Laura observes. "I would wear nothing that I thought suggested female clothing. I wouldn't even wear short pants because I thought they were feminine."

Curiously enough, Laura departs from this troubling memory to elaborate on her sexuality today. "I think I am a totally bisexual person. I have no sexual preference. I find a man's arm just as sexy as a woman's leg. There are no boundaries.... I know a lot of gay guys but I know more straight people. I think rigidly straight people are quite similar to gay people—they have their world and they don't imagine being outside it. When you live outside the box, life is full of surprises."

As a successful adult, Laura began to "live outside the box" in very small ways. When the wife was not at home, Laura might try on some of her clothes. "None of this was heading toward anything sexual," Laura explains but also notes, "I would say that perhaps 90% of the cross-dressers I have known would find the most exciting would be to have a sexual experience with *another woman* while dressed as a woman. I only had my first experience with another man six years ago. I never thought I would have a sexual encounter with another man when I started experimenting with wearing woman's clothes."

In the late 1980s, a massive recession caused a lot of cutbacks in the company Laura was working for. "I could see the handwriting on the wall," Laura says. "I got out of there and got a job in a smaller city not too far away. But I didn't want to relocate my family. We had a very nice home, and my children were happy in their schools. I left them there and only came home on the weekends from my new job. I suddenly realized I had the perfect opportunity to experiment. I started shopping, saying I was buying things for my wife—just a few things that I could keep in the back of my car. Finally, I had enough wardrobe so that I could dress in my hotel room—put on makeup, do the whole thing.

"The first time I actually went out, it took me an hour just to get out of my hotel room. All I did was leave the hotel. Get into my car. Turn the key, then turn the engine off again, and run back into my room. My heart was beating so hard I thought I was going to faint. That took the most courage of anything in my whole life.

"I believe, for every Laura like myself, there are a thousand men who don't have the courage out there. These are the admirers of transvestites. By having sex with a transvestite, they are coming as close to experiencing this as they can allow themselves. I now see that all my preconceived ideas about being a transvestite were completely wrong."

Soon after this first experience Laura's wife and children moved to the smaller city. Laura's opportunities to dress as a woman became more difficult to arrange and less frequent. But then Laura came upon *Tapestry*, a magazine for people like herself. In it were notices for clubs for transgendered people. Several were not far from where Laura lived. One was oriented toward patrons whom Laura calls "entry people." Husbands and wives could go there together, change into the clothing of the opposite sex (the husbands, that is), sit about and chat, and meet new people. In this particular club the meetings were on the first Saturday of each month.

Laura's first opportunity came when there was a family holiday scheduled in Fort Lauderdale, Florida. The plan was to drive down with Laura's wife's parents. Business required that Laura fly back home, while the family followed by car. That freed up time on a Saturday evening so that Laura could try out the club.

"The meeting was in a hotel banquet room," Laura says. "I rented a motel room, got dressed, and went to the hotel where the meeting was being held. I was sweating so profusely my earrings wouldn't stay on. It was my first experience meeting other people like myself. I was only there about an hour and a half, but it was a great awakening for me. I had done it! I had thought about it so much, and now my vision was much clearer. Now I knew what I wanted to do. How does that song go? 'How you gonna keep 'em down on the farm after they've seen Paree?'

"The local baseball team frequently played home games on Saturday nights. I would say I was taking a client to the baseball game and I would go to the transgendered meeting. I'd get home and wouldn't have a clue as to who won the game. I had to be very careful.

"My Laura White identity's first home was a 5-by-5 storage unit. I kept my identity and wardrobe there. With my two kids it was very important that they get no clue. After the meetings I began to go out to bars with the other 'girls.'"

At this period Laura's career entered a difficult period. The kinds of heavy equipment companies where she had worked were being bought out. Massive firings and corporate restructurings were the norm. Laura found herself being hired at an excellent salary to get a company pulled together and functioning at its best—only so that it could later be sold. And as soon as it was sold, Laura would no longer be needed. "I had heavy expenses," Laura says of those years, "and I had a daughter whose private school tuition alone was $20,000 a year. My high-maintenance family required a high income on my part. I had to do some thinking."

On the plus side, Laura's transitional jobs were sometimes in a fairly distant city, allowing time only for weekend visits to the family. In one of these cities Laura began to go to gay bars. "I had joined another transgendered club in this city, and with those acquaintances I began to go to gay bars because I would be accepted there. But this was a tough city where I was working. One of the big gay television shows is supposedly situated there. I can tell you it was nothing like that. You had to be careful."

After 14 months in this city, Laura's job once again petered out, which had become a pattern. It was now 1994. Laura was determined not to work for someone else again. Very expert in the world of big business, particularly the field of transportation, Laura conceived of a new kind of business to service this industry. With a partner she launched it city by city in her home state. Because Laura was such an excellent sales person, the entire state soon became a viable market for this new business, which was extensively written about in the press.

Thanks to this welcome publicity, a group in Florida contacted Laura's company and invited them to come to that state to provide the same kind of service. Laura's partner remained in the Middle West to supervise the company's business in that region, while Laura moved to Miami to launch the new division, which immediately became a success.

Having left her family firmly ensconced in the Middle West and only returning home on a monthly basis, Laura became freer to roam than ever before. At that time Laura was a big and muscular 230 pounds and made quite an impression at the "Whale and Porpoise," a popular gay bar in Fort Lauderdale. Very quickly, Lori grew friendly with Lori, a habitué of the bar, and they became very close friends. "There was a synergy there," Laura says. "We got along very well. And it took less courage to go out together rather than separately." For her new persona, Laura White lost 60 pounds. "It was hell. Building the Panama Canal must have been easier."

Lori's wife in Key Largo knows about the cross-dressing life her husband leads. When asked about Lori's relationship with his wife, Laura comments, "Let's put it this way. She isn't thrilled." But Lori's wife has nevertheless accepted her husband's lifestyle. Lori came to Miami every weekend when she first met Laura so that they could spend time together there. They soon became lovers. Laura claims, "This was my first male lover."

Actually, before meeting Lori, Laura had already had one sexual adventure with a man. After placing an ad in *Tapestry,* in which she described herself as a "tall, beautiful transvestite," she received a request for a meeting from a well-known writer, who also lived in the Midwest. Taking advantage of her family's absence in Europe, she drove to his house one afternoon. Thoughts that she might be encountering Jack the Ripper darted through her head as she drove into his garage and the door closed behind her. "I was so depressed," Laura reflects. "I thought, *What am I doing?* But he turned out to be quite attractive. We didn't go all the way, but I enjoyed it."

With Lori, Laura entered into a full-out relationship. "It wasn't a romance. It wasn't an affair. It was a very unique friendship and sex was part of it," Laura says, adding,"Lori is basically a top. I am a bottom. Well, she is top/bottom. But we have had many sexual episodes. We have gone to Club Hedonism in Pompano Beach, a sex club for basically straight men and women and bisexual women." There Lori and Laura took part in orgies. As her transgendered persona, Laura had sex both with men and women at the club.

Laura gives Lori—who appears in public as a retiring, long-haired, blond quasi–Marilyn Monroe persona—credit for having provided the impetus to get where she is today, even though their relationship is now waning. "Lori will come anywhere," says Laura. "A couple of times I've gotten into difficult situations and called, and she has come to the rescue. She's a policeman. She can handle anything."

Although Laura seems more outgoing during the twosome's public antics, Lori in fact has been the more dominant partner in their relationship. Lori has been the one who always decided where they will go and what they will do. And somewhat surprisingly, Lori was the seamstress who put together the voluminous ballerina tutus they recently wore during the Lincoln Road display of costumes at Halloween. "It was Lori who knew what she wanted," Laura says. "I didn't know where to go anyway. But gradually you reach a level where you know more about what next steps you want to take."

Now Laura White meets men on the Internet, which she claims has "made places like Club Hedonism obsolete." Of the dates she has made, Laura has found that about 50% of the men get cold feet and don't show up. Of those who show up, about one in ten don't like Laura when they meet her. And then there have been other mishaps. A recent encounter with an attractive man ended the moment Laura stood up. She was a good bit taller than her prospective date, who had already reserved a hotel room. He said, "Sit back down. Being tall is a turn off for me." And their rendezvous was over, much to Laura's regret.

"He was cute," She says. "But I'm in the business of rejection. If you can't handle rejection, don't get into sales."

Laura has now completed ten videos for Wulf Treu. Personal appearances in Germany and Austria are being planned As for her relationship with Wulf, Laura attests, "It has opened a whole new world to me. Parading around on Lincoln Road as some kind of showgirl is one thing, but you have to go somewhere from there."

Where this "somewhere" is remains highly conjectural. If Laura were to become some kind of media celebrity, the media would certainly ferret out her true identity as the president of a highly successful transportation company. Her wife and children would find out everything. Yet when this subject is broached to Laura, it is clear that something about the "cat and mouse" life she leads excites her. Will she or won't she be found out? Definitely, Laura likes the "secret identity" aspect of her existence.

Nor does Laura especially fear encountering someone from her hometown in the Middle West. "There was a women I know very well from back home, sitting only two tables away in the Da Leo restaurant not long ago," Laura notes. "I kept my voice down, and she never recognized me. And only two weeks later I was at a party with her in my hometown, and she was telling about what a great time she had in Miami Beach."

Laura White is approaching a kind of resolution for her complicated life, but it is a resolution that is not entirely of her own making. It will be interesting to see whether Laura's public persona carries her so far that there will be no turning back from the full revelation of her true identity—and what the results of that revelation will be.

Sexually, Laura finds herself becoming exclusively homosexual, because of the opportunities for lovemaking she has as a transvestite. "I love women, but I no longer can perform as a man with one," Laura says, adding in regard to her relationship with her wife,

"We discussed my interest in women's clothing before we married, so she's not completely in the dark. She knows something of my life, but we never discuss it. She probably has a life of her own back in the Midwest." When asked how she would react if she learned that her wife was in a lesbian relationship, Laura says, "I would be delighted. Whatever makes her happy. You must realize, we have been married over 31 years and we have known each other over 40 years."

Laura White continues to be a weekend celebrity in Miami Beach. She has even been hired to appear as a transvestite hooker in a MTV video, about which she quips, "Three hours of hot and horrible work for 20 seconds on air." Hot and horrible work notwithstanding, one gets the strong feeling that Laura has finally come into her own.

The Guilt-Free Generation: 30 to 40

Their older peers often complain that this group is not suffi-ciently interested in gay causes. This criticism may be apt. There seems to be a new mentality emerging in the 30 to 40 age group, which in large part can be attributed to the world they experienced as they grew up.

Many of these men have had difficulty coming to terms with being gay, because they have had to surrender certain goals they nurtured when members of their social groups regarded them as heterosexuals. But unlike men in the older group, loss of self-esteem seems to be a relatively minor problem for this younger group.

When counselors explain to them that sexual preference seems to be immutable, they accept this and move forward in an attempt to put their lives together in a new way. This generation shares a perception that long-lasting relationships are difficult and unending romance unlikely.

They seem to also share a perception that what is important is car-ing for and forming a bond with another person, even if that person is of the same sex. A kind of "Hey, that's the way it goes" attitude seems to take the edge off their acknowledgment of their gayness.

Using condoms for sexual protection is seen not as an intrusive defense against lurking disease but more as an accepted way that one has intercourse. It has always been a part of their adult lives. It is not a particularly gay phenomenon in their minds.

In this group are some men who seem to be truly bisexual.

Their claim is that they are attracted to personality, and the source of that attraction may be male or female. Having these kinds of feelings and being aware of them may be the result of diminished social stigma, at least as they experience it.

When homosexuality does not make a person a sinner, a criminal, or a social pariah, healthily self-regarding attitudes can emerge. Certainly it is important to note that some of these men married simply because they wanted to, not because they wished to please their parents or conform to society's standards.

Also important to note is that being openly gay is no longer a barrier against successful careers in medicine, law, public service, and other traditionally prestigious male careers. For this reason this group has every right to perceive being gay as an irrelevant factor in regard to social advancement.

This perhaps explains why they feel less called upon to defend gay rights and fight for acceptance. As far as they perceive it, the battle as it concerns them is largely won. Whether it will stay won in their eyes remains to be seen. They may become more politically active if the future requires it, and certainly many of them are in powerful and visible positions from which to do so.

Edward Edison:
ESCAPEE FROM A DREAM LIFE

Ed Edison's looks are deceiving. A clean-cut, New England type, he seems ill at ease in his new role as an out gay man. He does not dress to emphasize his broad-shouldered and narrow-waisted swimmer's body. Yet he was among the most cogent of all those I interviewed, and he comprehends all the aspects of his new situation with a greater clarity than most of the men who appear in this book.

And in the intimacy of an interview his usually inexpressive face opens up, his eyes become larger, and he seems aware of his appeal. He is clearly a one-on-one kind of person—at his very best in an emotional context, despite his rather aloof initial self-presentation.

Not so enigmatic as he seems at first glance, Ed Edison is from Maine, and he feels that this factor has had the most influence upon his personality, his life to date, and his behavior for most of his life.

Until he was 9, he had a relatively uneventful life. His parents met in high school, had been very much in love, and had gone through their 1960s hippie phase before they both launched successful careers: his father as a college professor and his mother in nursing administration.

Then suddenly his parents divorced. Although aware of their frequent quarreling as a child, Ed was taken completely unaware by this development. In the smallish town where he lived as a child everyone knew everyone, so when his mother saw the process server for the divorce at the front door she fled to a neighboring friend's home to hide. Not to much purpose: The process was finally served, and his parents separated prior to their divorce.

In a straight-out-of-television scenario, his father went to live only a few doors away, at the home of the woman who had sheltered his fleeing wife. Such were the complexities of life in the Maine childhood of Ed Edison.

An only child, he felt betrayed by his father. Particularly since his father was now living with his mother's former best friend. He saw his father every other weekend, but those visits did little to bring them closer. Fortunately, today their relationship is much closer, and they make contact at least weekly.

Ed was always aware of his attraction to other males, even when he was quite young, but he learned very little about it in his isolated Maine world. He saw there were "sissies" in his school world, and he didn't want to be categorized with them in any way. He didn't like contact sports, even though his father had been a football star in high school; he chose to be on the swim team. He was not particularly good at first, but he became determined to excel. He practiced more than other of the team members and won the state finals as a senior.

He says his years in high school were not particularly enjoyable, and he had little or no sexual contact with other boys. He remembers an outing for his mother's coworkers when he was in his mid-teens at which he realized while swimming in the pool that he was being watched. Seated by the pool was a college-age young man with a good body and a tight swimsuit who winked at him and indicated with his head that Ed was to follow him into the woods. Ed did so, quaking at his own daring.

But as he passed his mother she said, "We're leaving in five minutes."

All Ed could say to his new friend as they approached each other in the nearby woods was, "I have to go."

He says that later his team practiced in the pool of a small college near his school and that several times he saw this same man enter and sit in the bleachers to watch the practice. From this Ed surmises he must have been a student at this college. They never met.

In college he felt his life began to take off. He attended college in the South—the school his new stepmother had attended. It was a high-energy, very social university where fraternity and sorority life dominated. He immediately felt at home there when he visited, and he quickly decided to attend. It was far from Maine and totally different in atmosphere.

In school—where he majored in psychology—Ed met the woman who was to become his wife. The young woman, who was a year ahead of him in school, immediately took to him. Soon she had dropped her hometown boyfriend and was seeing only Ed. Although Ed had had little contact with boys or men, he'd had some experience with women. His first sexual experiences were at the age of 15 with a 22-year-old woman, and he had slept with some girlfriends during his high school years also.

When asked what his masturbation fantasies were during his teen years, he explains that the few he had were of men. Most frequent were wet dreams in which he observed a dark-haired Latin boy getting out of a swimming pool. It had no overt sexual content. This prefigured his great interest in Latin men.

Ed says now, "I had a real need to conform. I was from a very conservative Maine background. I was from a broken home. I was determined to have a life that was acceptable."

He adds, "My feelings for men were entirely a sexual thing. There was nothing emotional about it. I only felt emotions for women. Only later did I feel an emotional thing for men."

His fiancée was a very popular girl, had been a homecoming queen in her hometown, and was an excellent student. She was exactly the kind of woman he wanted to marry.

Toward the end of their college period she had returned home, decided she should be with her previous boyfriend, and broken off her relationship with Ed. He immediately began dating a sumptuous young woman and became the envy of all his fraternity brothers. When his ex-girlfriend got wind of this new relationship, she soon swept back into his life, forcing him to break things off with his beautiful and wealthy new interest. The engagement was back on.

After graduation, Ed proceeded to go to law school in Texas. His fiancée finished her graduate work as he completed his first year of law study, and they were married at that time. Ed says he had no misgivings about his marriage. He remembers telling himself, "I will make this work."

But also by this time, he knew more about his sexual interests. In his junior year of college he traveled to Florida over spring break to spend time with college friends at the resort home of his fiancée's parents. He drove with a fraternity brother, whom he suspected had yearnings for other men. On their drive back they picked up some pornographic magazines and read to each other from the magazines as they drove.

There was both heterosexual and homosexual material in the magazines, and Ed remembers that they were soon concentrating only on the homosexual letters and stories. They were planning to make an overnight stop at the Florida home of Ed's maternal grandmother. In her twin-bed guest room that night they found themselves looking again at the magazines, this time concentrating on the gay sex photographs. They then masturbated, watching each other, and in the morning they had sex on the bedroom floor.

Ed finished his law degree in Florida, where his new wife had an excellent job opportunity. His married life was not a brand-new experience, as before their marriage they had spent a summer living together. Of that time he says, "She became very obsessive about neatness. But we talked about it very seriously, and she sorted it out. And it didn't return after we had actually gotten married. Of course it ties in very much with the kind of work she does in hospitals."

When asked whether he had ever considered the fact that his wife did exactly the same kind of work as his mother, Ed pondered this for a moment and answered that it had crossed his mind but that he had not drawn any particular conclusions.

Once out of law school, Ed's world was complete. He quickly had an excellent job with a local law firm. His wife was advancing rapidly in her own profession. They began building a new home and in 1984 they had a child. Ed was 29. He had quickly gotten together all the parts of the life he had planned.

Their child was the center of their universe and also that of the baby's maternal grandparents, who lived nearby. But Ed's life started taking a kind of spin he hadn't anticipated. He found himself going to bookstores and hanging out in the gay sections. He says, "I put myself in places where I might meet men." He started having anonymous encounters and going to a famous nearby nude beach, which was largely patronized by gay men.

One day as he was arriving at this beach he saw a young man in a spandex swimsuit preparing to leave, brushing the sand off his feet as he stood by his car. Ed parked nose to nose with the other man's car and couldn't take his eyes off him.

The other man came over to Ed's car and started talking to him in Spanish. They each only had a few words of the other's language, but the man got into Ed's car and they talked for what Ed says was "hours and hours."

Ed's wife was out of town on a business trip and his child was visiting his grandparents, so he took the handsome young Latin-American home with him. This was something he had never done before. They carefully parked the young man's car in a nearby supermarket parking lot before going to Ed's home. Ed returned him to his car after they had made love all night.

Ed gave his new acquaintance his beeper number. He says now, "The more I saw of him the more I wanted to see him. I started having real feelings for him, and I knew I was in trouble." Once involved with his new love, he became less interested sexually in his wife, although they had always had very successful and exciting sex.

But then, Ed says, he started to wake up in the middle of the night with panic attacks. "What if I had gotten infected! What if I'd given something to my wife? I cried for hours. It was awful.

"My wife saw that I was under a great deal of stress but thought it was my job. I hated my job and wanted to quit. But what I really wanted was to 'fix me.'

"I thought there was some kind of behavioral therapy that could 'cure me.' I was so lucky. I went to a really good therapist. She told me that sexual orientation was immutable, according to the best current knowledge. The help you get is helping people to accept it.

"Once I was with a therapist it went very quickly. Once I realized that it was never going to change I knew I had to tell my wife. I said to her, 'Let's go to your parents' vacation home.' And I told her there. I couldn't really tell her. I started crying uncontrollably. She was stunned. It was not at all typical behavior for me. I couldn't stop crying, so she started to try to guess what was wrong. 'You're dying?' 'You're sick?' 'You've been having an affair?'

"Finally she got down to 'You're gay?' and I said, 'Yeah, that's it.' But she refused to believe me. 'No, I know you're not. We have sex all the time.' I really had to convince her.

"So I came out with it: 'This is what I've been doing.' I told her and she was finally convinced. But even then she said, 'I don't care. I don't want to lose you.'" Over several weeks they sorted through the possibilities.

His wife even considered sharing him with his Cuban lover. But at Ed's insistence, she started going to his therapist. He knew compromises were not going to work. They finally separated after a few more tortured weeks.

Ed says, "The weird thing was that during this time we had the best sex we had had in years." Their therapist said this wasn't unusual: When people know they have to let go, it heightens their desire to stay bonded.

So Ed moved out. His Cuban lover eventually moved in with him in his new bachelor home, but his jealousy became a very real problem for them. At a gay bar in Key West, when Ed was partially stripped by a drag queen in a nightclub act, his lover stormed out, outraged that Ed would let another man take his shirt off. This kind of behavior soon became wearing, and Ed was relieved when his lover found new employment aboard a cruise ship and had to move out.

Ed had a subsequent lover, commencing in 1998 and lasting for two years. Ed quotes a friend who says, "I believe all baggage should fit securely into the overhead compartment." Ed notes of this lover, "His baggage was so heavy that it was bringing the plane down."

Ed Edison presents an appealing figure as he leaves the interview. He stands firmly on his blue-jeaned legs and squares his shoulders. He loves his wife as a close friend, and he sees his child regularly. After a certain amount of trauma, his own parents and his wife's parents have come to accept the situation, and he sees them regularly as well. For himself, he told me he wants a man with whom he can have the kind of relationship he had with his wife.

Since this interview was concluded Ed Edison has resumed his relationship with his baggage-laden lover, and they are happily still together after more than a year.

Carlos Gonzalez:
A New Kind of Latin Lover

"In Latin America, being gay is seen as a sickness or a sin. Now in the States, you see being single and being gay as a possible lifestyle." Carlos Gonzalez is explaining why he is living in the United States and, more specifically, in Miami Beach.

Born in Caracas, Venezuela, Carlos attended private schools there through high school. His father died when he was 3 years old and he spent his youth in a close relationship with his mother and family members in the upper-class world of Caracas. Having good manners and doing the correct thing were powerful cultural influences for him as he grew up.

At the age of 23, in 1989, he went to Boston to study engineering for nine months and then returned to Caracas. In 1994 he returned to the United States to study for his MBA at the University of Michigan. Carlos has a very quick mind and is one of the new international entrepreneurs who thrive in the world of the Internet. Their business acumen and international know-how are essential parts of their lives and override the purely national influences of their backgrounds. Carlos is one of this new breed—more at home with other business persons than with people of his own culture.

Returning to Caracas in 1996, he created a sports marketing program in coordination with the Association of Tennis Professionals. A Venezuela tennis tournament was created, with a top prize of $100,000. As Carlos explains, "This didn't attract the top professionals, because they go after bigger money, but we had plenty of very good players, and the tournament was a big success."

Graduating with an advanced degree from the University of Michigan allowed him to obtain working papers in the United States for a year and a half after graduation. Upon completion of the tennis tournament, Carlos returned to the United States and accepted a job with a large American company based in Miami.

There was now a Mrs. Gonzalez also. Carlos was married, to a school friend and longtime sweetheart, after one year in Michigan. They both liked Ann Arbor very much but soon followed Carlos's new job to Miami. There his wife soon found work with an entertainment company that promotes and develops channel television. As Carlos's dependent, she was also entitled to working papers in the U.S.

After a year of almost nonstop business travel, Carlos left his company and took a job with the financial department of his wife's company.

Of his private and personal world Carlos says, "I got married, and I didn't know I was gay." He says that he had no sexual contact with other boys and men growing up; his experience had only been with women. Handsome, dashing, and certainly not at a loss for words, Carlos must have broken quite a few female hearts in Caracas before settling on the woman who became his wife, for whom he cares very much. But his life was to take an unexpected turn once he was living in Miami Beach and had some free time. Always an avid tennis player, he began playing on the courts in Flamingo Park and made the acquaintance of other players, many of whom were gay.

He says, "My sudden interest in men was very much involved with my becoming interested in being free. Wanting to be free was almost a stronger influence. I always had to go home after we played tennis, and they went off to do what they wanted—to sleep with whom they wanted. It was all very attractive." He ends his explanation by saying, "When you play with fire you get burned."

For some years he had felt an interest in other lifestyles. He explains, "I never thought about them as being real and never thought about acting upon them."

It was in 1997 that he began to feel a need to be free. Most of his new friends were not Latin American. He says, "I have always had and liked international friends."

That year, he separated from his wife for two months, telling her only that he had a great desire to be free and needed to live by himself for a while. This was a difficult time for him. He says, "I felt it was too late, I was too old to come out and play this game. Everyone I had met had been out since they were 22 or 23. They had a ten-year lead on me. I didn't know how to handle myself.

"I really didn't know where I was in that period. One weekend I would be with someone and want to go home to my wife. The next weekend I was very happy with what I was doing. I had had plans for my life and now I didn't know where I was going."

Carlos went back to his wife for five months and during that time occasionally went out to explore. "I felt that sex wasn't the most important thing. And I very much didn't want to leave my wife alone in life. So it took me some time to finally separate from her. When I told her, she was very angry. She said 'You knew it but you never told me.' But the hardest thing was explaining that I was not leaving her for something better, which was how she felt."

He went to a psychologist for a year and during that time went to Caracas to tell his mother and close friends about the direction his life had taken. His mother was outraged. She blamed his situation on the fact that he was living in Miami Beach. "She thought that I was crazy and that Miami Beach was hell," he says.

He adds, "So many married men I know in Venezuela are unsatisfied with their lives. They move to London, they move to Paris, they try this, they try that. But I believe that sex is at the core of everything. They are not fulfilled sexually, and they don't know it. And don't know what to do about it. And what really struck me is that when I told a close friend what was going on with my life, he immediately started telling me about *his* problems. That was more important to him than that I had announced that I was a homosexual. It was weird."

Now life has sorted itself out a bit for Carlos. After five months of refusing to speak to him, his mother relented, and she recently visited him in Miami Beach for Halloween. She observed the high-spirited goings-on, replete with many drag queens in a myriad of looks and disguises, and had nothing critical to say. Of Carlos's gay friends, she mentioned that "they seemed very nice."

His wife, who still works at the same company he does, sees him daily and is friendly with many of the men he sees. She even goes to the movies and discusses her own romantic problems with one of his boyfriends from time to time.

Carlos says, "You know, things are changing very rapidly, even in Venezuela, in the past six years. Or perhaps I just never noticed it before, when I was living there. Being gay is kind of cool in Venezuela now. People want to be associated with gay people. Women have always been at ease with it pretty much, but now only a few straight men are uneasy.

"This isn't true in other South American countries. Argentina and Chile are still pretty uptight. Argentina is supposed to be quite open about it, but it's not."

For himself, Carlos has set pretty high standards, but he is not certain about achieving them. He describes a man he met soon after coming out: "He had pretty much what I wanted, but it was too early in the game. All the guys I've dated for more than three months, they're not from Miami Beach. They're about my age, a lit-tle younger maybe, but they have other things on their minds, in addition to sex. They're professionals, they're smart, and they're going someplace.

"I like cool people, natural cool not artificial cool. Smart people who have strong personalities. I like people who are on top of things. They don't have to agree with me, but they have to under-stand me. That's all I ask."

Carlos wants a relationship that is at the same level as the one he had with his wife. He doesn't want to accept less, and he says, "My idea of a relationship is a person you live with and you don't sleep with other people. And I have to say that I'm not sure that I'm at that point yet.

"Yes, I'd be willing to support a lover if there was a real reason to, but I don't want someone in my life for whom I represent stability. I want them to be stable within themselves.

"And it has to be someone I can appear in public with, someone who can come to Venezuela and meet my friends and family, and who knows how to conduct himself socially."

Smart, handsome Carlos Gonzalez is unusual for a Latin American man in that he does not want a spouse in the traditional sense. He wants a freestanding, equal partner. This may very well tell us a lot about where our culture is going. He may be a prototype for many people in the century ahead: unwilling to conceal their sexual interests, incorporating them into a successful, guilt-free life, and wanting a partner who lives in the same way, not a partner who is subordinate. The rapid and life-changing steps Carlos has taken in recent years may be the same ones that the world will take also.

Tommy Conroy:
THE IRISH CATHOLIC WHO GOT AWAY

How would you like to meet a man who married a woman he had known for only six hours and slept with only once? That's Tommy Conroy.

He has quite a story. But the first thing you should know about him is that he is very cute. Just under 40, Tommy has a perfectly proportioned body, is of average height, is buffed just enough from his work as a trainer at a gym, and has a very welcoming Irish grin. In the new definition of a "hottie" he definitely qualifies.

I had seen him supervising various middle-aged women at my gym. The ladies all obviously adored him and did their best to please their Irish godling, who was usually attired in a white tank top and green shorts with white trim. Just in case anyone should forget he's Irish.

I think I really noticed him one afternoon on Lincoln Road Mall as he passed by a table where I was having iced tea with friends. Head up, in his gym togs, there was something about the way he held himself that me made think he was being brave. It seemed something of an effort for him to parade himself through the throng of male and female beauty that is the daily fare on the famous Lincoln Road pedestrian mile.

Friends at the gym, when I told them I was working on this book, said, "Oh, you must talk to Tommy Conroy. He was married. He has a child. He was in the Marines!" He did sound like the ideal subject, so I stopped him the next time our paths crossed. I explained the concept of my book, and he agreed to be interviewed.

Tommy Conroy's story is in many ways an Irish one. Often as he talked during the interview I thought, *This could easily have been the story of a young man in the 19th century, even the 18th.*

Tommy's father disappeared from the life of Tommy's mother and her three sons when Tommy was 13. They lived in Fall River, Massachusetts. They and their kin were descended from emigrants who had left Ireland 150 years earlier to escape the potato famine. Once settled in New England, the lives of these new Americans continued much as they had in Ireland. With less poverty and hunger perhaps, but with just as much drinking, battling, and noisy piety. Again and again I found it hard to reconcile that the story I was hearing was from a young man just under 40.

Tommy isn't quite sure why his father left. Perhaps he had impregnated the younger woman he soon married. Perhaps he had gotten tired of working for his own father. But Tommy was led to believe, particularly by his older brother, that their father had left because of him. Because he didn't play sports well enough. Because he didn't fit into the "little roughneck" Irish mold as well as his older brother did. The child of divorced parents often feels guilt, because he imagines he is somehow responsible for the rupture. Most children overcome this delusion, but in Tommy's case, his brother confirmed the farfetched idea for him regularly.

His mother and her children moved in with the boys' grandfather at the time of the divorce, but this was only a temporary solution. The old man, an important labor figure at the large factory where he worked, died within the year, leaving no will. Tommy's aunts and uncles felt little responsibility for their divorced sister and her children. They demanded the house be sold and the proceeds divided along with the rest of the estate.

This was a tough period for the family. They moved from cheap apartment to cheap apartment, leaving when they couldn't pay rent. His mother found work in the offices of a large Fall River company and began dating the owner. This man, who was fond of her and her children, was a high point for Tommy. His mother was a good-looking woman who did not lack for male attention. But she had a penchant for attracting men who indulged in shady business deals, drank too much, and were abusive.

Largely ignored and regularly reviled by his brother as a useless good-for-nothing, Tommy slid from honor roll to running with a gang, committing petty thievery, and doing plenty of drugs. His first experience with sex was with a very available girl in the back seat of a Cadillac parked in the garage of a house the gang had broken into.

His sex life with boys began at about the age of 14, with a neighborhood boy. They engaged in sex acts but never discussed it. He engaged in the same kind of sexual activity with a very close male friend when they were 16 and 17. "We never talked about it, and I never thought about it as romantic," Tommy says. "But Burt used to come over to my house in the night, and I would let him in the window. My mother and brother never even knew he was there. We would have sex, and then he'd climb back out again and go home. You have to remember that my mother's brother was a priest, an important one in Fall River. And my father's aunt was a big-time nun in our school. I liked doing it, but I was never going to admit it."

Tommy's school career petered out after tenth grade. His gang activities were taking up too much time. To avoid getting too deep into criminality, he joined the Marines when he was 18.

He says, "What else could I do? My younger brother married when he was 17. Now he has six kids and lives off workmen's compensation. That was what was waiting for me."

In the Marines Tommy Conroy was an immediate success. He was made a platoon leader in boot camp. When IQs were tested, he was immediately sent to electrical engineering school. After serving in Japan, he was stationed in Los Angeles, where he was introduced to cocaine and got very heavily into drugs. It was 1980. Tommy was 20.

Caught smuggling drugs onto the base, he went to military prison. Soon after he was released he was caught again smuggling drugs from overseas aboard military aircraft. Tommy went AWOL, to avoid being sent to federal prison. Appearing without notice in

Fall River, he was greeted with the news that his family knew all about his situation. They had already been notified by the authorities.

Call it bad luck, call it bad vibrations, or call it the will to fail. Tommy's life plunged into even greater complications during this underground visit to Fall River. One of his best friends was about to join the Marines and was celebrating his engagement before leaving. The engagement party was held at a local college's sorority house, to which the soon-to-be bride belonged. However, at the party her hopes were dashed as her fiancé and she broke up during the drunken brawl that the party became. She then proceeded to go to bed with a very drunken Tommy Conroy. Soon more mayhem would follow.

Tommy's family prevailed upon him to return to California, where he was promptly put into a federal prison. Nine weeks later there was a call from the young woman he had slept with the night her engagement was broken. She was pregnant. He was the father.

He asked her to get an abortion. She refused. He conferred with his mother. Every inch the Catholic mom, she said, "Do your duty."

When asked how old he was at this point, Tommy said, "I was 23, I was in the Marines five and half years altogether." Asked his wife's age, Tommy replied that she was 28. When it was suggested that this was somewhat mature for a sorority girl, he said, "She wasn't in love with me. She was just determined to be married and have a child."

Making Tommy available to marry his Linda was another story. Through family connections, contact was made with a local congressman, who fortunately was deeply involved with military funding in his congressional committee work. Through this congressman's string-pulling Tommy was released from prison, discharged from the Marines, and sent home to get married.

Before getting married he told his bride-to-be, "Look, I don't even know you. I am going to marry you, and I'll stay with you until the child is no longer an infant. But that's it."

He says, "Linda said that I wouldn't leave her, that I would come to love her. But the truth was that the more I saw of her the more I hated her."

Circumstances did not do much to improve their relationship. They lived in a trailer behind her parent's home. It was one of the coldest winters in Fall River history. They were both miserable.

What about Tommy's sex life? "I did sleep with Linda from time to time, but not much. We were spending every night together in the same bed."

Did he have any kind of sex life with other men? "Nothing, nothing, nothing in the Marines. That was very taboo. Two black guys were caught fooling around when I was stationed in California, and they threw them out a fourth-floor window. You just didn't dare."

And what about later? He breaks into a laugh and says, "Yeah, I fucked Linda's brother once in an old barn out behind the trailer. That was about it." He points out that that was the only time that he ever cheated on a partner with whom he was living.

From the trailer the couple moved with their new baby into a nearby apartment that had an extra bedroom. They were immediately encumbered with Linda's older brother, who was not mentally competent enough to live by himself. Her family consisted of seven siblings and a mother who consumed a gallon of rum every day, seated at her kitchen table. She unburdened herself of her slow-witted son by sending him to her daughter's spare room. This did not do anything to improve this thrown-together marriage.

Tommy had a good job finally as a manager of a local dime store. He says, "I took the job partly because it was very near where we lived and I could go home on my lunch hour and make sure the baby was fed and changed. Linda sat around most of the day watching TV and smoking pot. She wanted to be a mother, but she didn't want to take care of the baby."

He did his fair share in this relationship, and after two years he left his wife and their daughter. From his apartment with Linda he moved in with a couple who had been his witnesses at his wedding and had become close friends.

Linda in turn married a Coca-Cola delivery man. Four months later she was divorced from him.

Before marrying her delivery man, Linda made Tommy's life difficult by manipulating him with their child. She would hide the baby when he came to visit and made any visitation almost impossible. She was trying to force him to reconsider his departure. Once it was clear that he was truly gone as a financial support, their paths separated permanently.

In his new situation Tommy soon found himself in a new romance with Monica, the wife of the couple with whom he was living. They slept together after six months of flat sharing and then moved out to live together for five years.

When asked whether he loved her as much as he has loved a man since, he says no. Tommy says, "I wasn't in love with Monica."

Of this period in his mid-20s, he says: "I was still very attracted to men, but I kept telling myself, 'You're not a homosexual.' I thought it was just a phase. That I'd grow out of it. I had fantasies about men, but I thought I was sentenced to living my life as I was living it. And what did I know? I had no contact with it. I had no contact with a gay community. I thought the gay community was a bunch of 50-year-old male nurses somewhere in a basement wearing dresses and sipping martinis."

He adds here that he thinks his father, despite a second marriage and more children, may have struggled with being gay himself.

In this state of self-imposed repression he began dabbling with drugs again, which quickly became more than just dabbling. He remembers thinking, "Stay numb. Just don't feel anything." Monica finally told him he had to clean up or clear out.

A clinic for the very rich was selected for the process of kicking drugs. The fee was $55,000 for 33 days. Tommy came out of the clinic clean and went to AA meetings.

While he had been with Monica he worked as a high-powered salesperson for an international electronics company. His relationship with Monica and drugs occupied what time he had left. They had no friends and saw nothing of their families.

In the clinic he made a new friend: the witty, intelligent, and undoubtedly homosexual scion of a wealthy New England family.

Tommy remained in touch with his new friend when he left the clinic, and he also began to see his mother again; she had come to see him in the clinic. Having gay friends and seeing his family became possibilities.

The months after he left the clinic were difficult, particularly since Monica resented the time Tommy spent away from her at AA meetings. Tommy refused to attend Monica's office Christmas party, as he steered as clear of alcohol as much as he could. However, some acquaintances convinced him to go after the party had started, swearing they would make sure he had nothing to drink. The party was being held in a suite of hotel rooms, and when he arrived Monica was not in evidence. Nor did she appear as he sat in a bedroom drinking endless amounts of 7-Up. The bathroom door in the suite was locked, but finally he forced the door, needing desperately to use it after his many soft drinks. In the tub was Monica with the 18-year-old mail room boy. Tommy stormed out.

He immediately went to a bar, drank a lot, and ran into Timmy Thompson, his first teen sex partner. He drove Timmy to the apartment he shared with Monica and parked in the driveway. While they were having sex, Monica arrived and rapped on the car window. "It wasn't a good moment," Tommy says. He continues, "My sobriety had already killed our relationship. I wasn't totally dependent upon her anymore, and she didn't like it."

Tommy kept their apartment, Monica returned to her parents, and he began drinking heavily. He would frequently drink himself unconscious, a state in which his mother found him on one occasion. She promptly put him back in treatment.

Tommy stayed sober for 14 months. In that period of slightly over a year he started working out frequently at a local gym and began dating Andrea, a young, single working mother he met there. He enjoyed being a surrogate father to her little boy, and soon they decided to get married. He also became very friendly with the gym's aerobics instructor, Andy.

Andy ran around with a crowd of young gym instructors, and they spent many evenings out. The other men had dates, Andy was always there with his sister, and Tommy was there with Andrea.

Andy obviously had a crush on Tommy, and he created as many opportunities as possible for them to see each other. Finally they made a date to have dinner with each other alone. Andy selected a well-known Boston gay date restaurant. At dinner Tommy slipped off the wagon, both men became drunk, and each man came out to the other.

The next day Tommy decided to come out to everyone. His girl-friend, Andrea, did not mind having her engagement broken. She had been about to enter therapy as she felt there must be something wrong with her because Tommy rarely wanted to have sex.

Tommy and Andy did not become lovers, because Andy already had a lover. This left Tommy free to hang out for several years. He made many new friends and decided to return to school to study law. He worked part-time in a law firm and on his summer vacation went to Provincetown to work as an assistant manager at a guest-house. He loved living in this gay community and quit his job to take up full-time residence in Provincetown.

In his new completely gay life he encountered a male couple who had a weekend home in Provincetown. First dating one of these men, he concealed the crush that he had on the other man. But soon he found that his interest was reciprocated, and he had his first great romance. "This was the first time I really experienced sex truly with another man."

Theirs was a true romance. They were together constantly, and Tommy was finally living the life he had not even imagined possible only a few years before. But his new lover, Henry, blew it.

Tommy was scheduled to attend a convention in Miami Beach. Henry had business in Palm Beach and decided to go at the same time. There was talk of meeting in Key West, but Tommy decided against it. However, the last night of the convention he awoke in the night and was deeply disturbed. He returned to Boston, where he had been living with his lover, to await Henry's return. He prepared a romantic reception. He filled the trunk of the car with helium bal-loons and bought roses, which he spread across the entryway of their apartment.

He met Henry at the airport, and when the balloons flew out of the trunk Henry burst into tears. As soon as they were home he admitted that he had gone to Key West from Palm Beach with friends, which he had not planned to do, and there had sex with eight men in a hot tub. "But I didn't come so it doesn't count," he finished.

Tommy left immediately. He packed everything that was his in their Boston apartment and tried to live temporarily in Provincetown. "I couldn't stand seeing Henry in the streets in Boston," he says.

Tommy's solution to the dissolution of his happiness was to take a long driving trip the entire length of the East Coast. He began in Montreal and spent 11 weeks on the trip, stopping in every major city and managing to have a love affair in each one. He finally arrived in Miami Beach and has remained there since.

For a year he also worked as a dancer at the famed Warsaw Ballroom two nights a week. Tommy had come a long way from the ex-Marine married to a wife he didn't love, living in a trailer behind his in-law's house.

Although very attracted to beautiful Latin men, which abound in Miami, he had no real relationship for some time. As he explains, "I can't be around people every day who drink and do drugs."

Four years ago he met a young Hispanic man who came into the North Miami fitness center where he was working. The young man was job hunting. Tommy says, "I seduced him and then we went into a relationship." The young man proceeded to get a job at the reception desk at the center.

Their tempestuous relationship broke up very recently. The young man, who was 24 when they met, decided he wanted to be free. Tommy, who was 36 when their relationship began, took this news with some equanimity. Of the young man he says, "He saw sex as a kind of a favor you bestow on someone when you want to reward them. Or when you want something. He never really got excited about sex for sex's sake."

Tommy's Latin lover didn't like that fact that he accepted their parting calmly. At the fitness center he got into a screaming fit, shouting, "You were supposed to lay down and die when I left you! How dare you have a life after me!" He topped his hysteria by trying to run over Tommy in the parking lot.

Tommy has lived in Miami long enough to accept this kind of behavior as a testimony to his own attractiveness. He still has an appreciative eye for good-looking young Latinos, despite the theatrical end to his latest romance.

A sensible man, Tommy Conroy doesn't despair. He has fought his way through to a life that is entirely consistent with who he is. Now he must find the man who has discovered his own stability, the man who can love him and whom he can love. Having survived all he has, he knows this isn't the impossible dream.

Rachid Douri:

A MARRIED MAN IN MOROCCO

Rachid Douri is 39. A tallish, dark, good-looking man, he has three children and has been married for more than 12 years. He is also the official lover of a retired American military man, Jeremy (known as Jerry) Stuart. All Rachid's friends envy him his good luck.

Both Rachid and Jerry live in Tangier. For Americans of a Judeo-Christian religious background, their relationship is a no-no. In the Muslim world, however, it's a way for an adult male to take care of his family and have a little fun in the bargain.

Although strictly forbidden by the Koran, homosexuality in countries that follow Koranic teaching is not regarded as a sin and certainly does not lead a person down the road to hell. It is considered as an appetite or a thirst, to be slaked where and when one feels like it. And if bettering oneself socially and financially is part of the deal, so much the better.

Morocco is a very poor country. A person who is considered middle-class has an income of about $500 per month. This makes Morocco a very attractive retirement destination. A Social Security check of $1,000 a month will go a long way in Tangier.

Although once a center of glamorous and lecherous chic in the 1950s and 1960s, when Woolworth heiress Barbara Hutton was installed in a home in the Casbah of Tangier, the city has declined greatly since those free-wheeling years. Then a free port, it has been incorporated into the economic system of Morocco now, which has gravely affected its fortunes. The Jewish community, which was largely composed of merchants, found themselves unable to do business under the new system and departed. This has left Tangier a floundering, dirty place and has only enhanced its already notorious reputation for easily accessible drugs and boys.

The foreign community is skewed heavily toward older expatriates, many of whom were in middle age when they came to Tangier. For the most part they live in gated enclaves on the hills above the city. Servants and swimming pools abound, and the indolent rich devote themselves to their social lives and their pleasures.

Jerry Stuart was attached to the Armed Forces in Europe, serving in many cities until his retirement. Vacationing frequently in Tangier, he decided to settle there when he was no longer working. He rents a very sizable apartment overlooking a main street in the Casbah, for which he pays the equivalent of about $200 a month. Jerry, still a well set-up man, is 70.

Rachid Douri spends two or three nights a week with Jerry and seems to enjoy being the co-host when friends drop in for a drink. Jerry and he communicate in French, for the most part, although he knows some English and Jerry understands some Arabic.

The other nights of the week Rachid spends with his wife and children. He is unhappily married, but this, too, is commonplace in the Arab world. His marriage was arranged—he had never met his wife before they were married. In the bargain he got three children, to whom he is devoted.

He also had the luck to encounter Jerry Stuart. Jerry brings Rachid's children gifts of American sports clothes when he comes back from his annual stay in the United States, and he welcomes these children when they come to have a weekly shower and watch television at his apartment.

Rachid supposedly works in import-export, which usually means smuggling, but his gentle and agreeable nature probably does not suit him very well for this kind of enterprise. More often Jerry arranges for him to chauffeur friends about, to be helpful in any

way he can, and he earns small sums in this way. Jerry is both solic-
itous and mindful of boundaries. He is willing to be helpful with
Rachid's life, but he will not overstep certain self-drawn lines that
determine how much he will do financially for his lover.

Jerry had a previous Moroccan lover, younger than Rachid,
whom he installed in a home he owned in London and whom he
sent to school there. That young man now has a job in London and
only recently has moved out of Jerry's home there. His relationship
with Jerry allowed him to escape the poverty of Morocco, work in
a first-world country, make financial contributions to his family in
Tangier, and generally improve himself and his life immeasurably. In
speaking of him there is something parental in Jerry's tone. He is
both proud of his protégé's success and strict about how the young
man must now adjust to living in a less grand apartment in a less
swank part of London. He wants the young man to get on with the
creation of an independent life.

Rachid is obviously not going to follow this path. Educated in a
minimal way, faced with the absence of any decent jobs, probably
unwilling to do menial or manual labor, he has the same dilemma
as thousands of other young men in the country. And he lives in a
city where thousands of homosexual tourists visit every year looking for readily available sex.

Writers such as Joe Orton and Paul Bowles have covered this
subject thoroughly. The sidewalks and sidewalk cafés are full of
young and youngish men keeping a wary eye out for passers-by. The
promenade above the Hotel El Minzah, Tangier's only first-class
hotel, is crowded with wandering young men as evening falls. And
empty as one returns from dinner. "They're all taken," Jerry Stuart
says as the promenade is traversed.

In this kind of world Rachid is fortunate. There is obviously real
affection between Jerry and him, and there is a pleasantly domestic
warmth in the home they share. Jerry has a second home in the
United States, where he spends the winters, which can be harsh in
Tangier. Interestingly, he does not give a key to Rachid, who does
not use the apartment in his absence. But he monitors Rachid's

financial situation when he is away and makes sure that he has enough. He has many friends who remain in Tangier year round, and Rachid is available to help them also, which he frequently does. All of these other friends, largely men, have household staff who have functioned as lovers at one time or another, so there is an understanding and support network among the expatriates and the Moroccan men who work for them and live with them.

Visiting an American woman at her villa, one man said of her major domo, who was waiting on table, "Isn't that so-and-so's old lover?"

Jerry replied, "Yes, he's married now and has a child and Amélie (our hostess) likes him very much." Still young, the major domo had a certain air of sexual availability about him but was brisk and efficient in the discharge of his duties.

Jerry says that at first Rachid would only permit oral sex to be performed, but now he involves himself in the full range of sexual activities possible between two men—and enjoys himself thoroughly. His youngest child, only 3, was born long after Jerry and he were involved. Jerry, teasing him, said, "But I thought you didn't like your wife."

To which Rachid replied, "But you were away in the United States, and I had to do something."

Visiting the Arab countries, one has the feeling that some of the deep-seated attitudes toward relationships between men have their roots as far back as the Greeks and the Romans. Much remains the same. Women are still confined to their homes and have little presence in the social life that is conducted in public. Men walk hand in hand, fondle one another, and kiss on the cheeks as a matter of course. Teenage boys, who are denied any contact with girls, hold hands and touch one another in ways that clearly suggest that their contact does not stop there.

In these old cultures, men finding pleasure in one another is not dismaying or forbidden. What is required is the establishment of a family. There is no moral squeamishness about what orifices can be used for what.

In this way, Rachid Douri lives a life that suits him and makes things comfortable not only for himself and his family but also for Jerry Stuart. If his wife is unhappy about the situation, that is not Rachid's concern. She is taken care of, and as far as he's concerned she has no right to an opinion in the matter.

From an American point of view, Rachid Douri is a homosexual living with a man. But if accused of being gay, he would find it difficult to understand the point that his accuser is making. From his perspective he is living his life in a way that injures no one and benefits many. It is a life that originates in very ancient ways and customs, and it allows people to manage with a fair amount of dignity in the difficult circumstances in which fate has placed them.

Carlos Hernandez:
A Long Trip in a Short Time

How many of the men interviewed for this book were themselves the children of gay men? This question has come up repeatedly through the course of the narrative. Often these men told stories of fathers who deserted their families when their children were young. We have met fathers who derisively, or perhaps ashamedly, called their little boys "faggot" when they weren't good at sports or were interested in girls' things—art, music, and literature. Some of these men committed suicide, like the father of Carlos Hernandez. Perhaps he was unable to face the censure of society and the particular macho horror the Spanish-speaking world has of homosexuality.

Carlos Hernandez is one of the youngest men interviewed for this book—he was 32 at the time he told his life story. A tall, good-looking, dark-haired man with an excellent smile and a good bit of self-assured charm, he made my acquaintance when I was in Philadelphia on a book tour. A friend came to my reading, planning to have dinner with me afterward. He had Carlos Hernandez in tow, and as we were waiting for our meals in a restaurant not far from the bookstore I mentioned casually that my next project was a book about gay men who had married women. Carlos said with a big smile, "Well, then you can put me in it."

I was a little taken aback, as he looked at least half a decade younger than his years, and he certainly in no way had the manner of a young man who was unfamiliar with the gay world. But married he has been, and divorced quite recently.

Carlos was born in the Dominican Republic and was brought by his mother to Puerto Rico when he was 5. In the Dominican Republic he had lived in a small town, of which he remembers little. Nor does he remember much of his father, who deserted Carlos's mother for another woman when Carlos was very small. Carlos was the only child of this marriage.

While Carlos's mother was supporting herself and her child in the Dominican Republic, she struck up a correspondence with a man who lived in Puerto Rico. Through their letters they came to know each other better, and her "pen pal" asked her to come to Puerto Rico and marry him. Carlos feels there is little question that this was not a love match but that it was the only sensible move for a woman who had the responsibility of bringing up an only child in the grinding poverty of her homeland.

Carlos was 10 by the time she had reached her decision, and it was another year and a half before the necessary papers were completed and they were able to move to San Juan to live with their new husband and stepfather. Carols left behind his scarcely remembered father, who sired more children, and then killed himself.

It wasn't an easy transition for Carlos, with new friends to make, a new school to fit into, and a new stepfather to reckon with. Carlos says he and his stepfather were never close, but the man was always a good provider, so it was never necessary for his mother to work. His stepfather died only last year in Philadelphia, where he and Carlos's mother had moved to be near him just two years before.

Carlos had come to Philadelphia to complete his studies and is now involved in HIV case management, work for which he has lengthily prepared, with a bachelor's degree in psychology and a master's degree in social work.

His ex-wife does very similar work. They met while both were students in Puerto Rico.

Carlos sexual history did not begin early. He was brought up in the Baptist church, which he remembers as not too repressive, though sexual matters were never discussed. Before her second marriage, Carlos's mother had been a not very seriously practicing Protestant, but her new husband was very religious. Fervent religious faith charged the atmosphere of Carlos's teen years.

In his high school years he did not date girls; he was very involved with his studies. Only when he was 17 or 18 did it come to his attention that he found other boys attractive. He felt close to one good school friend and says that relationship was very "emotional," but he never considered having sex with other boys.

However, before he left high school, Carlos did have sexual contact with an older man who lived nearby. On his way to school he passed in front of this man's house—every day the man was seated on the front porch. A regular exchange of greetings eventually led to the suggestion that Carlos come inside and let the man give him a blow job. Carlos did this a few times, and on one occasion the man tried to enter him, but the attempt was neither successful nor enjoyable.

The following year, when he entered the university in San Juan, his sexual life began to expand. He says, "I was nervous, but I was ready to do something. I used to go to the bathrooms and watch what other guys did. But I had four or five straight friends I hung around with. I was still living at home, so there wasn't much I could do."

Soon he started a pattern of going out with his friends in the early evening and then going out again after they dropped him off. "In the early evening I was straight and after 1 o'clock I was gay."

His partners were always one-night stands—tourists or closet cases he says. He never encountered anyone who might want a relationship, which Carlos believed impossible for him then. He was also fearful of being seen in the company of effeminate men.

He was making his parents proud at the university, and while he was finishing his master's degree a counselor encouraged him to consider entering a Ph.D. program at Temple University in Philadelphia.

He went to Philadelphia, found a job, and never really worked on his thesis. He was quickly caught up in the gay world of the city.

Feeling that he was wasting his time, he left Philadelphia to return to Puerto Rico and to devote his time to learning English. With that accomplished he returned to Philadelphia and began a serious campaign to get a job as an HIV case manager with a social service agency. The agency dallied in making any hiring decisions until finally Carlos forced the issue, claiming that he had another job offer and had to have a response. He was hired. He had only $20 left in his checking account when he got his first paycheck.

During this period he developed a close friendship with a young woman he had met while back in San Juan. As his English improved, much of their relationship was carried on over the telephone. He felt an attraction for her and, assuming that eventually they would marry and have children, he returned to Puerto Rico to be with her. This didn't work out, but because of his job experience in Philadelphia he was able to get a job in HIV case management in Puerto Rico. His first day at work he met his future wife.

They had a conservative and conventional courtship. They became close friends. They fell in love. They started dating, but there was no sex. After six months they began making plans to get married and they became occasional physical lovers. Carlos was living with his parents, and his fiancée was living in a university dormitory.

At the end of a year there was an elaborate wedding. Relatives came from all over the world. Both the bride and the groom were happy with the choice they had made. Carlos remembers, "I thought I wasn't gay anymore."

Things looked as though they were going to work out well. Shortly after their marriage the young couple moved to Philadelphia, where they were both hired by the agency Carlos had worked for previously. They rented an apartment and worked together at this agency for five years.

After two years of marriage Carlos began to feel strong cravings for sex with men. He says, "I began to feel I wasn't getting what I wanted. I wasn't happy. I began to have dreams, which became nightmares. I became terrified that I was going to yell, 'Juan, fuck me, fuck me!' in the night. And when I saw men in public urinals I would think, 'That's what I want at home.'"

Though they tried to become parents, his wife miscarried three times. This misfortune added to the tension of their marriage.

Finally, Carlos says, "I started fooling around. And I didn't like it. So I made myself sit down and tell my wife about my life before I met her. We both cried. It was hard, but I felt so good when I got that out of my mouth."

His wife was compassionate—probably more so because of her years of social work. She wanted to continue the marriage and try to make something of it, but Carlos said no.

He moved out and launched himself into a year of one-night stands. He continued to see his wife during this time, they began to sleep together again, and finally, Carlos says, "I decided to go back to being straight." His interest in his marriage continued for a year and a half, in which time his wife and he bought a house together. Then his need to be with men reemerged, in exactly the same pattern. He began having erotic dreams and found it impossible not to have liaisons with men he met casually. Once again he had to sit down with his wife and tell her, "I think this has been a mistake. I'm having the old symptoms."

His wife was less sympathetic this time and moved out, leaving only with her suitcases and taking no furniture. Carlos remained in his new house alone.

They broke off completely this time, only contacting each other when there was mail to be taken care of. Complicating things even more was the fact that Carlos's parents had moved to Philadelphia by this time and had taken an apartment close by. Upon his wife's leaving Carlos felt he had to explain to his mother.

They met on Thanksgiving Day for dinner and Carlos told his parents that he wanted to make it clear that his divorce was in no way his wife's fault. He went on to tell them he had no plans to marry again or have children. With this, they cried. They'd had no inkling. Despite his confession, his mother found his situation impossible to comprehend. Carlos had fathered children, even if they had ended in miscarriages. A man who could father a child was not a homosexual, in her mind.

Despite their great unhappiness they were very supportive, even with their strict religious beliefs. They assured Carlos they would always love him. His stepfather said "I'll pray for you."

Carlos says, "It was the best Thanksgiving day I ever had."

Carlos went into therapy with a gay therapist. This therapy lasted for three months, at the end of which his therapist said, "Carlos, I think we're done."

Carlos replied, "Are you giving me a certificate that says I'm 100% gay?"

Carlos started dating after this, and in this same time period his stepfather died. This brought his wife back into his life. She had been very supportive while his stepfather was ill, and they became close friends again.

The funeral was a big turning point in Carlo's life. He says, "Everyone was there: my friends, my coworkers, my family, and my boyfriend. My entire life was present. Frankly, I didn't know whom I was supposed to kiss. Who was I supposed to sit with? Finally my mother and I sat alone, as it was impossible to sort it out."

Now, two years later, Carlos is finding that a long-term relationship with a man is not easy thing. He feels comfortable that his ex-wife has a life of her own with new friends and an apartment that she likes, but he doesn't see too clearly into his own future. He says, "When I tell men that I'm serious about a relationship and that I would like to consider adopting a child, it scares them away. I liked being married. I liked the intimacy of it, even though the sex was wrong. I really miss that."

Tom Ryan:
GYMNAST ON THE REBOUND

Is there really such a thing as a true bisexual? Most homosexuals will say no. Most say that men who claim to be bisexual take that appellation in preference to being called gay. And some men interviewed for this book have confirmed this attitude in their own statement about themselves. They had first referred to themselves as bisexual before fully coming out.

And yet, and yet. There are men like Tom Ryan who seem to have undivided personalities that are truly drawn to both women and men, if only on an entirely physical basis.

And Tom's life is about physicality. Not yet 40, he has spent the greater part of his life as a professional gymnast and teacher of gymnastics. He has a natural athlete's body, not too tall, with muscles that are strong even without training.

From a military family, Tom was brought up at various points on the globe, including the Philippines, Japan, and Alabama. When he was high school age his family resettled in his parents' hometown in Ohio. During these years, during his summer vacations, he channeled his abundant energy and natural athleticism into gymnastics school at Ohio State University. His abilities as a gymnast were well developed by the time he attended college.

In his freshman year at college he followed a sports program, but a television show he saw diverted him into pursuing a career as a paramedic. These two activities were to shape his collegiate career as well as his later life.

Tom's memories of the time he spent in gymnastic training camps include a relatively strong gay atmosphere. "I'd say about 40% of the male students were gay. We used to call Bart Connor 'Butt Connor.' There were two guys who were roommates who were inseparable. We always called them 'The Couple.' I never had any homosexual experiences in the training camps, but I'm sure there were men who did. My sexual experiences were with girl students who attended."

Upon graduation from college he asked the director of the last camp he had attended to help him find work. Through this contact Tom found work at a school in South Dakota. He disliked the environment, where very young girls were pushed hard to be competitive by trainers and parents. "There was just too much crying and sobbing all the time. It wasn't good." He only remained there a few months before returning to Ohio, where he founded a gymnastic program for men at a large and successful sports school. Because the wife of a major football star owned the school, Tom soon found himself hanging out with many famous football personalities. His new pals were twice his size, but he matched them in his enthusiasm for a life in sports.

He augmented his meager income from teaching gymnastics by working as a paramedic with ambulance services, which he has continued to do throughout his adult life.

He then moved to another club in Virginia, where the team turned out to be greatly successful. Although there were complaints from parents that "he looks too young," Tom became a very popular teacher; many boys who had been trained by him in summer camps followed him here. For the first four years at this club he turned out the top team in the state in their age category. Every year the owner was very pleased with him, but in the fifth year, when the team only took second place, he was fired.

His enviable record gave him many opportunities to find a new job, and he chose a spot with a major training club on the East Coast. A number of boys followed him there from his previous post, and the son of the man who fired him wanted to be among them. His father refused to let him go.

Tom's private life in this period included sleeping with both men and woman, most of them athletes he was meeting through the training he was doing. Tom is quick to point out that they were not his students. A very serious mentor to the young gymnasts he trained, many times he made a home for some of the younger students who had left their own homes to study with him. These young men were never in any way subjects of Tom's sexual interest or activity.

While in Virginia, Tom did allow the mother of one of his students to treat him very well. A married woman, she bought him a car, and they spent a lot of time together, which went unnoticed by her businessman husband.

He met his wife while on paramedic duty in Virginia. She was a helicopter nurse. Tom says, "When she jumped out of that helicopter at the scene of a car crash, I noticed her body immediately."

He pursued her, they dated very intensively, and they were married in a short period of time. They were not married for long before Tom's wife gave birth to their daughter.

The reason for their divorce? "I'd found her in bed with someone once before during our marriage, but we agreed to rise above it. We had the baby, and I wanted to make it work.

"I was working nights part of the time, and one night the next shift came in early and told me to go on home. There was no reason for us both to be on duty. So I arrived home two hours ahead of schedule—6 o' clock instead of 8 o'clock in the morning. And there she was in bed with one of my best friends. I went crazy this time. I just packed up the baby and some of my things and got in the car and drove all the way back to Ohio to my mother's."

As with a number of other men in this book, Tom's divorce had nothing to do with his being gay. Rather, it was about a wife who really couldn't stay within the boundaries of marriage. His daughter returned to her mother, but now spends long vacation periods, including the entire summer, with Tom's family. She has a number of cousins, children of Tom's brother and sister, and is well integrated into the Ryan family. Tom spends as much time as he can with her during these vacation periods, and she visits him regularly in Detroit, where he is currently living.

Tom now lives with a man some ten years his junior, whom he met in a gay bar. Of his life after his divorce and before beginning this relationship, he says, "Generally, I go through phases. It's 'guy' month. Let's see what I can find."

The fact that there is a low-key gay bar not far from his suburban neighborhood may have played a factor in his lifestyle. His youthfulness and abundant energy could only make it easier for him to meet men there.

Reflecting on the difference between his marriage and his present relationship with his lover, Sean, he says, "I can trust Sean." He uses the word "trust" frequently in talking about his lover. As for his marriage, he says, "I wasn't proving anything. I think I got married to have a child. I don't think I basically wanted to get married. But once I was married I didn't want a divorce. I was reluctant. But it just had to happen."

Although Tom lives openly as a gay man in his home with friends, he is not as open about it at the club where he trains young gymnasts. His feeling is that it would be a source of trouble for parents and the gymnasium owner. He also has never discussed it with his mother (his father is no longer living) or his siblings. His mother has met Sean and stayed with them. But they have gone to some length to convince her that she is staying in Sean's room and that Sean is only temporarily sleeping on an inflated mattress in Tom's room. One wonders whether she is really taken in by this subterfuge or simply appreciates being allowed to bypass a discussion of her son's homosexuality.

In addition to his paramedic work and his training of young gymnasts, Tom Ryan has in recent years worked for major clothing manufacturers, planning the display of clothing in store windows and interiors. Tom seems to have an innate gift for selecting merchandise that will sell well and has enjoyed this work very much. It has also allowed him to be in daily contact with the world of fashion, where his sexuality is of no consequence.

As his body begins to suffer from the stress placed upon it through his years of gymnastics, work in the clothing field looks more and more appealing to Tom. As he approaches 40, he faces the next wave of the future, with a partner who seems well suited to him and a variety of possible directions for a career.

He says, "I think this is the turning point in my life. I share a lot of responsibility and love with my partner, and I don't think this will change. Should he leave me, who knows? I might look for love again with either a male or female."

At no time does Tom seem to have been unduly stressed about his sexual choices. He seems to feel that it is in his nature to respond to both sexes—for now he is content to be with a man. This is, perhaps, how sexuality will develop in the century to come: without excessive guilt, without great explanation, simply following one's true feelings without undue concern for reprisals.

E.D. Armstrong:
THE FAIRY STORY THAT CAME TRUE

The presence of E.D., or David, Armstrong in this book is in itself unusual. He is black—the only African-American in the group. Finding gay men who were or had been married to women was not in itself a difficult task. Every dinner table turned up an interviewee or someone who knew somebody. Usually there were several prospects. But even in the very mixed cultural environment of Miami, there was never a black subject for this book.

Even the male hustlers on Biscayne Boulevard, who cater to a masculine clientele and who are predominantly black, would only cautiously admit to having been married and never agreed to an interview about being gay.

Does this mean that the percentage of gay men among the black population is smaller? Or does it mean that homosexuality is an even greater taboo in African-American culture? Having no statistics, only personal contacts, this writer would guess that percentages remain pretty steady in all cultures, but that in the very macho black society, being gay is difficult to reveal, particularly for the purposes of publication.

One black man I interviewed for another book project revealed that he had had a married black lover for many years. He could not be interviewed about this now-deceased lover because "the family would never, never allow it." Evidently the man's wife knew that her husband had such a relationship but would never accept it, even though she was often in social situations with her husband and his lover. The married man's children were able to accept him, the lover told me, but the wife never could. There was stress in his voice when he repeated that he could not be interviewed on the subject.

E.D. Armstrong, however, is a different story—and a different kind of person than has perhaps existed before. A professional photographer, he uses "E.D. Armstrong" as a business name. He is known to his lover, friends, and family as David.

David Armstrong was born in Chicago to parents who had spent much of their marriage not getting along. He has four older siblings, and there is an eight-year difference between him and the next oldest in the family. When his parents separated he was 2 years old, and he moved to Bellevue, Washington, with his mother.

He graduated from high school in Bellevue and went to the Cornell Art Institute in Seattle with a plan to be a graphic designer. He also studied photography there.

After one year of study in Seattle he transferred to Pasadena City College to concentrate on the study of photography. In Pasadena he renewed a friendship with his older sister's best high school friend, Ramona Vasquez. He had known her since he was 11 and she was 18.

There had been a good deal of moving back and forth between Bellevue and Los Angeles during David's teen years because, as he says, "My mother was a nomad. She couldn't make up her mind between Seattle and Los Angeles. Right now she's in Seattle with my sister."

As a student in Pasadena David had run into Ramona at a mall. She was looking for a roommate and asked David whether he would like to move in with her. He did, and their friendship became romantic.

David says, "I knew I was gay when I was 5. But I grew up with three older brothers and a dad in my life, playing sports and bedding every girl I could get my hands on. I was always trying to prove to myself I wasn't gay. But I was always going from girl to girl, and I guess I thought people were getting suspicious.

"Before Ramona I had always had gorgeous girlfriends. And I

was always finding out they had cheated on me. Ramona wasn't really gorgeous. She was attractive, she was a trained nurse, and she would be a good mother. And actually we had a lot of fun together. We started out as roommates, and throughout our marriage there was always something of that quality. When it started we'd go shopping, we'd go dancing, she'd come on to me, and I'd back off. That never really changed.

"The urge to be with men got stronger and stronger, and I stopped sleeping with her. It wasn't fair to either of us. I was about to discuss the whole thing with her and leave, and then she got pregnant. So I dropped out of school, got a job as an accountant, and we stayed together for 10 years. I was miserable.

"During that time our sex life was kind of a 'by appointment' thing. Every Tuesday night. To avoid her I took two jobs so I could arrive home very late. She'd be asleep. The baby would be asleep. I'd slide into bed, and then the little fingers would start.

"But I had a kind of gay sex life. My best friend was in Los Angeles. We'd known each other since I was 7. We used to take baths together. Finally my mom said, 'Maybe you guys are too old to bathe together.' I was 14. He taught me to masturbate when I was 12, and after that we'd masturbate together. This went right on throughout my marriage. Before marriage, we'd double date, drop the girls off, and go home and jack off together. I'd hang out with him after work or on weekends when I was married and then we'd do it together.

"I was very impressed with the stuff Robert Mapplethorpe was doing, and I'd do pictures of young Tony. Our whole relationship was sort of 'It's OK for straight guys to jack each other off as long as they don't suck each other off.'

"When my wife was in the hospital having the baby he came over and we had a three-day porn and jack-off fest. And I did the same thing when his wife was in the hospital having her baby.

"I started feeling guilty. Ramona was thinking, 'I'm too fat, too ugly, he doesn't want to sleep with me.' She didn't get it. It was kind of obvious. I did the cooking. I did the shopping. I did the color coordination and the decorating. I painted the nursery.

"And at the same time I had a friend at work, Michael Hadley, who was an out gay man and made no bones about it. I used to say to him, 'You're a fag.' I made fun of him, but he never got angry, and through him I began to find my way out of the life I was in. We still are associates, and I have a lot to thank him for.

"I saw *The Lost Language of Cranes,* where the father hangs out in gay porn movie houses and the son discovers it, and I decided I had to take action. I didn't want to be an old man having spent my life pretending to be someone I wasn't.

"It made me think. I was always someone who had been different. They'd say, 'Why don't you go play ball?' And I wanted to cook, design, and decorate. I thought I was a freak, and then hanging out with Mike Hadley I realized that gay men weren't just the swishy queens on TV. Just like all black people are stereotyped on television, gay people are, too. That was a tough time for me. I contemplated suicide. I thought I was going to burn in hell.

"You know, black men don't eat pussy. They of course don't suck cock. There are no gay black men. Growing up in a world that thought that way, you already had three strikes against you."

At 31 David Armstrong began a double life. The first thing he did was come out to his friend Tony. "Tony said, 'I knew it,' and I thought, *What gave it away, Tony? When we were sucking each other's dicks?* He still hasn't come out, and he's turning 40.

"For ten years I had felt guilty, and I wasn't even doing anything wrong. I thought I'd go to heaven having had two jobs and a mortgage, and that would be it. So I took Ramona out to dinner and told her. She cried, and she stopped me from telling her everything. She said 'I thought it was my fault. I'm sure it's just a phase. I'll always be here when you want to come back.' But I wasn't planning to come back.

We had moved three times in our marriage, two apartments and then a house. Finally Daddy had his own bathroom. That's where all the magazines were. I had to have release. Though Ramona caught me out once. She said, 'I was at the video rental store and they gave me a printout. What are all these videos, *Bi-Bi Baby* and this other stuff?' I don't know what I told her, but I didn't tell her that was how I stayed sane.

"Anyway, now I had my own place, and it was completely different from where I lived before. Ramona always wanted carpets, draperies—all those things. I got an apartment with bare floors, French doors, and a mattress on the floor. I just took off my clothes and danced around, I was so glad to be there. I was free. No more rushing to grab a phone for fear of it being some guy. Now I was counting on it being some guy.

"But I didn't really come out at work or with my straight friends. I just added new gay friends and cut myself off from my family and my straight friends. Nobody knew what had become of me. Finally, about three months ago, I went to the computer and came out to all my friends."

David Armstrong's resolve to finally come out to everyone he knew was very much prompted by his relationship with filmmaker, writer, and painter Clive Barker. He says, "I met Clive five years ago, when I was 33. I had quit my job as a bookkeeper, and it was just too hard leading a double life. Part of me was still ashamed, and I just had to give up the American dream for a lifestyle where the risk of HIV was greater.

"Shortly after I got my new apartment I also got my first real boyfriend. I really fell in love—this was the first time. Unfortunately this was a guy who wanted to fuck everyone, and I just thought we were going to live together until we were old men. He was just the wrong one.

"I was with him for two years. Then I went back into the closet. I thought all men were pigs. When you met men they were quick to judge you, and it was hard to meet anyone anyway. At the same time I just let my gay side run wild. Partying, sleeping with all kinds of guys. This was great, but I just burned out. I was working for a trucking company as a bookkeeper and dispatcher with a bunch of ball-scratching guys. My life was full of contradictions.

"Then I met Clive at the Fault Line, a leather bar. It was the night before Easter Sunday. I was about to park and suddenly this guy in a green Lexus just pulled into the space. I jumped out and went over to his car and yelled, 'You motherfucker, you just took my parking spot!' And then he looked around. I said, 'But that's OK.' He was cute. We went into the club and watched what people were doing and talked about what they did.

"When I found out I was with Clive Barker, I was very surprised, I expected him to look like Anne Rice or Stephen King. We laughed and had a good time. I said, 'You can never really meet someone in a bar. I'll give you my number.' So we made out and then went outside to say goodbye. Clive wanted me to stay, but I said, 'I can't, I have a ham in the oven.' And Clive said, 'Maybe I could come home with you?' And he did. When we came into the apartment he said 'What's that smell?' I said, 'That's my ham.'

"And we made a pact. We decided to date, then if it's not going to work we'll fuck each other's brains out and say goodbye. But I told him, 'First you have to pass the spooning test. We have to fit together like spoons when we sleep, or it's no go.' And that part was easy.

"Meeting this man, I finally realized that it's all right to be gay. He made me *proud* to be gay. So I moved in with him after about three weeks. I called my siblings and they all asked, 'Where have you been?' And I said 'I didn't call because I'm gay and I didn't want to tell you. But now I'm with someone who makes me proud to be gay.' I told everyone except my father.

"Then Clive had a book signing in Chicago, where my father was living with my stepmother. Clive said, 'Don't you think it's time to talk to your dad?' We flew to Chicago and planned to take my father and stepmother to dinner and tell them everything. My stepmother made it easy. She said right away, 'We know why you're here. We may not agree, but we want you to be happy. You have our blessing.' I thought that was easy and that I had gotten away with murder.

"But when no one had said anything further on the subject, Clive said, 'Should we get down to basics? I've been married to your son for two years. So what are your feelings about this?' I wished the earth would just open up and swallow me. My father turned to me and said, 'What's your thought on this?' I said, 'This is really good soup, what do you think, Dad?'

"He said, 'As long as you treat each other right I don't have problems with it, do you, Willie?' And I realized it was my step-mother who had the issues. She didn't say anything, and my Dad said, 'Well, then, let's eat.' And I realized that if your family is going to love you, they're going to love you no matter what.

"With my ex-wife it was another matter. When I moved in with Clive, there was a custody battle immediately. My daughter was 8. Ramona realized that I was definitely not going to come back, and I was frightened she would try to take Nicole away from me because of my lifestyle. Ramona became bitter and took me to court. I guess she felt the only thing she could do was take away the thing that was dearest to me

"In court the judge asked, 'Does he pay child support?'

"Ramona said, 'Yes.'

"'Does he abuse the child?'

"Ramona said, 'No.'

"'Does he spend time with the child?'

"Ramona said, 'Yes. But he's one of those gays. He's gay.'

"The judge said, 'OK. What's your point? If that's all you have for me, lady, you have no case. Next!' And then he added to Ramona, 'In California, that's no reason, if he's a good father.'

"I didn't want Nicole to grow up being too aware of gay men's sex, since she was spending a lot of time with us. Like, Who's the top? Who's the bottom? I mean, you don't ask some straight guy, 'What do you do when you fuck your wife in your own home?' He's going to say, 'That's personal.'

"So we played roommates when Nicole first started staying with us. We finally pointed out that we were roommates sleeping in the same bed. That was OK.

"When she was 9 I sat down with her and said, 'If you had to tell your friend something very personal, how would you do it?' Nicole said, 'I guess I'd take them out to dinner.'

"Then I took my ring off, which was inscribed with 'Clive and David' and the date of that Easter Sunday we met, handed it to her, and said, 'I've been married.'

"She said, 'Who to?' and then read the ring and ran out of the room. I called after her, 'Where are you going?' and followed her to the next room, where Clive was sitting. She threw her arms around him and said, 'Welcome to the family. I'm so happy for both of you.' Clive is crying, we're both very emotional. Nicole starts out of the room and then turns back and says, 'Would this be a good time to ask for an iguana?'

"A while ago, Nicole had a conversation with her mother and Ramona said, 'Do you know your dad is gay?' Nicole said, 'Yeah, man, he told me two years ago. Why are you tripping?'

"Nicole wants to spend more time with us. We're more of a stable family environment. She told me that when her mother asks prying questions she says, 'Mom, they never ask questions about you.' She calls Clive 'Dad,' and I have to make her go when she has to spend every other week with her mother."

David Armstrong's photography career has grown greatly since he has embraced his new life. He does a lively business in stills for actors and actresses and also does commercial work, photographing weddings and bar mitzvahs. He had a downtown Los Angeles studio for a number of years, where he did fashion shoots and other jobs.

Most recently he has been concentrating more on his male nude photography, which began years back with his friend Tony. Magazines have recently been more and more interested in his work, and Rizzoli recently published a book of his work.

Of his male nude work, David Armstrong says, "I guess it's my gay flair coming out. I wanted to make the beautiful body even more beautiful. I have always liked the black body. Some of my family members are much blacker than I am, and I always wanted to be so black I was purple. So I began to paint my models so they were *really black*. I think these are some of my best pictures."

In conclusion, about his life Davis Armstrong says, "I found my prince, and I have my princess, and I have my dogs, too. My fairy story has come true."

Joseph Fulton:
BOY IN FLIGHT

Joseph Fulton has just turned 30, but he still looks very much as he must have in his teen years. Even as a young child he was enamored with flying; he soloed at the age of 16, well before he had a license to drive a car. At 17 he was licensed to fly a plane, and he has never had any plans for himself other than to be a commercial airline pilot, which he is today. Of all the men interviewed for this book, he was certainly the youngest when he set out upon his career path and the most certain in his choice.

Although Joe was born in Arizona, most of his life was spent in Michigan in a small town in the lower part of the state, where his father founded a very successful business. The youngest in a family of seven, he was an obedient child and pursued the goals his father established as worthy ones.

He was an able but not outstanding student in the small school he attended. His interests in art and music were not well supported by his school or his family. When he expressed interest in playing in the high school band, his father refused to purchase an instrument for him, as he considered playing music to be a waste of time.

Despite a lack of interest in the arts, his father was very successful in his business and could afford a private plane, in which he took Joe on flights. Joe says, "I sat in the back and loved it." From those early experiences he developed his love of flying.

His mucho-macho father never discouraged this interest and

never objected to Joe's plan to become a pilot. Several of his older brothers worked with his father in the family business, but Joe was not pressured to do this. However, he was required to work in the business as a teenager before going to college.

At 18 he enrolled at Northwestern Michigan College in Traverse City for a course in aviation, which he completed in two years. He then returned to his parents' home and worked as a flying instructor. At the same time he continued to attend a local college, studying medical courses, and received a final graduate degree from the University of Michigan, largely through extension programs. One can guess it was his father's frugality that required him to work and attend college at the same time.

Upon completing his education he took a job as a pilot flying cargo jets. After this he was employed by a large corporation and flew private jets all over the world. His determined climb through the ranks of piloting possibilities resulted in his becoming a pilot two years ago for a commercial airline, flying out of southern Florida. He was 28 at the time he achieved this, completing the path he had set out upon as a very young boy.

In his private world Joe remembers being interested in exploring sexual experiences with other boys at a very young age, and in his early teens he began a relationship with another boy his age that continued throughout his high school years. But when asked whether he had been in love before his present relationship, he says, "Only with my high school girlfriend, who treated me badly and broke my heart." But he adds that during this period of teen romance, which included sleeping with his girlfriend, he continued to have sex with his male buddy.

During his college years in Traverse City he explored more sexual relationships with both men and women. He says, "It was a time when lots of guys were trying things out to see if they liked them, so it wasn't very difficult." It was also during this time that he dated the girl who was to later become his wife. He says of her, "She rejected me any number of times until I wasn't interested anymore, and then she decided she wanted to marry me."

At the same time that he began working as a corporate pilot based in Texas, the young woman whom he had dated in college told him, "I want to come along." They were married soon thereafter.

Of his marriage he says, "I loved my wife as a person. She's a very fine human being. But I was not *in* love with her. I guess I felt compelled to be married and live a heterosexual life as my brothers and sisters have, because my family expected it." The marriage was not very long-lived. During the nine months they were together Joe came to realize that he was not going to be able to live his life as a heterosexual. His sex life with his wife was sporadic, and he frequently avoided it, claiming he was too tired. His wife complained of this. When he was employed by a commercial airline and sent to Miami for training, he decided he had to get out of his situation.

Like the steady and stable stock from which he comes, he felt he had to make his position clear and come out to his wife and family. All parties concerned received this news unhappily. His oldest sister, a veteran of three divorces, was the most understanding, and his family has reconciled themselves to the truth about Joe. They have also had to accept that he has a male lover, a young man he met online while in Miami training for his job as a commercial airline pilot. Younger by eight years, but mature for his age, Joe's new lover, David, has introduced him to the multicultural and multisexual life of Florida's largest city. Their relationship has blossomed, and Joe now feels comfortable in this world.

His marriage at 28 followed a number of years in Michigan when he continued to encounter men and have sexual relations with them. Although he never went to gay bars, he says he feels he has explored and experienced the world as a gay man to the point that he does not feel any compulsion for further experimentation.

Joe Fulton may very well exemplify the gay man and the gay world that we will see develop in the century to come. Although eager to commit to a career and a degree of social responsibility, Joe and his cohorts know that happiness lies in pursuing who you are, rather than who your family and society want you to be. Joe has done this. He has steadfastly followed the only career path he felt was possible for him, and although he first tried to do what was expected of him in his private world, he has since struck out bravely to find his own way.

Of his future he says, "Pilots are a different kind of people. You fly and you love it. It gets in your blood. You desire to do it. I should retire in 30 years, but I will probably fly privately long after that. And I can imagine that I will be with David all those years. He is nervous about such long-term plans, but that is the way I see it."

Conclusions

What conclusions can we draw about these men, whose reasons for marrying have been so varied and whose experiences have been so different?

Certainly one conclusion that can be drawn is that a human being's sex drive can obviously be repressed or subverted for social reasons. Among the men I talked to, there are a number of common motivations: They wanted to fit into society. Their ambitions were within the more conservative regions of the heterosexual world. They wished to please their parents. They sincerely felt a strong need for parenting. They wished to create a kind of home life they themselves had been denied. For whatever reason, these men were willing to set aside their own instinctive sex drives and strike up an alliance with a woman for whom they had a lesser or nonexistent physical attraction.

And one cannot say that heterosexual men would not be capable of this, for there are many instances in the gay world of men who are essentially heterosexual making a career in gay porn or lending their bodies to other men for the purpose of payment.

One must also conclude that Alfred Kinsey's concept of an arc of sexual orientation, with exclusively heterosexual at one end and exclusively homosexual at the other, seems to be a handy tool for understanding many of these men. Many of them felt some degree of attraction to women—some were even very strongly attracted to the opposite sex. And one certainly cannot blame anyone for wishing to follow the path of family and social integration that is so esteemed in our American culture as the only acceptable way to live.

Comparing our own period in time to earlier ones, it would seem that the 18th and 19th centuries certainly allowed for a greater degree of individuality in one's life choices. Remaining unmarried was not considered a disaster: There was room for maiden aunts and bachelor uncles in the extended family units and living patterns of those times.

There was also a greater acceptance of eccentricity and a bemused acceptance of alternative lifestyles. Only as the Victorian period intensified were aberrations from a generic way of living considered shocking. But this earlier period was, of course, also a time when alternatives to earning money and becoming rich were considered acceptable ways to live. There was a certain admiration for someone who was intent on learning, inventing, creating, or devoting his life to spiritual endeavors. Many of the men presented here felt that in today's society they had no alternative to the competitive heterosexual world where the drive to make money governs everything.

I was able to find almost no men under the age of 30 to interview. This is perhaps partially due to the fact that gay, married men in this age group are in the early stages of their passage through life and are not yet at a point where they are convinced they have made a mistake. Another important consideration is that, with the increased presence of openly gay men in the worlds of business, communication, entertainment, and journalism, many men do not have to marry to have a successful life, even in the newly conservative nation that the United States is today.

Even for those who have a great wish for parenting, there are now many options. Take, for example, Mark Rutherford and Tom Davis, who make their home in West Palm Beach, Florida. A gay couple, they have joined forces with a lesbian couple to parent two children, a 5-year-old boy and a 1-year-old girl. The two couples live near each other, and the children spend three and a half days with each couple. The children are always together, and they will grow up with the love of four parents instead of just two.

This is how it came about. Mark Rutherford is a native of southern Florida, having been brought up in a community near West Palm Beach, where his mother, a teacher, still lives. After local schools he attended Florida State University in Tallahassee, where he obtained a degree in communication. Handsome, with dark hair and intense blue eyes, his excellent singing voice led him to a job performing on cruise ships. He left that gig in 1990, when he was in his early 20s, to become a case manager in an AIDS support organization in West Palm Beach. After two and a half years of this work, during which almost all of his clients died (the advanced protease inhibitors had yet to arrive on the AIDS treatment scene), he returned to school and attained his masters degree in social work from Boston University.

He had met blond Tom Davis while working in Palm Beach. Mark was singing at a church where Tom was a newcomer. Mark saw Tom in the congregation, sought him out, and they began a relationship that has had its tempestuous moments.

Tom, originally from North Carolina, graduated from the state university at Chapel Hill with degrees in business and economics. He moved to West Palm Beach with a boyfriend and launched a career in real estate, which he still pursues.

After the two met, their relationship was interrupted by Mark's stint at Boston University. They saw each other regularly, but Tom says, "We were breaking up about every six months, and then we'd get back together again."

When Mark returned to West Palm Beach they were once again a couple, but he was soon offered a world tour aboard a cruise ship at a very desirable salary, and left for what would be about a year. It was planned that Tom would visit at various ports of call, but they did not see much of each other during that time. Tom, meanwhile, had made a close friendship with a lesbian, Ember Cariana, who was embarking on motherhood. She had a partner, Mimi Waddel, but felt strongly that her child should have the important influence of male parenting as well. She asked Tom

Davis whether he and his partner would share this parenting role.

Ember was six months pregnant when Mark returned from his world tour. Mark was unsure what his role would be exactly, as he felt Tom would be the primary father and Ember the primary mother. In discussions Tom and Ember told him that his involvement would depend entirely on how he involved himself. And there seems to have been a successful creation of a family module that is a true original.

Their children spend half of the week with their fathers, and return to spend Saturday with them as well. The other half of the week and Sunday are spent with their mothers.

As an infant, their son Cristofer spent most of his time with his mother. Tom says, "We were afraid we wouldn't know what to do if something happened." However, a few years and a lot of practice later, they felt confident of their ability to care for Sofia. When she arrived, both couples began sharing the responsibilities of caring for a newborn.

Mark jokes, "I would personally like to thank whoever invented the breast pump. It's made all of our lives a little easier."

Ember, who is a naturopathic physician, and Mark, who is a psychotherapist in a private practice, are both able to work part-time. Mark's mother, after some reluctance, has accepted that she has grandchildren by her son and is a regular presence in their lives. Quite spontaneously Cristofer started calling her Grandma, which seems to have sealed the deal.

There seem to be few difficulties in the time-sharing arrangements. Mark says, "If anything, we call each other and say, 'Could you possibly take them a bit earlier?' from time to time. A 5-year-old and a 1-year-old are no joke. They're exhausting!" Tom and Mark have time to socialize with friends, but find themselves leaving social events early because they know they have to be up early the next morning with their children.

Mark says, "Occasionally Tom and I are visiting a gay couple in their beautiful home and they're talking about the great trips they've made and are planning, but we have no regrets. None. We would much rather have the life we've got."

After much discussion, the couples, who already lived in the same city, made the decision to move into the same neighborhood. They felt their closer proximity would make the shared parenting easier as well as create a more unified environment for their children to grow up in.

Both still under 40, and both still very youthful-looking and handsome, Tom and Mark have embarked upon a completely original life plan. They carefully checked out the school their son attends to make sure he would be welcomed there. They say that the presence of other children of gay and lesbian couples in the school ensures that Cristofer will have children from similar backgrounds among his playmates.

They know of no other gay male couples in the area who have attempted to have a child. Mark says, "We hope our coparenting arrangement will open peoples' eyes to the possibilities. Gay guys have the best potential allies in their lesbian counterparts. You can create any situation you want. There are no real boundaries. Some of the heterosexual parents are very friendly, and one father said he envied our arrangement. We could schedule nights off, so as to enjoy the time we had with them even more."

Solutions like the one that Tom and Mark have found with their coparents Ember and Mimi will undoubtedly be used as role models in the century that lies before us. It will be fascinating to see how alternative ways of living develop as both gay men and lesbians learn to live comfortably with their own emotions and to be fulfilled in their own desires for homemaking and parenting.

As the pressure to conform to the prototypical norm of Mom, Dad, and the kids diminish, it may also well be that many people will not choose to follow this path. Gay men will be able to choose from a wider variety of lifestyles, as will many heterosexual men and women. It will be possible to elect serial monogamy as a way of life, not as a prelude to a more permanent arrangement. One will be able to create a home with another person regardless of sex, and some people will elect to create a home with nonsexual intimates in a kind of mutually selected family. All of these will undoubtedly become possibilities.

In the creation of this book I found it impossible not to think often of how many men must still be living in marriages where they are feigning emotions and concealing their true selves from those who are the closest to them. This nexus of painful self-deceit has been the focal point of this book. These men were cut off from their true selves because of perceived pressures from a variety of sources. I hope these oppressive social forces will diminish in the years ahead.

It has taken a lot of strength for the men interviewed here to deal with their lives—and a lot of strength to agree to be candid in an interview. To the men who shared their stories with me, I offer many thanks. This is really their book. Their lives have been their victories. They cannot be praised or admired enough for their bravery, their fortitude, and their ability to find themselves in a world that has done little to make their journey of self-discovery easier.